Silent America review

SILENT AMERICA: Essays from a Democracy at War.

Posted by Mr. Natural on December 23, 2002 05:47 PM:
This should be required reading for every school-age child and for every school teacher. As long as we have voices like this, we will prevail over the forces of darkness and evil.

Posted by Steven Malcolm Anderson on December 23, 2002 07:45 PM:
Thank you for defending my freedom and the honor of my country. You embody what is great about America, which is now the heart of our Western civilization.

Posted by julie on February 15, 2003 08:52 PM:
My heart is beating so fast! What a great essay!

Posted by Erbo on February 15, 2003 09:18 PM:
Oh. My. God. You *rock!* Undeniably and without question.

Posted by Greg on February 16, 2003 01:36 AM:
I turned my stereo off once I started to read COURAGE; your essay was musical in its own right.

Posted by F. Davis, Capt., USNR (Ret) on February 16, 2003 09:16 PM:
This is simply the best piece of writing about the American Spirit I have read in many, many years.

Posted by SallyVee on February 18, 2003 12:39 AM:
Marvelous. Dazzling. I know nothing, for instance, about flying machines or lawn mowers for that matter. But under the spell of a grand concept, in the hands of a superb writer, I was gripped by mechanical details and pilot-speak, and could even imagine being an astronaut! Bill, you've got a gift.

Posted by MunDane on February 19, 2003 09:27 AM:
Words fail me, as much as they did not fail you. Thanks.

Posted by Scott on February 24, 2003 11:34 AM:
That was amazing. In fact, I think it even cured my hangover.

Posted by Ben Carter on February 25, 2003 04:34 PM:
I've never been so proud to be an American. And I'm a Canadian.

Posted by pbird on March 29, 2003 07:43 PM:
It helped so much to read HISTORY. You, sir, educate us in why it is in fact right to fight this evil and that we ourselves are not evil to do so.

Posted by Andy on March 29, 2003 08:39 PM:
I envy your "Situational Awareness" and wonder how one person can enjoy its insight in more than one subject. How you can be so possessed of such insight for all of the subjects that you write about is beyond me. You must be one hell of a pilot.

Posted by BillRay on March 30, 2003 12:07 AM:
I'm reminded of a story: when the trumpeter Miles Davis first heard the jazz pianist Keith Jarrett play, he asked, "What's it like being a genius?"
The same interrogative applies here.

Posted by Eric Sivula on March 30, 2003 07:18 AM:
I may have to read HISTORY every week, just to remind myself that the brave, inventive, and above all else *good* people who made America what it is today have not completely disappeared.

Posted by bob in the hills on March 30, 2003 09:33 AM:
You may single handedly be the "renaissance" of the essay, long overdue and greatly undervalued. Your observations and perspectives on history may themselves become history of note.

Posted by Roy on May 19, 2003 01:15 PM:
Look at those subject titles – HONOR... COURAGE... FREEDOM... Obviously this man lives in dimension other than us mortals and we mustn't listen to him. He's going to cripple us with common sense and we won't know what hit us, we'll end up better citizens, informed voters, useful producers and heaven forbid - intelligent.

Posted by GreatHairySilverback on July 4, 2003 02:22 PM:
TRINITY is a graduate level education in adult thinking, and just the slap in the face I needed to see just how good I've got it here.

Posted by Beth in Kansas on July 4, 2003 05:18 PM:
What talent, what heart, what smarts!!!

Posted by Ofc. Krupke on July 4, 2003 09:24 PM:
More of the usual. Which is to say, it's freaking *astounding*.

Posted by Chris Whittaker on July 5, 2003 10:53 AM:
Every time I hear someone crow about what is wrong with this country, I would love to smack them upside the head with this essay, a couple of times, then insist that they read it. Even in the worst of times, the optimism you spoke of, along with the wonderful people in my life, sustained me.

Posted by TB StLouis on July 5, 2003 11:15 PM:
I laughed, I wept, I got up and hugged my poor, confused dog. As much as I abhor unrestrained adulation... You are a titan!

Posted by BigD on July 7, 2003 03:36 PM:
I am not often speechless. This is almost one of those times.

Posted by John on August 20, 2003 06:10 AM:
RESPONSIBILITY is another fine piece of clear thinking. A republic like ours survives on minds like yours.

Posted by BAM on August 20, 2003 01:55 PM:
When I saw RESPONSIBILITY was posted I worked through lunch just so I could have a free hour to read it before I left work.
Now I'm going to walk home.
It's not a short walk,
but I feel strong.
Thank you Bill.

Posted by aliestar on August 20, 2003 02:12 PM:
RESPONSIBILITY is simply the best essay I've ever read. Period. What you've done is beyond outstanding. In my wildest dreams I never could have stated so perfectly what our problems are, who's responsible for them, and where the solutions can be found. I applaud you, sir. Simply brilliant.

Posted by Lerraunt on August 20, 2003 04:36 PM:
Wow. That was an hour very well spent. However Mr. Whittle, I am afraid I must now hate you, for the excellence of this essay will force me to spend several hours reading everything else you have written.
Bastard.

Posted by Black Oak on October 1, 2003 07:40 AM:
WOW. WOW. Wow. Wow. *deep breath* Wow.

Posted by twisterella on May 22, 2004 12:24 PM:
Wow...I absolutely and unequivocally agree with every word, and that's pretty damn rare! Bill Whittle, you are cool to the chromosomes, dude!

Posted by bolivar on May 22, 2004 02:11 PM:
Bill, I would love to meet you and shake your hand and buy you a beer! You magnificent son of a bitch!!! You are MY kind of patriot - not a bible thumping egotist but, an honest to God patriot who only cares for the general good and not himself. Thank you from the bottom of my heart and as I look at the flag from my WWII era fathers funeral I know that this country will survive and prosper as long as people like you keep the candle, nay *blowtorch* of Liberty and freedom and Love of fellow man alive and in people's hearts.

Posted by Michelle Y. on May 22, 2004 03:20 PM:
Bill, I am a dual citizen of Taiwan and the United States, and I'm used to just saying I'm Taiwanese. But your many essays make me *proud* to say that I'm American. No hyphens, no qualifications, just an American.

Posted by CB1100Rider on May 22, 2004 09:04 PM:
This. Is. *IT.* This is common sense in it's best form. This is what the population needs to see and hear. Your book will be a primer for people who feel the need to speak out about the greatness of this country, yet lack the words or eloquence. Until they find them, they can proudly hand a dog-eared copy of this book to someone and pass along your words. Nuthin' but Net!

Posted by Kevin Baker on May 22, 2004 10:37 PM:
I just sat and read STRENGTH. About four pages into it I felt the need to read it out loud. It *demands* to be read out loud. On television. On radio. On street corners. In auditoriums on college campuses and in high schools. In Madison Square Garden before a capacity crowd. In Carnegie Hall.
Before Parliament, by Tony Blair.
Before a joint session of Congress. By *the author.*
Bill Whittle goes to *eleven.*

Posted by Bonnie on May 24, 2004 07:07 AM:
Wonderful to see some off-the-cuff Whittle chainsaw work. Whirr, sparks, ice chips, sculpture. Wow!

Posted by Rainking on October 6, 2004 07:07 AM:
Just like always, just when I was beginning to waiver and loose the slightest amount of faith, you have restored it.

Posted by Opinionated Bastard on October 6, 2004 10:28 AM:
Bill, you're the best argument I've ever heard for gay marriage. Because I love you. (Please don't tell my wife.)

Posted by atrophied462 on October 6, 2004 01:07 PM:
I started out being impressed by your passionate writing. Then I became downright moved by your sense of history. What a great tragedy that we should have to look for essays of this quality on - with all due respect - little-known weblogs, when they should be published in your nation's greatest newspapers.

Posted by He Who Broods on October 13, 2004 09:36 AM:
Thanks for this excellent essay. The opinion front is a crucial front in the war on terror. Thanks for fighting it.

silent america
essays from a democracy at war

by
Bill Whittle

Published by Aurora Aerospace, Inc.
Los Angeles, California

Cover design and execution by
Buster O'Connor / Eye4
Gainesville, Florida

ISBN: 0-9764059-0-3 $29.95 Softcover

For Dad,
Who started me down this path, yet never got to see the first
letter I sent home. Even today, I find that every time I finish
an essay, I want to call him first.

How many of us wish for such a telephone...

FORWARD

These essays are the result of two years of thoughts and observations that first appeared on my weblog, *Eject! Eject! Eject!* They began on the plane ride home from my father's funeral at Arlington National Cemetery in October of 2002, and they end – it has to end somewhere! – with the reelection of President Bush in November of 2004.

On one level, they mark a sort of photo album, a collection of mental snapshots. They are the pictures of events frozen at the time they were written. Some of these dramas – such as the 2004 Presidential elections – loomed large at the time and have now been resolved. Others, like our presence in Iraq, have outcomes that have yet to be revealed as this – another snapshot – is being written.

I have left them as they were at the time they were written and I am shocked and surprised at how well they seem to hold up, and at how relatively few errors they seem to contain in hindsight. Luck is not always with me; yet it was with me here, most of the time. Of course, I repeatedly said in this collection that I believed Osama Bin Laden was killed in 2001 at Tora Bora, and recent events have shown me to be pretty spectacularly wrong in that regard. But he's still dead in a cave in these essays. That's just how things looked to me at the time. Perhaps those things we got wrong, as well as the things we got right, will have some value to those in the future trying to make sense of these *interesting* times.

Several of these essays start out connected to some event concerning the conflict in Iraq. But re-reading them, I am continually surprised at how superficial that original intent ended up becoming. **CONFIDENCE** became – quite to my amazement – a tribute to a man I had mocked and misunderstood so terribly in my sleepwalk through adolescence. **VICTORY** too started as another look at the events in Iraq, but very quickly morphed into an examination of the State and the remarkable, almost supernatural experiment to overturn that Iron Giant. Only one essay deals exclusively with the Battle of Iraq, with no detour, and that was written, I might add, in a fit of anger after driving home and hearing on KPFK that the LA City Council had "condemned" U.S. intervention in the weeks leading up to the invasion. I live in LA. I never voted on such a resolution. The result was **WAR**. It's still the one I like least in this collection for it's jackhammer approach. You can thank the ultra-leftist Pacifica Radio for that one.

COURAGE, on the other hand – well, that one was from the heart. I love to fly, I *live* for it – that's in there, I think. And my passion for the Civil War still shines unabated, and that glow, I hope, permeates **HISTORY**, another essay I am very proud of.

I think **TRINITY** is a corker, too – just a lot of fun to write and structurally far and away my favorite. **MAGIC** is also a favorite – near and dear to my heart. And **EMPIRE** was just a kick to write. I'm very fond of that little essay. It was the first all-new thing I wrote at *Eject! Eject! Eject!*

One of the most remarkable things about this journey was the constant realization of just how little I thought about things prior to cobbling together this little soapbox. **FREEDOM** started out as a series of comments posted on Rachel Lucas' weblog. She'd said she had a friend who wanted some good arguments about gun ownership. I'd never really given it much thought before.

As a matter of fact, I'd never really given *any* of this stuff much thought before. These things seem to come not from me but *through* me. It's very unsettling sometimes, and why I am always so embarrassed, and indeed, feel quite unworthy of the mind-blowing comments I continue to receive. Thank you all, and I am asked to pass on thanks from who or whatever actually comes up with this stuff.

Finally, I did make one change in the chronological order, and that was to put **POWER** last, even though it was written before both **STRENGTH** and **DETERRENCE**. It's a much more timeless piece of work, that – and a far, far better ending for this collection.
Let me now shut up and get out of the way. We'll talk again briefly at the other end. But take this with you as you wander down these pathways with me:

I have always felt that I am nothing more than a lucky photographer, taking pictures of this magnificent country we and our parents and grandparents have built, and our children, too – all of us, together. These are not my stories. These are *our* stories. And these letters and compliments I have received over these two years do not belong to me. I put them there because they belong to you, that voice of Silent America I have been fortunate enough to hear and amplify. All of you, who do not appear on *Good Morning America* or *Nightline* or *Larry King*. You who get up every morning and remake this amazing place every day: pharmacists and secretaries and soldiers and hairdressers. I estimate I deserve about 1/290,000,000th of the credit. The rest belongs to you.

These are *your* stories.

It's been my great, great good fortune to be allowed to help tell some of them.

See you in the Epilogue.

Bill Whittle
Veteran's Day, 2004
www.ejectejecteject.com

HONOR
December 15, 2002

On October 7th, 2002 I returned to Los Angeles from Arlington National Cemetery where we interred my father, 2nd Lt. William Joseph Whittle, who died from what may have been sheer joy during a fishing trip in Canada.

My dad served in the US Army in Germany, from 1944 through 1946. He was an intelligence officer, and was responsible for recording the time of death of the convicted War Criminals at Nuremburg after the war. He saw them hanged – he stood there with a stopwatch. He was 21 years old.

My father spent two years in the U.S. Military. He spent a lifetime in the corporate world. After twenty years as a world-class hotel manager, turning entire properties from liabilities into assets, he was let go without so much as a thank-you dinner or a handshake. Twenty years of service. He was a four-star general in the corporate world for two decades, and that was his reward.

Monday afternoon, at 1 pm, I stood underneath the McClellan arch at ANC. There were 13 family members there. There were also 40 men in uniform, standing at attention in the cold. Forty strangers. Thirteen friends. I was ashamed of all the thousands I had seen pumping his hand and patting his back over all those years. Where were they now? And who are these men, who have stood here at silent attention for almost an hour as we gathered ourselves?

They took my dad's ashes, in what looked like a really nice cigar box *(what a little box for such a big man, I thought at that moment)*, and placed it in what looked like a metallic coffin on the back of a flag-draped, horse-drawn caisson. His ashes were handled by other twenty-one year old men, men as young as he had been, men whose fathers were children when my dad was in uniform. Everything was inspected, checked, and handled with awesome, palpable, radiating reverence and respect.

As we walked behind the caisson, the band was silent but for the click of sticks on the rim of the snare drums, and the hushed, clipped whisper of commands spoken so low that it seemed only the dead could hear.

And then came a moment I shall never forget, the moment I started on this journey as my father was ending his. For as the silent band stepped out from under the canopy of trees and into the cold, comfortless sunlight, there came an eruption of sound, of trumpets and drums, that knocked the cynicism and snide irony out of me like an explosion.

For that Army band played not a dirge, but a *march*...a tune that left me searching for the right adjective, which I didn't find until the flight home. It was **triumphal.** It was the sound of Caesar entering Rome; the sound of a hero coming home in trumpets and glory.

My sunglasses were no help after that. The tears rolled out from under them and I no longer cared.

My dad served for two years. He wrote on the back of his Army officer class graduation photo that he expected to die fighting for his country within a few months. Most everybody who signed his photo wrote the same thing.

My father received a military funeral: the folded flag, the 21 gun salute, the honor guard, and a Chaplain named Crisp who declared a grateful nation was welcoming their brother William home to rest among heroes.

The chaplain knelt, looking my stepmom in the eyes like this was the first time he'd ever uttered the words, and said that the men and women buried here had agreed to lay down their lives for their country and each other, and that *this*, not rank, or social status, or length in service, is what entitled them to be buried in America's most sacred ground.

Before the ceremony, I was looking at the headstones, and it's sad how each area of Arlington is like a forlorn vintage: here are buried the veterans who died around 1995, there is the 1982 pasture, the mid-fifties crop over on yonder hill. And standing between a Major and a Brigadier General, I saw a headstone for a PFC who was born in 1979, the year I entered college, and who had died in 1998. This young man, not even twenty, couldn't have been in the service for more than a few months, and yet there he lay, with the same marker as colonels and generals and the many, many sergeants that cover those fields.

That is American honor, and nowhere else in the world does it exist in such a naked, magnificent form. Each of these men and women, this band of brothers, receiving exactly the same heartfelt **respect**. For my father, who died at age 77, it was the honoring of a contract he had signed more than half a century before, a man who was by no stretch a war hero, who never saw combat, but who fully expected to never return to hunt deer again in the Pocono Mountains after he signed on the dotted line for Germany. That is a lot to ask of any teenager, whether they were born in 1925, or 1979, or 1846.

The corporate world gave my dad comfort and prestige; day to day life in the Army seems designed to eradicate every vestige of these things, but bestowed them in multitudes a half century later, when they were needed the most and when business glory had long, long faded and grayed. It was a contract paid in full, one that has given my family and me an indescribable sense of comfort and pride.

As we were leaving, it dawned on me that the ugly brown-grey building I had been looking at across the road looked suddenly familiar. I asked the funeral coordinator if that was, in fact, the Pentagon, and he replied that it was...indeed, it was the side that the aircraft struck.

On September 11, 2001, this man was about to conduct a morning service on a hill about 1/2 mile from that brown-grey wall. He heard a roar and a whine, saw a silver blur fifty feet above his head, and watched as a 757 immolated itself against the side of the Pentagon. It was my unpleasant duty to inform him that a book claiming that the plane crash never happened, but was rather an intelligence service plot, had become one of the best-selling books in France, the country my father and millions of other Americans were willing to die for in order to liberate as young men.

My mother remains, to this day, a proud British Subject, the daughter of a man Awarded the Order of the British Empire in 1954 for his service in the Royal Marines. She, my grandfather and uncle were nearly murdered by Egyptian mobs during the Suez crisis, and she is fiercely proud of both her native country and the one she married into. Yet she said that nowhere in the world do ordinary servicemen or women receive anything like this level of honor and respect and reverence, and she is right. All nations honor their generals and heroes. This nation honors privates and sergeants in indistinguishable fashion.

Walking behind the flag-draped caisson of an Army 2nd Lieutenant that day, I felt that my father was receiving the funeral of the President of the United States. And, number of people on the parade route aside, as a matter of fact, he was.

FREEDOM
December 22, 2002

When I was a little kid, I asked my dad about an image I had seen of really huge numbers of prisoners being marched to their execution in a forest clearing, guarded by perhaps five or ten men with rifles. I wanted to know why they didn't just rush the guards. I mean, it's one thing if they were heading to another miserable day at work camp, but these people were being led off to be killed, and they knew it. I mean, for God's sake, *what did they have to lose?*

I was six. My dad looked at me. He had served in the latter days of WW2 in Europe as a U.S. Army intelligence officer. No parachuting onto the decks of enemy U-Boats at night to steal Enigma machines – just newly-minted, 2nd Lieutenant grunt work. He'd been to the camps though, seen some horrible things. When I asked him why they didn't fight back or run for the woods, he said, without any arrogance or contempt or jingoism, "I don't know Billy, I can't figure that one out myself." Then there was a long moment. "But I can't imagine Americans just walking off like that, either."

Now when he said he couldn't imagine Americans marching off to their deaths, he meant, obviously, *Americans like the ones he knew.* Kids who grew up hunting, kids who got a BB gun for their fifth birthday -- tough, adventurous, American kids whose mom's never gave a second thought to them shooting their eye out with a Red Ryder air rifle.

Before we go any further, I want to be crystal clear about something: I don't believe for an instant in any genetic nonsense about slave races or nations of pure-bred heroes. That's a deadly trap, and the end result of such thinking is a place on the watchtower machine-gunning starving prisoners. But humans are the most successful species this planet has seen not for being ferocious or fast or strong or even intelligent, but for their malleability. Humans can, and do, adapt to anything. It is their **culture** that determines what is in their hearts.

Consider the case of Jews in Germany, during the 1930s: Here was a people who had been so tormented and prosecuted and psychologically beaten down that they came to believe the outrageous slander that they were guests in their own country. Behind their shuttered doors at night, they created cocoons of astonishing culture and beauty, a symphony of violins and cellos and poetry and literature. They were far over-represented in occupations we rightly esteem as among the most noble of our species: surgeons, musicians, teachers and scientists.

By any measure of human decency, these were the people that should have been helping to lead a ravaged Germany back to respect and prosperity. Yet they were massacred in their millions by brutes and sadists who sent infants to their deaths while listening to symphonies.

If it is possible to write a clearer lesson on human nature, then I cannot imagine it, nor can I imagine the amount of blood it will take to convince people unwilling to look reality in the face; that reality being that compassion, culture, law and philosophy are precious, rare and **acquired** habits that must be defended with force against people who understand nothing but force. The great failure and staggering tragedy of European Jews is that they could not accept that some of their neighbors were not as decent, humane and educated as they were. A culture that learned to survive by turning inward simply never was willing to face the reality of what they were up against; namely, that hoping for compassion and humanity from the likes of the Nazis was akin to reading poetry to a hurricane. This denial – and that is the only word for it – is, in the final horrible analysis, a form of *arrogance*, almost: the refusal to see things for what they are. A people of astonishing internal beauty simply could not look into the face of such ugliness without turning away.

And now they are dead.

And there are many intelligent, enlightened, gentle and good-hearted people today who believe exactly the same thing. If we let this self-inflicted blindness continue to gain ground, then they will get us all killed, too. And then who will put their boot on humanity's neck for the next thousand years?

I recently visited a website that featured a picture of *Star Trek's* Mr. Spock, with the caption: *My hero! Someone who thinks his way out of trouble!* The implication, of course, is that force and violence are universally to be rejected and despised as unworthy of thinking people (or Vulcans).

Well bucko, Spock carried a phaser as well as a tricorder, and he used it when he had to. If the *Star Trek* future represents a hope for our species at its most reasonable and open-minded best, it would be well to remember that the *Enterprise* carries a hell of a lot of photon torpedoes because the cause of human decency cannot be advanced if all the decent humans lie dead.

Freedom is preserved by free people. Our 40th President wrote that *"no weapon in the arsenals of the world is so formidable as the will and moral courage of free men and women."*

Free people know in their heart that they are free. Back again for a moment to a culturally rich, bathed in literature and opera, non-*simplisme* culture like 1940s Germany: I also asked my father what would happen if the Gestapo came for us one night. He said he couldn't stop them from taking us, but he could damn sure take a few of those bastards with them, and I decided right there that I'd do the same thing.

In the Warsaw Ghetto, in Solzhenitsyn's Gulags, in countless other miserable, terrifying pits of murder, some people woke up to the idea that resistance is *not* futile.

Which is why that old saw, which in my terribly, tragically misspent liberal youth I used to sneer at as the mark of a real idiot – *"they can have my gun when they pry it from my cold dead fingers"* – suddenly makes a new kind of sense to me.

That is not the statement of someone who doesn't want to give up a snowmobile or a Beemer. That is a statement that draws a line in the sand for the government, or any other oppressor, to plainly see. You want to take this freedom away from me? **COME AND GET IT.**

I believe gun ownership is the truest form of freedom, and here's why: It says you are your own person, responsible for your own actions. You are not willing to be collectively punished for the misdeeds of others. In fact, those that abuse this freedom by committing crimes are thought of and dealt with much more harshly by gun owners, as a rule, than Hollywood celebrities, precisely because a free person understands the responsibility that comes with freedom.

To the many thoughtful and intelligent Europeans and Canadians who scorn the 2nd Amendment of the US Constitution as the dangerous plaything of illiterate, mindless oafs who enjoy loud noises, let me simply refer you to that great unbiased and incorruptible teacher: History.

Ask yourselves why intellectual elites so love totalitarian states where people are unarmed and dependant sheep. Look at the examples of Hitler, Stalin, Pol Pot, Mao, and Saddam, and the horrors they have inflicted at will on their own people. And when contemplating your ever-so-sophisticated foreign policy, ask yourselves what compassionate and non-violent options you are left with when facing a determined, heartless bastard like Hitler, Napoleon, Genghis Khan or Attila.

Some say that the time for real evil like that has finally gone. I hope you are right, I really do. I don't want to go fight those bastards; I'd rather barbeque and watch the Gators. I'm sure the Jews in 1930 Germany thought such things could never happen again, not in the heart of European culture and civilization. I'm sure every bound and beaten musician, surgeon, philosopher and painter being lined up at the side of a ditch thought exactly that.

The Transnational Progressives who believe that the age of human brutality has come and gone should try and understand this about Americans like myself and others who can look such horrors in the eye: *We are not going out like that.* Get it? We'll put up with handgun murders if we have to, but we are not going down that road. As a general rule, we are quiet, peaceful, decent people with better things to do than referee endless bloodbaths abroad. But it is possible to get our attention. And believe me, you have it now, and I believe the time will come when you will regret calling us cowboys and Nazis and idiots, because the day may come when you once again need the help of a free and determined people, fighting forces you ignore not from superior sophistication but from sheer moral cowardice.

Great Britain, the philosophical home and mother to this nation, has responded to a horrible shooting tragedy by essentially disarming their entire population. Their crime rate has skyrocketed; London is now more dangerous than New York. Maybe this is a correlation without a causality. It is, of course, their decision alone to make, and history will record whether it was a wise one or not. But consider this:

A Marine Corps officer wondered to himself whether such an order to disarm law-abiding citizens would be carried out in the United States. He discovered that most of his men would not follow an order to disarm the populace by force.

This, to my mind, is the fundamental difference between the Europeans and the U.S.: We trust the people. We fought wars and lost untold husbands and brothers and sons because of this single most basic belief: **Trust the people.** Trust them with freedom. Trust them to spend their own money. Trust them to do the right thing. Trust them to defend themselves. To the degree that government can help, great – but TRUST THE PEOPLE.

It would take an army – not an army of celebrities or trial lawyers, an actual *shooting army* –to forcibly disarm this nation. Who will do the dirty work? Volunteer citizen soldiers, that's who – and the first guns they'd have to turn in would be their own. See, we don't have shock troops here, boyo. No Republican Guards, Special or otherwise; no Hussars, no Cossacks, no SS; we lack Praetorian elites, Napoleonic bodyguard units - any of that ideologically inculcated poison. Just kids serving their country, making some money for college. You think those people would fire on a crowd of American citizens fighting to preserve a right declared at the top of the Bill of Rights, when they themselves have taken an oath to defend that same document? Think again.

Unlike those poor, unarmed, psychologically battered Jews, Poles, homosexuals and uncounted other souls lost in the mid 1940s, *no one* is pulling *any* kids out of this crowd's house at night and going home fully staffed, ready to try again tomorrow. Understand? That is the point.

Here is a sociological experiment that might have something to teach us:

Kick down 100 doors of self-proclaimed French pacifists, grab the women and kids, and haul them away. Then try again in Texas, with 100 NRA members. Collate, or rather, have a surviving relative collate the results. Extrapolate the abductors' rates of casualties to determine the total number of murdering swine needed. See what percentage of jackbooted thugs have a suicide wish and then determine the number of men you will need to disarm, kidnap and murder 50 million armed people.

You will need a lot of men. More than you can raise.

These *trust the people* freedoms are so deeply engrained in the fabric of America as to be almost hereditary, I think. I used to worry that we'd bred that out of us, and then along comes Todd Beamer and company on United Flight 93, who, first among us that day, realized they were being marched to their deaths and decided to do something about it. Not for themselves, because by taking that action they knew they were doomed. They did it for **us**. Not only to save the lives of those on the ground for whom their aircraft was headed, but to remind us of who we are as a people, to add to the list of ordinary Americans who can gather extraordinary courage and resolve because they have been *trusted* all their lives by their government and their fellow citizens.

We are a nation of unruly immigrants, self-selecting people who placed bold action above endless suffering, sold what little they had and bought passage to take a chance on a place they had never seen except in their quiet hopes, a land our 40th President, Ronald Reagan, described as *"a beacon, a magnet for all who must have freedom, for all the pilgrims from all the lost places who are hurtling through the darkness, toward home."* Intellectuals have called Ronald Reagan a moron, but that is to be expected from people incapable of being moved by anything other than the sound of their own bitter and small voices in a world too full of hope for them to grasp.

We are, and remain, the descendents of people who had had quite enough of being told what to do by inbred aristocratic fops and unelected, intellectual sadists. When Europeans call us *simplisme*, they show themselves incapable of recognizing the difference between **intelligence**, of which we are amply endowed, and **intellectualism**, that circle-jerk of coffee table revolution and basement politburo planning that we have never had much patience with.

To those who doubt our mental sophistication, I would remind you that our *grandparents* walked upon the moon. And why is it that of all we produce and all we exult, the only things that seem to have caught on in Europe are McDonald's and *Baywatch?* That says much more about them than it does about us, and none of it good, I'm afraid.

We as a nation suffer an appalling number of handgun-related deaths each year – perhaps 11,000 of them. The number is not important; each is a personal tragedy and those lives can never be replaced. If we attempt to reduce this horrible number by banning handguns, we are taking away the property of a person who has broken no laws by a government whose legitimacy is determined by a document that specifically allows that property, namely guns.

Destroy that trust by punishing the innocent, by pulling a plank from the Bill of Rights, and the contract between the government and the people falls apart. Once the Second Amendment goes, the First will soon follow, because if some unelected elite determines that the people can't be trusted with dangerous guns then it's just a matter of time until they decide they can't be trusted with dangerous ideas, either. Dangerous ideas have killed many millions more people than dangerous handguns – listen to the voices from the Gulag, the death camps, and all the blood-soaked killing fields through history.

The Framers, in their wisdom, put the 2nd Amendment there to give teeth to the revolutionary, unheard-of idea that the power rests with We The People. They did not depend on good will or promises. They made sure that when push came to shove we'd be the ones doing the pushing and shoving, not the folks in Washington. And by the way, gun rights supporters are frequently mocked when they say it deters foreign invasion – *after all, come on, grow up, be realistic: Who's nuts enough to invade America?* **Exactly.** *It's unthinkable.* **Good.** 2nd Amendment Mission 1 accomplished.

But back to the undeniable domestic cost: When confronted with the idea of banning handguns to reduce this horrible toll, many handgun defenders are tempted to point to the numbers killed on the highways each year --- perhaps four times that number --- and ask why we don't ban cars as well.

The logical response is that bans on travel – cars, airplanes, etc. – are a false analogy compared to banning guns because cars have a clear benefit while guns don't do anything other than kill what they are aimed at.

While that is exactly true, I think it misses the point, which to me is simply this: We'd never ban automobile travel to avoid thousands of highway deaths. It's clearly not worth it in both economic and personal freedom terms. We choose, reluctantly, and with many a lost loved one in mind, to keep on driving.

Here is my dry-eyed, cold-hearted, sad conclusion: I believe that the freedom, convenience and economic viability provided by the automobile is worth the 40,000 lives we lose to automotive deaths each year – a number made more horrible by the fact that perhaps 40% are related to drunk driving and are therefore preventable.

By the same calculation, I accept that the freedoms entrusted to the people of the United States is worth the 11,000 lives we lose to gun violence each year.

I wish I could make both those numbers go away. I will support any reasonable campaign to make them as low as possible.

But understand this: 11,000 handgun deaths a year, over four years is very roughly 50,000 killed. In Nazi Germany, an unarmed population was unable to resist the abduction and murder of 6,000,000 people in a similar period: a number 120 times higher. Throw in the midnight murders of the Soviets, the Chinese, the various and sundry African and South American genocides and purges and political assassinations and that number grows to many hundreds, if not several thousand times more killings in unarmed populations.

Visualize this to fully appreciate the point. Imagine the Super Bowl. Every player on the field is a handgun victim. All the people in the stands are the victims who were unable to resist with handguns. Those are historical facts.

I, myself, am willing to pay that price as a society – knowing full well that I or a loved one may be part of that terrible invoice. I wish it was lower. Obviously, I wish it didn't exist at all. But any rational look into the world shows us places where the numbers of innocents murdered by their own governments in unarmed nations are far, far higher.

Of course, many societies have far lower numbers. Japan is a fine example. I'm sure if the United States had 2000 years of a culture whose prize assets are conformity and submission then our numbers would be a lot lower. Alas, we are not that society. Thank God, we are not that society.

It is abundantly clear that the rate of handgun murders in the United States is not uniform. Very large murder rates can be observed in small, exceedingly violent populations of every race in this country, and these rates seem to be more related to issues of education and the breakdown of families; specifically, the absence of strong, rational and *restrained* father figures . Certainly guns are freely available in areas where our murder rates are appallingly high. They are also found in very large numbers in communities where handgun crime is virtually nonexistent.

Doesn't that tell us that there is something deeper at work here? Could it be, perhaps, that the problem is not with the number of guns in this country but rather in the hearts of those who we allow to wield them, repeatedly? Could it really be as simple as apprehending, and punishing, those that would do harm to innocents and to civilization? Rather than banning guns, should we not attack the moral rot that infests these small, violent populations of every color who put such horrible numbers at our feet?

Assume for a moment you could vaporize every gun on the planet. Would crime go away? Or would ruthless, physically strong gangs of young men be essentially able to roam free and predate at will?

The history of civilization shows time and time again how decent, sophisticated city dwellers amass wealth through cooperation and the division of labor – only to be victimized by ruthless gangs of raping, looting cutthroats who couldn't make a fruit basket, sweeping down on them, murdering them and carting away the loot, to return a few years later, forever, ad infinitum. Vikings, Mongols, desperadoes of every stripe – they are a cancer on humanity but there they are and there they have always been.

If civilization is worth having – and it is – then it has to be defended, because the restraining virtues of justice, compassion and respect for laws are products of that civilizing force and completely unknown to those who would do it harm.

Therefore, since I believe in this civilization, in its laws, science, art and medicine, I believe we must be prepared to defend it against what I feel no embarrassment for calling the Forces of Darkness. Those forces could be raiders on horseback, jackbooted Nazi murderers, ecstatic human bombs or some kid blowing away a shopkeeper.

For the gun-ban argument to be convincing, you'd have to show me a time before shopkeepers were blown away, hacked away, pelted away or whatever the case may be. You would have to show me a time in history before the invention of the firearm, when crime and raiding and looting did not exist, when murders and rapes did not exist. We may lose 11,000 people to handguns a year. How many would we lose without any handguns, if murderers and rapists roamed free of fear, ignoring reprisal from citizens or police? I don't know. You don't know either. Maybe it's a lot fewer people, and maybe, in a world where strength and ruthlessness trump all, it would be a far higher one.

You may argue that only the police should be allowed to carry guns. Consider this carefully. Do we really want to create an unelected subculture that views itself as so elite and virtuous as to be the only ones worthy of such power, trust and authority? Have we not clearly seen the type of people drawn to such exclusive positions of authority, and the attitudes and arrogance it promotes?

Furthermore, I can't see any moral distinction between a policeman and a law-abiding citizen. Policemen are drawn from the ranks of law-abiding citizens. They are not bred in hydroponics tanks. They are expected to show restraint and use their weapon as a last resort. Millions upon millions of citizens, a crowd more vast than entire armies of police, do exactly this every day.

If all of these horrors had sprung up as a result of the invention of the handgun I'd be right there beside those calling for their destruction.

But clearly, this is not the case. In our cowboy past we used to say that *"God created Man, but Sam Colt made them equal."* This is simple enough to understand. It means that a villager, let's say a schoolteacher, can defeat a human predator who may have spent his entire life practicing the art of war. Firearms are what tipped the balance toward civilization by eliminating a lifetime spent studying swordplay or spear play or pointed-stick play. The bad guys have always used weapons and they always will. The simple truth about guns is that they are damn effective and easy to operate. They level the playing field to the point where a woman has a chance against a gang of thugs or a police officer can control a brawl.

I don't see how vaporizing all the guns in the world would remove crime or violence - history shows these have always been with us and show no signs of responding favorably to well-reasoned arguments or harsh language. I wish it were not true. I wish the IRS did not exist either, but there it is.

Criminals, and criminal regimes ranging from The Brow-Ridged Hairy People That Live Among the Distant Mountains all the way through history to the Nazis and the Soviets, have and will conspire to take by force what they cannot produce on their own. These people must be stopped. The genius of the 2nd Amendment is that it realizes that these people could be anybody - including the U.S. Army. That is why this power, like the other powers, is vested **in the people.** Nowhere else in the world is this the case.

You can make a solid argument that the United States is, by almost any measure, the most prosperous, successful nation in history. I'm not claiming this is because every American sleeps with a gun under the pillow – the vast majority do not. I *do* claim it is the result of a document that puts faith and trust in the people – trusts them with government, with freedom, and with the means of self-defense. You cannot remove that lynchpin of trust without collapsing the entire structure. Many observers of America never fully understand what we believe in our bones, namely, that the government doesn't tell us what we can do – *we* tell *those* bastards just how far they can go.

Of course, all of this is completely whimsical, because, like nuclear weapons, guns are here and they are not going to go away. You cannot just vaporize them. Honest people might be compelled to turn in their weapons; criminals clearly will not. So what do you propose? Forget the moral high ground of gun ownership. Again a simple truth, often maligned but demonstrably dead-on accurate: *When guns are outlawed, only outlaws will have guns.*

The American Revolution surely is unique in the sense that the ringleaders – Washington, Jefferson, Adams, Franklin, Hamilton, etc. – were men of property, wealth and prestige; in other words, men with something to lose. Compare this to any other revolution in history, where the ringleaders were outsiders; plotters staring in through the windows of prosperity, powerless. The Russian Revolution, French Revolution, etc – these were joined by desperate people fighting mind-numbing poverty and severe political repression.

And yet the Founding Fathers were men who were as well-off as any men on earth at the time, and furthermore, any of them could have been (and were) political leaders under His Majesty's government. The average colonial farmer likewise led a life far more comfortable than those of his cousins in Europe, to say nothing of Asia or Africa.

For all practical intents and purposes, these people had absolutely nothing to gain, and everything in the world to lose, by taking on the greatest military force the world had ever known. Why would they do this? What possible motivation could well-off, comfortable people have?

Militarily, they seemed certain to lose, and they knew before they started – and Patrick Henry made that abundantly clear – that they would be hanged as common criminals if they failed.

Of course, the answer is, they did it to be free. And they did it to make the rest of their nation – the poor, the disenfranchised – free as well. And it is clear as crystal from their collective writings that they took that risk to make Noam Chomsky and Michael Moore and the rest of us in their unseen posterity free, too. They could look down the dim, moonlit riverbanks of the future and see a society worthy of their sacrifice and determination.

They knew that God, (or for me, chance perhaps) had put them together in a time and place where bold, courageous action followed by much suffering, doubt, blood and fear could, perhaps, unleash in mankind an energy source the likes of which they barely imagine.

So for me, a child of that bet – that guess, that commitment, that roll of the dice – for *me*, I owe them the defense of that freedom, and I will do my poor mite to pass it on as best I can. These men pledged to each other their Lives, their Fortunes and their sacred Honor. They pledged that to *me*. I owe them. I **do not** have the right to take away someone else's freedom and property – it is offensive to me to even contemplate it. Of course, if someone breaks the freedom/responsibility covenant by committing a crime, then all bets are off. To that extent, I view handgun murderers not just as criminals but as traitors as well.

I hate seeing our kids get shot on the street, I hate it, *I hate it*. But that is the cost of freedom. People get horribly killed on Spring Break road trips to Florida at age 18. They're driving drunk. We could prevent them from going. We would save lives. Enron and MCI steal like the worst characters from Dickens, taking people's Christmas dinners so they can have gold plated toilets. We could regulate more, make things harder for the millions of honest businesses that build and trade honorably each day. The day may come when someone flies a Cessna into a stadium. We can ban the airplanes. Ditto for pleasure boats. We can ban and confiscate and regulate to our hearts content, a*nd we will undoubtedly save many, many innocent lives by doing so.* All for the price of a little freedom.

I believe we should punish the perpetrators. I will not agree to restrict the freedoms of the vast numbers of people who abide by the concomitant responsibility and live lives of honesty and decency.

And there is more than the physical restriction of freedoms: There is the slow erosion of self-reliance, self-confidence and self-determination among a nation. The more your government restricts your options, the more you psychologically look to government to keep you safe, fed, clothed, housed and sustained.

There is a word for people who are fed, clothed, housed and sustained fully by others, and that word is SLAVES.

If Congress were occupied by angels and Michael sat in a throne of glory in the Oval Office, I would listen to what they said for my own greater good. But I have noticed that no government is made of angels, and that many seem to be exclusively staffed by members of the opposite persuasion. So who determines how much freedom we trade for how much security? *People* do. People are not unknown to place their own interests above those of others. There is even a vanishingly remote chance that a moral titan like Jacques Chiraq has at some point perhaps put personal interest above those of his constituents. The real genius of the Founding Fathers was that these great and good men had the foresight and the courage to look into their own darker motives, and construct a system that prevents the accumulation of power.

The Constitution they created could only be torn up by force of arms. And that is why the Founders left that power in the hands of the people, who together can never be cowed by relatively small numbers of thugs holding the only guns.

As PJ O'Rourke points out, the U.S. Constitution is less than a quarter the length of the owner's manual for a 1998 Toyota Camry, and yet it has managed to keep 300 million of the world's most unruly, passionate and energetic people safe, prosperous and free. Smarter people than me may disagree with that document – I'm for not touching a comma.

So as a proud son of those brave men, I'll take freedom – all of it – and because I accept the benefits of those freedoms, I'll solemnly take the responsibilities as well. I may someday lose a child on a trip to Spring Break, but I'll never lock them in the basement to keep them safe. And I'll accept the fact that living in Los Angeles puts me at risk for being shot to death because I feel the freedom is worth it. I breathe that freedom every day, and hey, we all gotta go sometime. I'll continue to fly experimental airplanes because I am careful, meticulous, precise and responsible, and yet the day may come when I am out of altitude, out of airspeed and out of ideas all at the same time. Oh well. I have seen and done things up there that you cannot imagine and I cannot describe.

Freedom.

Our failures and disgraces cruelly remind us that we, like every other government, are composed of fallible men and women with no divine ability to read the future or foresee all outcomes. But these failures are failures of *action*, action borne of confidence and a belief in our way of life, and come all the more painful for their contrast to the everyday standards to which we hold ourselves as a people and a nation. For it is an undeniable fact that no great nation in history has held a shadow of our measure of power, and yet exercised it with such restraint, nor does any time in the bloody history of warfare reflect a people so magnanimous in victory against enemies sworn to our murder and destruction. From our first hour, we have been, and remain, the beacon of hope and freedom for a world desperate and longing for such an example, and we can measure our success in building such a place by the numbers of those who are literally dying in an attempt to come and be part of it.

Our ancestors made their choice and here we are. I respect anyone's right to chose differently. I only speak up to defend the choice we Americans made as a deeply spiritual one, borne of reflection and danger and a spectacular triumph against all odds. I will not stand idly by to hear people denounce our freedoms as the dimwitted macho posturing of a mob of illiterate uncultured idiots who are so vulgar and uncouth as to still believe in Hollywood myths manufactured for our simple, complacent, unsophisticated nature.

From the Revolution until today, the choice for full freedom with all its accompanying excesses and failures is a profoundly well-reasoned, moral and ethical choice, and the result has been national and personal success unparalleled in the history of this world.

I am deeply proud to be a member of such a magnificent group of people.

I hope to God I can give back as much as I owe.

EMPIRE

December 27, 2002

Many, many years ago, I heard second hand a true story that still makes me smile. It was the story of an American walking down the Champs-Elysees in Paris. He was enjoying the day, going nowhere in particular.

After a few moments, he came upon a small knot of people clustered in a tight circle, and as he drew nearer, he heard the sound of a guitar. Even from a distance he could tell that most, perhaps all of the group were Americans – from just-off-the-plane tourists to seasoned, long-term ex-pats. They were smiling as they clustered around a street musician, who was strumming away energetically. Many in the audience had tears streaming down their faces as he sang:

Come and listen to my story
'bout a man named Jed,
A poor mountaineer
Barely kept his family fed.
And then one day
He was shootin' at some food
When up from the ground
Come a-bubblin' crude.

Then, with all the passion of Bill Travis and Davy Crockett calling the Alamo defenders to the ramparts, this crowd of Americans hollered at the top of their lungs: "OIL, THAT IS! BLACK GOLD! TEXAS TEA!"

Shocked, mystified and undoubtedly worried for their safety and those of their children, the Parisians continued walking by, no doubt giving them a wide berth and that expression we see so frequently from their waiters and maitre'Ds. To the Americans, they and the rest of their city no longer existed, and the unknown musician – God bless him, whoever and wherever he may be – grinned like a monkey and picked up the pace:

Just sit right back
And you'll hear a tale
A tale of a fateful trip…
That started from
This tropic port
Aboard this tiny ship.

The smiles, the group singing – you can just take that for granted. But the tears, the weeping – we can understand that too. The loneliness, the longing for the simple comfort we find in a kindred spirit, far from home. The instant camaraderie – *"Pittsburgh?* **Go Steelers!"**

And there's something just so damn carefree and glorious about a bunch of oblivious Yankee tourists making complete idiots of themselves, surrounded by two thousand years of culture and art, banding together to sing about the *Modern Stone-Age Fam-i-lee!* and think about home…

You want to go where people know
People are all the same
You want to go where
Everybody knows your name.

In '98 I spent a terrific three months in Brisbane, Australia. OZ is home to the nicest, most fun-loving people who ever walked the earth. I went boogey-boarding in the Coral Sea and walked on white beaches so fine and clean that the sand squeaked like new sneakers on polished hardwood with every step you took.

But the night I got up and sang a karaoke Danny Zuko to an adorable, blonde, Australian Sandy and a mob of fifty drunken Aussies torturing "Summer Nights" from *Grease*…well, to be perfectly honest, I was just so damn proud. That American accent really sold it. My money was no good in the joint after that.

For those of us paying attention, it looks like the world is getting to be not the same cozy place it was when I swam in the Coral Sea or The Unknown Musician put his hat down for a few francs. Something has happened. We all know what that something was, and there's nothing worthwhile I can add about that clear, blue, fall morning.

Something has happened to us as a people, too – most of us, anyway. And the rest of the world looks at us the same way those Parisians did that harmless afternoon on the Champs Elysees: nervous and apprehensive and deeply concerned. We have already deeply shocked and surprised our enemies – those that are still alive. But from those we thought friends we have heard a growing stream of bitter invective and shrill hysteria that has risen in pitch above the range of human hearing and is now audible only to the neighborhood dogs. We are called unsophisticated, swaggering cowboys who have somehow stumbled upon vast power, and many of our erstwhile allies have taken to talking to us as you would a four year old holding a loaded gun.

Our critics watch us with an intensity most of us cannot believe or perhaps even imagine, and they are looking carefully, waiting to see what the American behemoth will do next.

At home and abroad, there have been renewed charges of American Imperialism, of cultural and economic hegemony, and of determined efforts on our part to subjugate and dominate the people of the world through our greed, our ignorance and our cruelty.

Once again, events not of our doing have thrust the United States into a position where military engagements on the far side of the world seem inevitable, and no less inevitable are the charges of American Imperialism. If we are to be worthy of the manifest blessings and freedoms we enjoy, we must take these charges very seriously and be as ruthless in our self-examination as we are on the battlefield.

Unlike the miserable, poorly trained, ill-fed and disgracefully led legions of conscripts we will face on that battlefield, our soldiers are citizen volunteers, and such free people need, and deserve, a cause worthy of their hardships and sacrifice.

And there is no disputing the fact that it is *we* who are going over *there*. To the degree that there are civilian casualties (and there will be), it will be their civilians, not ours, that are dying. There *are* justifications for such a course of action, justifications that tower above the base and criminal plunder of territory and resources. So if we are about to go and inflict such violence, we had better be damn sure we check our motives before we go.

Accusations of "Imperialism" are flung at us so frequently, and met with so little defense, that it is actually shocking to see how easily such a *simplisme* charge can be overturned.

To be *Imperial* is to possess, or hope to possess, an Empire, and these slanders have been made for about a century now. The Cambridge International Dictionary of English defines "empire" as "*a group of countries ruled by a single person, government or country.*" Oxford paperback dictionary calls it "*a large group of states under single authority.*" Cambridge goes on to define "imperialism" as "*a system in which a country rules other countries, sometimes having used force to obtain power over them.*"

Any rational person can see that the United States does not meet these qualifications by any stretch of the imagination. What nations do we rule? Whose legislative bodies can we overturn with a wave of the hand? Where on this planet do people live under an American flag who do not wish to? And as Jonah Goldberg correctly points out, where are our governors and our tax collectors so that we can siphon off the meager wages of our Imperial Slaves? What kind of empire does not have these imperial mechanisms?

At the end of World War II, America stood astride the world as the unchallenged military and economic power. The terrible might of Germany and Japan lay crushed in smoldering ruin. Great Britain, bled white by the near-total loss of two successive generations of their best and brightest, was in barely better shape. China was a collection of pre-industrial peasants fighting a bitter civil war, and nowhere in the rest of Asia, Africa and South America did there exist anything more than local defense militias.

Only the Soviets remained as a potent military force – and that force was essentially tactical, not strategic, in nature. While strong in tanks, artillery and men, it had no navy to speak of, and an air force consisting mostly of close support ground-attack aircraft such as the Il-2 Sturmovik. While effective against ground targets, the Soviets in 1945 had nothing resembling US heavy bombers such as the B-17, the B-24, or the magnificent B-29.

On the other hand, the United States not only had what was far and away the world's preeminent Navy; we also had large numbers of long-range strategic bombers and swarms of highly-seasoned fighter escorts. We had a Marine Corps flush with victories: battle-hardened men who had invented through blood and horror the means to go ashore on enemy beaches **and stay there.** We had an Army whose courage and skill in battle was unsurpassed, and whose critical supply and ordinance staffs were, by far, the best in the world.

And, of course, we had the atomic bomb, and the will to use it.

History has never, *and will never*, record a time when such unchallenged power existed in the hands of a nation, nor of a time when opposing forces were so weak and in such a state of disarray and abject surrender.

And these feared and ruthless Americans, a people who had incinerated cities in Europe and Japan and whose ferocity and tenacity on island jungles and French beaches had brought fanatical warrior cultures to their knees – what did these new conquerors of the world do?

They went home is what they did. They did pause for a few years to rebuild the nations sworn to their destruction and the murder of their people. They carbon-copied their own system of government and enforced it on their most bitterly hated enemy, a people who have since given so much back to the world as a result of this generosity. They left troops in and sent huge sums of money to Europe to rebuild what they all knew would eventually become trading partners, but also determined competitors. Then they sent huge steel blades through their hard-earned fleets of ships and airplanes and came home to get on with their lives in peace and quiet.

Oh, and some of the islands they had visited had asked to remain under the American flag as territories and protectorates, free to leave whenever they chose.

We are still too close to our actions in those critical years to fully grasp the meaning of what we did. Distant history will show it to be the most magnanimous act in human history, a test of national character passed with such glory and distinction that it baffles and amazes both our friends and enemies to this day.

Of course, many of our critics will claim that those were the actions of a better, simpler America, a place long gone and nothing like the cruel monstrosity we have become today. But isn't it odd that those who call us Imperialists are the first to point out our overwhelming strength – a relative strength that is starting to approach once again that which we held in 1946? Surely, with the political, economic and military power we command today, we could safely assume the mantle of Imperialism – *"a system in which a country rules other countries, sometimes having used force to obtain power over them."* -- pretty much at will. And yet we do not.

Once again we see the posters calling for NO BLOOD FOR OIL. Putting aside whether or not oil is indeed worth fighting for, let us look at a past so recent as to be indicative of the people we are today.

In 1991, NO BLOOD FOR OIL had an actual point to make, for during the Gulf War we were indeed fighting to keep oil supplies out of the hands of a madman who would, perhaps – and eventually did – try to hold the world hostage to his ambitions by trying to control or destroy this vital resource.

After handing him the worst defeat in modern history, and once again with vast numbers of battle-hardened and victorious troops in place, the United States could have simply claimed the Iraqi and Kuwaiti oil fields as spoils of war. It was clearly the Imperialist thing to do.

Furthermore, it was a *fait accompli* – already done. There was no further risk to us. The Republican Guard was running as fast as their stolen Mercedes-Benz's would carry them. We had achieved such a total and spectacular victory that our pilots – men called baby-killers, sadists, murderers and worse – refused to drop their weapons on legitimate military targets because the victory was so one-sided that they in their decency could no longer continue to do what they were ordered to do.

And so what did these American Imperialists do with the spoils of such victory, with the precious, *precious* oilfields completely and totally ours? We sent our best people over there to put out the fires. And then we came home. **Again.**

How many times will we have to do this before our critics are able to discern a pattern? How many provocations and taunts and slander will we have to endure before anti-Americans wake up to the simple truth that brings us home time and time again, which is simply this: **For the first time in history, a nation powerful enough to rule the world has simply refused to do so.** It is a moral and ethical choice we make as a people. More than that; it is *data*. It is *evidence*.

People who ascribe to us the most base motives imaginable, using ancient rhetoric from 80 years of Marxist failure have, as usual, had to confront the fact that everything they believe in is demonstrably and spectacularly **wrong**. Despite their shrieking words and foaming mouths, the history of our actions makes liars of them all. It is a truth so *simple*, written so large and so clearly, that even the most liberal among us can understand it.

Don't let them use that word, "imperialism," unchallenged again.

There is no American Empire. There is, however, the possibility of American *Hegemony.* Back to the dictionaries:

Oxford Online is shockingly direct: "Hegemony: noun. *Leadership.*" Clearly, by Oxford's definition, we are an Hegemony.

But it gets more complicated. Merriam-Webster defines it as *"preponderant influence or authority over others,"* while Cambridge weighs in with *"the position of being the strongest and most powerful and therefore controlling others."*

"Preponderant influence" and *"the strongest and most powerful"* are hard to disagree with. Those seem indisputable facts as applied to the United States, whether it be in the area of culture, politics, science and engineering, or our military prowess. Where the term comes into question lies in whether or not we use "authority over others" and are "therefore controlling others."

We are widely criticized among Europeans for what they call our cultural and economic hegemony. They decry our pop culture as vulgar and commercial, and in fact, it often is. McDonald's are now everywhere on the European continent, and we are reminded what horrible, fattening food it is. Agreed.

What doesn't seem to get through their anti-populist, anti-American blinders is that basic economic principle of supply and demand. I suppose we shouldn't be too shocked to hear this. The birthplace, intellectual home and last bastion of Marxism has always had a tough time with economic reality.

They also have a tough time with democracy, and the idea of people – you know, *the masses* – making their own decisions. And the thing that breaks the heart of every European elitist is the inescapable fact that McDonald's and *Spider-Man* are huge in Europe, because *their own people* can't get enough of it.

I have never been to France myself, but I would presume that daily life there does not consist of squads of heavily armed US Marines rounding up the terrified population, herding them into McDonald's at gunpoint, and shaking their last euros out of them. When France passes laws saying that some minimal percentage of their television programming must be produced in France, then that is an admission – and it must be, if you will pardon the pun, a *galling* one – that huge numbers of their people prefer our culture over their own.

Fact is, dreadful or not, McDonald's is not subsidized by the US Department of World Hegemony. They are a business concern. The day European customers stop eating at McDonald's, the McDonald's *will* go away.

But they do not. They are growing like mushrooms. American television programming has to be legally constrained. I suspect that *Spider-Man* out-drew more Europeans in a weekend than all of the films of Truffaut's did in the United States over forty years.

This is telling them something, and what it is telling them is that our culture has a greater hold over the imaginations of their own people than theirs does.

To the Average French Citizen, I imagine *Spider-Man* and McDonald's represent more or less what they do to Americans: a fun couple of hours, a few laughs, and something quick to scarf down when you're in a hurry. Big deal.

But to the deep-thinking elites of Europe, these trends are catastrophic, and terrifying. For it shows them, yet again, that a mob of boorish, unsophisticated, common brutes – that'd be us – is able to produce art and music and *culture* that cleans the clock of any nation that lets it in the door.

Spider-Man and McDonalds, and the long lines of their own countrymen waiting eagerly for a taste of them, prove to them daily that the European cultural superiority that they so deeply believe in is...*how do we say this delicately?*...uh, **wrong.**

And of course, being unwilling to face these unpleasant logical inferences, the blame has to be put somewhere. And who better to blame than a blinded, staggering, idiotic Cyclops, smashing all the delicate china in its drunken, obnoxious rampage?

So, are we being an hegemony? Are we using some "authority over others" to force our cultural and political will on unsuspecting, defenseless people? Or do those people, from their own free will, choose to enjoy American movies and food and music and television because it has somehow managed to tap into the human spirit, into a sense of playfulness and freedom and above all, *optimism* – things that all people crave, and that their own dark, brooding, pessimistic outlets have failed to deliver? Are these common Europeans being brainwashed by the orbiting Yankee Mind-Control Ray, or is the idea of a place where *everybody knows your name* or a beat-up teenage kid who can fly through canyons of skyscrapers on gossamer webs something that just about everyone wants to be a part of?

I studied film in college. I sat through *Jules et Jim, The Bicycle Thief, 1900, Satyricon* and *The Grand Illusion*. Watching them was **work**. I enjoyed just about all of these and many other mov – sorry, films – and I am a better person for having seen them, but some of them – like a recent Polish entry in the Academy Awards, *"Life as a Fatal, Sexually Transmitted Disease,"* well, that approached prolonged oral surgery in terms of its enjoyment value.

You don't have to have the vast intellectual reserves of a French Minister of Culture to understand why our movies and music have such appeal abroad. They are, more often than not, each small ambassadors of freedom and optimism. From James Dean to Brad Pitt, Americans are cool; cool because they don't spend their evening sitting around bumming cigarettes and discussing global warming. They have bad guys to fight and motorcycles to ride, vast stretches of open road to get lost in and a disdain for any authority whatsoever. Where the European hero is a deeply conflicted soul lost in an existentialist nightmare, the American counterpart is a member of a rag-tag group of Rebels flying out to destroy the Death Star. Or a no-nonsense cop who plays by his own rules. Or an ordinary person, who, as the result of chance (*Spider-Man*), determination (*Batman*) or accident of birth (*Superman*), uses amazing personal power to aid the weak and fight evil.

These are our myths. They lack the patina of history that elevates those of the Greeks and Norse and countless other mythologies. But they are not created in a vacuum. These stories come from our common heritage and our common beliefs. Our heroes are what we make them, and for this country, the most successful have been young men and women thrust into extraordinary circumstances, who fight evils and monsters and never, *ever* use their powers for personal gain.

Yes, these are fantasies. *No,* of course real Americans are not so altruistic. But these are the standards we create for ourselves, and these American heroes represent what we represent as a nation. Action over endless discussion and moral paralysis. Rebellion against authority. Defense of the weak and helpless. And most of all, the optimism of the happy ending.

We get a lot of criticism from our betters about how shallow and mindless the Hollywood ending is. Fair enough. It does turn its back on the untidiness of reality. But it is also an expression of how we would have things turn out in a perfect world, a world where freedom and justice triumph and reign. These are the things we believe in, and these are, not surprisingly, *immensely* attractive to the rest of the world.

Much of that world is now going through a state of cognitive dissonance regarding America and her people. In some places, this split-personality disorder is so intense as to cause us real concern.

Talk to the vaunted "Arab Street" about America. Watch as their eyes glaze over with hatred and loathing and a desire to see us wiped off the face of the earth as criminals and infidels. Then something amazing happens. Time and time again, after expressing their view that there is no higher calling for their sons and daughters than to kill as many Americans as possible, watch what happens when asked if they want to visit the US.

On a table, place a $100 dollar bill, keys to a nearby Mercedes, a steak and lobster dinner and a US green card, and see which one disappears first.

These people, common people who spend their entire day sipping coffee and fantasizing about our violent demise, want nothing more than to go to Disney World (presumably they will blow themselves to pieces *after* they get through the lines at *Pirates of the Caribbean.*) They want to live in nice houses and drive nice cars, just as we do. They want to live in affluence and security – like the Americans. They want everything we have, and admit it cheerfully. And then, some of them revert to planning how to blow up, shoot, poison or infect every last one of us.

How do they sleep with this contradiction? I personally find Islamic fundamentalists revolting, violent, ignorant and cruel. I have no desire whatsoever to visit Cairo or Damascus or Amman. To the extent that they want this fight I am ready to give it to them, with no schizophrenic mental contortions.

Mohammad Atta spent some of his last days in Las Vegas. *That* must have put the zap on the head of that murdering, smug bastard. He could have despised it from a distance and kept his Muslim soul pure for the butchery ahead. But he and his colleagues did not. They drank alcohol and cavorted with strippers. They could not resist the temptations. Even they, the most committed haters of what we are, could not stay away from what we have to offer.

To be honest, I think the very presence of America drives these Jihadists insane.

Promised world domination from their God and their holy Koran, they see around them nothing but failure and frustration and humiliation; while on the far side of the world lies a nation which, in their minds, has no culture and no history, and is populated by 300 million people bound and determined to break every one of their prohibitions on sexuality, drinking, gambling, and trade. As Steven Den Beste has pointed out brilliantly and often at www.denbeste.nu, our very *existence* calls to lie everything they believe in.

Again, paraphrasing my friend Steven, they look out from under a repressive, brutal government and a religion that demands obedience, conformity and denial of all natural desires...and see in us a society so free and comfortable with ourselves that we had the nerve, the *audacity* to include *"life, liberty **and the pursuit of happiness"*** as inalienable rights!

I have no trouble understanding why such fanatical elements of Islam want to see us destroyed. What I do find hard to understand is how so many of them love us with the look of little children promised a trip to The Magic Kingdom. For many, many people on "The Arab Street" the very idea of coming to the US fills them with visible glee. I don't think I will ever understand how they can turn this inner argument down enough to be able to sleep at night.

In one sense perhaps, we are, in fact, an Empire. **We are an empire of the mind**, a place whose dreams and ideals have colonized the world. We are a black hole of desire upon which billions place their unfocused hopes. And yet, to them it seems as if we turn them away. We dangle freedom and hope and comfort in front of them with a glimpse into our everyday lives though television and movies. They want what we have, desperately. And they hate us for not giving it to them.

Well, sooner or later they are going to have to grow up a little and face some unpleasant truths. These people want the fruits of our success; they want our freedoms and our wealth and our confidence. But they are not willing to do the work. They are not willing to pay for it.

They wonder why we do not come and set them free from their own governments, why we don't send our sons and daughters around the world to get killed in order to break their self-imposed shackles. They wonder why we don't let all of them into the Magic Kingdom. They do not see, because they do not *wish* to see, that these freedoms and ideals cannot be dispensed like Hershey bars from a passing Jeep.

No one gave us our freedom – *we earned it*. We fought and died for it. We have paid a terrible price in blood and treasure to keep that freedom. We fight and die to this day to preserve it. Right now, at this instant, American kids have **chosen** to be sitting in foxholes or cooped up in the bowels of ships, trading the liberty of their youth for poor pay and drab conditions to allow us to keep these freedoms. We will again ask some of these people to die for us, and some of them will.

To those poor suffering billions out there who want what we have, our refusal to hand our success to them on a platter makes us cold and inhuman and uncaring. But freedom is not a gift, it is an idea which only becomes a *right* when it has been paid for, and to that extent our edifice of prosperity and success is built on a deep and strong foundation that they simply do not have.

These foundations are well known to all who care to pay attention. Freedom of speech, no matter how reprehensible or challenging. Respect for law. Racial, sexual and religious equality. Respect for work and education. Tolerance. We have been hammering on these principles daily for almost two and a half centuries, and we still have a long way to go.

These and a thousand million small webs of trust and interdependency simply do not exist in the countries we find ourselves at odds with, nor do they seem in any hurry to develop them. The millions who stare wide-eyed at all we have accomplished refuse to do the dirty, unglamorous work that makes it all possible.

The founding legal document that we revere with the same passion that they do their religion is not a secret known only to a robed cabal. It is available for study in millions of places, quoted daily and debated in thousands of publications. It is the key to our success, prosperity, and outlook.

But adopting it is not easy. It means abandoning the easy satisfaction of blaming others for one's own failures. It means forgoing *fatwahs* and murdering people who express opinions you find abhorrent. It means enduring the stress and strain of finding a way to make compromise with people you dislike. It means treating women and homosexuals and Jews and much more that they hate with respect and dignity. More than any of these lofty and essential habits, it means nothing more or less than getting out of bed each morning, slugging through traffic and putting in an honest day's work – five days a week, fifty weeks a year.

But they don't want that. They just want the Gold Card, and they want someone else to make the payments.

There are a few writers out there who have been responsible for teaching me not what to think, but *how* to think. Carl Sagan was one of the first; Victor Davis Hanson and Steven Den Beste are two of the most recent. But of them all, the one who has been the most fun has been P.J. O'Rourke. He toured the world pondering why some places work, and some don't. His book, *Eat the Rich*, is just simply brilliant – brilliant in how it shows success not to be the product of geography or the accident of national resources, but rather the culture and attitude of the people and the way they view themselves.

PJ ends this really excellent and very funny work by pointing out that while nine of the ten commandments deal with such primal, elemental rules as *"Thou shalt not kill"* and *"Thou shalt not steal,"* God and Moses added at the end one that is somewhat startling in concept, namely: *"Thou shalt not covet thy neighbor's house; nor his wife, nor his male servant, nor his female servant, nor his ox, nor his donkey, nor anything that is your neighbor's.'* "In other words," writes PJ, **"go get one of your own."**

I believe this Republic will weather the threats we face today in the same way we have for 250 years. I believe we are already a stronger, better place than we were on September 10th, 2001, for we have once again had to take stock of who we are and what we believe in.

And I believe that the power of our American Dream will, in fact, eventually cast off the ignorance and fear that have held so many in bondage for so long, because it is ultimately a fight you are free to join or walk away from. It represents a choice to join a ragtag group of Rebels fighting a desperate battle against tyranny and oppression – and who would want to walk out on a movie like *that*?

WAR
January 26, 2003

The internet is a wonderful place. I almost wrote "invention," but it is, in fact, a landscape, a space to explore. We have, at our fingertips, all of the combined wisdom (and idiocy) of our species throughout our long struggle up towards enlightenment.

The internet is also a horrible place, for there are dark rooms and hidden sewers where all of the festering evil we humans commit upon each other are exposed for those with the stomach to witness it.

I have spent much time in these disgusting realms in the days since September 11th, 2001. I have forced myself to endure many videotaped nightmares. I have seen Africans hacked to pieces with machetes, watched mere boys shot in the street and left there like dogs by other Kalashnikov-wielding children. I've seen a mass execution by firing squad, men tied to poles set against a gorgeous beach while picnickers cheered and danced. I've seen a man's hands cut off in front of his very eyes.

I've seen photos of blackened lumps in a morgue in Bali, the charred and twisted remains of happy young men and women in the prime of their lives. I've seen the unimaginable carnage in the few seconds after a suicide bombing in Israel, dead and dying old men and women looking down at their shattered bodies in disbelief, and yonder the head of the perpetrator smiling joyously on the sidewalk. I've seen the rage and joy of pre-teen children as they throw stones at their murdered neighbors accused of collaboration in Palestine.

I've seen emergency workers with shovels cleaning up what's left of people after a Serb mortar attack on a marketplace. I've seen the almost unimaginable cruelty of Chechens screaming *Allahu Ackbar!* as they decapitate a Russian civilian with a small axe in a forest clearing, and I have watched them cut the throat of a Russian boy soldier with such horror and disgust that I was sick for the rest of the day. I have seen these things, and more.

There are two images I will never forget, and I expect I will think of them often in the days and weeks to come. For in the front row of this parade of horror and depravity, I have watched a fundamentalist Islamic crowd stone two women to death. They were covered head to toe in shockingly white linen – the better to see the bloodstains. Taken into a field and buried up to their waists, they looked like odd white sails on a sand horizon, until the stones began to fly, leaving red carnations where they landed. One of the women just crumpled, bent at the waist, and I still pray that this person was knocked unconscious within the first minute or so. The other did not go peacefully into that good night. She died fighting and struggling, enduring the most sickening lurches as the unseen stones fell on her, twisting under that now-scarlet hood, trying to protect her face as best she could, as hundreds of her friends and relatives vented their rage, calling out the name of their god as we would cheer on the Tampa Bay Buccaneers.

Allahu Ackbar!
Allahu Ackbar!
Allahu Ackbar!

I will not forget that image.

And I will not forget another one, either. As long as I draw breath, I swear I will never forget the sight of two people holding hands, and leaping from 108 stories above the hard concrete sidewalks that I myself have walked, gawking skyward at one of the wonders of the world. I *will not* forget them. I will not forget their fall, the spin that finally tore their hands apart as they fell forever, *forever* down that quarter-mile. I will never stop wondering what they said to each other in that last moment, or their cries to each other as they launched themselves to their deaths, having watched their friends take the same leap a few moments before. I will never forget what an unimaginable hell that their cozy office, full of coffee mugs and pictures of grandchildren, had become in order for them to make that choice, with the ruins of their friends visible on the streets so far below them.

Now let me explain why I have sought out such despair and horror, endured again and again the rising bile, the nausea, the sickening unclean sense that is cured only by a long, hot shower.

I do it because I want to see what is, not what has been fed to me. I have worked as a scientist and a television editor, and both of these professions have driven me to seek out the *reality*, the *raw data*, the *source footage*. I want my worldview and my opinions to reflect facts, not wishes – no matter how unpleasant the facts, or how comforting the wishes.

One of the reasons that September 11th remains so shocking and clear to us today was that it was all raw and unedited during those first few hours. Bland, chatty newsmen were rendered speechless, a tough-as-nails mayor broke down and wept, congressmen spontaneously broke into *God Bless America* because they didn't know what else to do, and people sent in video of jets flying into buildings, broadcast unedited as their friends screamed *Jesus F------g Christ!!* on network television. It was raw. It was real. It stayed that way for perhaps 48 hours, until people like me (but not me) got a hold of it and turned it into *America Mourns* with slow-mo flags snapping and moving dissolves of weeping bystanders super-imposed over somber musical chords.

Now that awful, enraging footage is being held back, so as not to *inflame public opinion*. We are about to launch a war in which people will die at our hand, and we have done a dreadful job of making the case for such an action. No cold-blooded, clear-eyed look at what we oppose in this conflict could do *anything but* inflame public opinion.

Those who criticize the United States from within clearly have not seen any of these horrors I have mentioned, for if they had it could not but mitigate their rhetoric, and put some perspective into their arrogant and affluent lives. Those who actually *endure* such daily horror as can be found in the world want one thing and one thing only: *they want to come here.* They want to come here **now.**

We never see these grotesque realities on US television, and yet our news media has not been shy about reporting the effects of US bombing campaigns, never missed a chance to show us the weeping civilians wailing over children lost in US air attacks, never blanched at showing charred Iraqi soldiers hanging out of tanks destroyed by our weapons.

However, by showing only *our* actions, by showing only what we did to Iraqis without presenting the horrors they inflicted on Kuwait, we have made an editorial decision, that being: The US is the cause of, and not the remedy to, much of the suffering in the world.

That said, in a democracy we are responsible for the actions of our military. Reporting on the consequences of our actions is disturbing and demoralizing, and yet it **is well and proper that they do this.** We *cannot* turn our backs on the actual consequences of our actions as Americans. We need to see and hear the result of our military operations, for *if we do not* we will lose the shock and outrage, the human compassion and decency that so often stays our hand. We, as a nation, have learned that war is not jingoistic glory. It is also not a videogame. It is concentrated, unleashed pain, agony, grief and horror, and real people, people who love their children as much as we do, are going to suffer and die because of the actions we are about to take.

Unlike our political opponents both here and abroad, we need to fully and completely understand and accept the consequences of our position. And those consequences, when making war, are the most solemn and heavy responsibilities we can bear as a people.

Those protesting this war do not seem to get this at all. Not only have they failed to make an argument based on fact and historical precedent, they have stooped to the most childish and infantile posturing and rhetoric imaginable. Their chanting has all the mindlessness and cruelty of a kindergarten cabal; their slogans and slanders and taunts seemingly exclusively *ad hominem*. Watching them on C–Span for as long as you can bear, you rapidly become convinced that they have no point to make at all, other than that the United States is, by definition, the source of all evil and injustice in the world.

Conscientious liberals admit in private, and indeed, more frequently *in public*, to the paucity of thought, the irrationality and sheer *lunacy* of those who march in our streets in opposition to war with Iraq. I see the absurd posturing of these suburban socialists, listen to the inane chanting from these mall Marxists, watch them return to their Lexus' and their minivans and their SUVs and find myself stuck with *Life During Wartime* running over and over in my head:

This ain't no party
This ain't no disco
This ain't no foolin' around
This ain't no Mud Club
No CBGB
I ain't got time for that now

As we enter the eve of this war, I am myself torn by a paradox in human nature that has confused and baffled minds far greater and more refined than mine. *How can human beings be both so good and so bad? How can the SS and the Salvation Army be staffed by the same species? What exactly* is *our nature, anyway?*

This has been debated for ages, but to me the most cursory look at the world can quickly and clearly provide a powerful clue. The single definitive trait of Homo Sapiens, or greatest – indeed, only – strength as a species, is our limitless adaptability.

No other creature before or since can live anywhere, (or eat anything) and *thrive*. From the bleached sands of the Sahara to the ice floes of the poles, we can adapt and prosper. We can be found in every latitude, in the far reaches of space, and at the bottom of the ocean. We appear to be infinitely programmable, and so we adapt to anything.

In societies where cruelty and domination rule, we are capable of the most unspeakable acts of torture, repression and murder. In the streets of revolution-torn Africa, in torture chambers in South America, in the killing fields of Asia, the Gulags of the steppes, the European death camps and the Confederacy's cotton plantations we see refined and perfected barbarism and inhumanity.

Some say this is just human nature. And yet, *and yet*, in those few historical moments where freedom and prosperity and democracy are allowed to flourish and grow, we are startled by the near total absence of such plagues. No democracy has ever declared war on another. They may have endured hunger, but no true democracy has ever faced actual famine. *Individual* crime and atrocity have sadly not been banished, but bloodshed and massacre in the streets day after day are unimaginable. Entire communities and nations have been built and survive on deeply cherished ideals of liberty and freedom.

Where the people rule, soldiers do not come jackbooted in the night. Decency, trust, respect and cooperation are the coin of such a realm, and their by-products are equality, prosperity, and happiness. And by any measure, the most free and prosperous and inventive of these societies may be found in the United States of America.

We have managed, as a nation, to build and maintain what might best be thought of as a bubble of freedom, safety and opportunity. We have paid for this privilege through two and a half centuries by wars that have taken the best of our sons and fathers, and now our mothers and daughters as well. We have for two hundred and fifty years found our voice and our memories intact, and now stand at the doorstep of a new millennium facing a world that has once again largely chosen to ignore the lessons of history.

We and two or three other nations, old and true friends who have stood by each other in the presence of such enemies before, now face an adversary in the full bloom of romance with death and destruction; an enemy willing – *eager* – to spray our cities with a virus it has taken armies of scientists and doctors, working diligently through centuries of research and learning, to eradicate from the blood-soaked rolls of history. We face fanatics who would bring down the entire world, themselves included, in a radioactive Armageddon, secure in their own twisted souls of the heavenly rewards of sexual gratification and revenge for their many abject failures. We face people such as this, people who are so far beyond the pale of human mercy and so corrupted by black and bitter rage that they *must* be killed, for nothing else will stop them, *nothing* – as they tell us at every opportunity.

We have blithely ignored them for many years, turned a deaf ear to their warnings and *fatwahs*, turned an even more blinded eye to their procession of assassinations, massacres, bombings and attacks. Despite our recent and proven record of aiding and defending innocent Muslims in Kuwait, the Balkans, and elsewhere, we have been singled out as a Satan, a nation of sub-human infidels, and been the target of slander and incitement to murder that would have shamed the most fanatical Jesuit in the Spanish Inquisition.

There are those of us who have the courage to actually listen to their unedited rhetoric, view the video records of their atrocities, and face the fact that these people are sworn to kill as many innocent civilians as they possibly can. Some of us, in the months since September 11th, 2001, have chosen to take them at their word.

So let us gather the moral courage to take a factual, cold-hearted look at the reasons why this war with Iraq is the necessary next step in this conflict; one that needs to be undertaken without delay.

First, and most importantly, we can plainly state the prima facie cause that makes up our first argument in favor of invasion:

1. The impending military action is not the pre-emptive opening of hostilities against a sovereign nation, but rather the continuation of hostilities begun by Iraq in 1990 with their invasion of Kuwait; said resumption being a direct result of repeated and flagrant violations of the ceasefire signed by Iraq in 1991.

So much for the 'pre-emptive' attack criticism. This upcoming military action is indeed the product of a pre-emptive attack on a sovereign nation…that nation being Kuwait. Saddam Hussein took his country to war in a naked grab for oil and glory. He was handed the worst military defeat in modern history, a defeat so complete and total that US forces began to hesitate to fire on Iraqi units that were so spectacularly and completely routed.

The United States acquiesced to international law in the form of the UN resolution limiting military action to the removal of Iraqi forces from Kuwait. The Iraqi leader, facing complete and total ruin, entered into agreements as a condition of ceasefire, and has failed at every turn to honor those agreements, bringing his country to ruin and starvation by doing so.

It's really just that simple.

Second, the current resolution is clearly worded so that the burden of proof regarding disarmament is on *Iraq*, and *not* on the success of the weapons inspectors. UN 1441 makes it clear that anything less than full and complete cooperation – this means things like meeting us at the airport and handing over the uranium-enrichment centrifuges that we know they have – is a material breach of UN1441 and will be met by "serious consequences" (and we should perhaps rename the *Nimitz* the *USS Serious Consequences*.)

So:

2. Failure to turn over known WMD components, and not the failure of UN Inspectors to find them, puts Iraq in material breach of UN Resolution 1441 and authorizes the US and her allies to enforce previous UN resolutions by means of military force.

So much for the legal niceties. Now let's get down to brass tacks.

On Tuesday, September 11th, 2001, the United States was suddenly and deliberately attacked by forces of Islamic extremism in an act of barbarity that stunned the world.

In order to grasp the full meaning of that attack, we would do well to change our terminology to better reflect the reality we face. We should be thinking and discussing the upcoming conflict not as the War on Iraq, but as the *Battle of Iraq*. For it is indeed that: a major – hopefully, *the* major – battle against Islamic fundamentalism and the tactic of terrorism that they have employed against the US and others in their rage and shame at their own manifest failures.

Let us then examine the evidence and motivation that firmly places Iraq as the key component in an alliance of terror directed against the West in general and the United States in particular.

We should begin by having the honesty and integrity to admit that the direct connections between Iraq and Al Qaeda prior to the events of 9/11 are tenuous and murky at best. We should also acknowledge that despite feverish claims to the contrary, Saddam Hussein is a totalitarian dictator exclusively concerned with his own power and in no way is he the Muslim Saladin he makes himself out to be. It does indeed seem likely that Osama bin laden and Saddam detest and hate each other (and soon we shall be able to refer to *both* of them in the past tense.) But to say that this is enough to prevent them from allying themselves against the United States is self-delusion of the highest order.

For the full horror of a terrorist nuclear attack upon the United States to come to fruition, our enemies need both the *means to produce* an atomic bomb and *a delivery system* for it.

Anyone who doubts the willingness and ability of Al Qaeda to deploy and use such a weapon has frankly not been paying attention and is unworthy of this debate. They have, in public statements, on web sites, in training videos and operations manuals, shown a persistent and desperate attempt to obtain such a weapon. We have only to look back to that clear blue morning should we have any doubt whatsoever that such people would do everything in their power to kill as many of us as possible. Let us not forget that without the heroism and professionalism of our police and firemen, and the most well-managed, success-ful emergency evacuation in history, that death toll that day could have easily reached twenty or thirty thousand. There is a great deal of evidence that other terrorist teams, both here and abroad, were thwarted by the quick grounding of the commercial fleet by the FAA. Who knows how many others might have been killed that day, and where? Or how many unsung victories we have won in the months since that terrible day?

A small nuclear device can be fit into a suitcase. We need to face the stark, brutal fact that in a free society there is no defense against such a weapon. This war can-not be won, and our cities and people saved from nuclear annihilation, *by playing defense.*

Fortunately, constructing a nuclear weapon is not easy. In fact, it took the United States the better part of several years and billions of 1940's dollars to construct an operational nuclear device, using the full resources of the world's richest na-tion and the best theoretical and practical minds on the planet. Not only must the bomb maker get his or her hands on large quantities of a rare and tightly controlled substance – uranium or plutonium – they must also overcome huge engineering problems in terms of hardened materials and exquisitely timed explosions needed to implode the fissile material to critical mass.

A finished nuke can fit in a suitcase, but to *build* one takes a factory, indeed, takes a nation: money, massive equipment, large work areas, armies of scientists. These things, unlike suitcases, can be found, targeted and destroyed.

There can be no question whatsoever that Saddam Hussein has been desperately seeking the means to build such a weapon. Let's make sure everyone heard that: **There can be no question whatsoever that Saddam Hussein has been desper-ately seeking the means to build such a weapon.** Really astonishing piles of independent records and sources confirm this without question. From Iraqi defectors who actually had hands-on experience with the programs, to intelligence reports of the import of the required equipment and raw materials, to the reams of evidence that prior inspectors discovered in their seven years of investigations, to the unabashed statements of Saddam Hussein himself... *Saddam has brought his country to ruin for no other reason that his obsession with owning a nuclear bomb.*

Had the Israelis not bombed the Osirak reactor in 1981 (and endured world condemnation for it at the time), then without question Iraq would have had a nuclear weapon during the 1991 Gulf War. It is impossible to imagine a man such as Saddam not using such a weapon when faced with the greatest defeat in military history. Whether he used it in a Scud attack on US troops, to contaminate Kuwaiti or Saudi oilfields, or, more likely, to use against Tel Aviv to ignite a holy war against the hated Jews, the result would have been catastrophic, indeed, in the likely case of a nuclear response from Israel, *unimaginable.*

We can therefore sum up the next argument for attacking Iraq as follows:

3. Saddam Hussein has the means and the motivation to develop nuclear weapons, and there is irrefutable evidence that he has tried to do so. He has shown staggering errors in judgment and a belief in his own personal infallibility by attacking Iran, Kuwait, and Israel. Iraq attaining nuclear capability therefore provides a potent and immediate threat to our allies in the region and the vital interests of the United States.

Like all dictators, Saddam runs a state apparatus ruled by fear. There is no one in his military command structure, or indeed among his party or even his sons, who are willing to give him real information, because most of that information will be bad news. This, coupled with his clinical paranoia and narcissism, have led him to absolutely appalling errors in judgment, such as assuming the Iranian people would join him in his war with Iran, the miscalculation over Kuwait in 1990 and the subsequent evasion of his obligations in the years since.

Furthermore, the people who have had first-hand contact with Saddam Hussein all speak of his messianic complex. He cares not a whit about world opinion, and indeed seems preoccupied with how the people – particularly the Arabs – of 500 years hence will record him. Saddam, to put it plainly, plans to make a big splash on the pages of world history. In this he is no different than Hitler, Stalin or Pol Pot. There are no legal or behavioral inhibitions on totalitarians such as Saddam. He does whatever he wishes, and every action is met by terrified praise and false adulation from a population cowering in fear.

Therefore, it is not only likely but probable that Saddam will be tempted to use such weapons to strike back at those who have committed the unthinkable crime of embarrassing him before the world. And this is where Al Qaeda can provide him with not only the delivery mechanism, but also, to Saddam's irrational and misinformed mind, a form of plausible deniability.

His success with The Big Lie these past 11 years has emboldened him to believe – with ample justification – that there are legions of useful idiots ready to rally to the defense of anyone who dares attack America.

So we may summarize our fourth cause as follows:

4. Saddam Hussein shows irrefutable signs of mental impairment in the form of Clinical Paranoia and Narcissistic Disorder. Given control of nuclear or other weapons of mass destruction, his temptation to use them against the US on American soil is not mitigated by normal behavioral inhibitors, and indeed is amplified by his aberrant mental state. This poses a potent, immediate and intolerable threat to the safety and security of the people of the United States.

A close corollary to this argument can be made from the fact that Saddam routinely tortures, murders and gasses his own people. We may disagree violently with the Chinese, the Russians, the Pakistanis and the French, among others, but we do not unduly fear nuclear attack from such nations because each of them can be deterred by the unimaginable rain of destruction we would unleash upon them in return.

A self-absorbed Narcissist such as Saddam does not see people – even his own people – the way we do. They are objects to men like Saddam, props and extras that enhance the panoply and glory of their own lives. Brave German generals disobeyed Hitler's orders to destroy everything that remained intact in Germany during the final weeks of the Third Reich. Like all dictators, Hitler saw the impending end of his own life as the final curtain on his nation's history…and what happened to the extras in his biopic was completely irrelevant.

Saddam has taken the cradle of civilization, one of the most enlightened and educated populations in the middle east, and driven it to utter ruin in the service to his own vainglorious ambitions. The money designated to feed and care for his people under the UN sanctions he has used to build mad palaces of sickening opulence under the noses of his starving children. And yet there are those that say the threat of reprisal against his nation is sufficient to keep him in line.

Nonsense. Saddam has to die someday. And when he goes, he clearly means to take whatever he can with him.

Therefore:

5. Saddam has repeatedly shown his contempt and bitter disregard for the welfare of his own people. He has totally neglected all of the misery they have endured since his ascension to power, and is therefore undeterrable and immune to fear of reprisal against his nation and his people.

No one disputes that nuclear weapons are dangerous. No one disputes that Saddam is dangerous. So why do legions of people argue that Saddam with nuclear weapons is somehow *not* dangerous?

Those, as I see them, are our primary *causus belli*. Now let's deal with some of the reasons why people oppose this war.

Innocent people, innocent children will die in this war.

That is true. Innocent people will die at our hand. But let us never forget that *action* is visible and direct, but that *inaction* also bears consequences.

We will do everything in our power to limit civilian casualties in this war. In fact, during the days and weeks ahead, we will see something unheard of in military history: a campaign designed not only to minimize civilian casualties, but one aimed at killing *as few enemy soldiers as possible.* We have already dropped leaflets on Iraqi regular army units, telling them that if they remain in their positions they will not be harmed, but if they mass for a counterattack, we will destroy them. The Iraqi army has recent experience in this matter, both with our destructive capabilities and our generosity and kindness to prisoners of war.

Saddam's miserable, poorly-fed and disgracefully-led conscripts have no love for the man. That is why he consolidated what loyal soldiers he had into the Republican Guard. This body, too, became understandably unreliable after Saddam's bloodthirsty and paranoid purges, so he created the *Special* Republican Guard, a further decimated cadre that may in fact fight for him, since they are the predators at the top of this dictatorial food chain, and therefore have the most to lose and, certainly, the most to fear from an outraged and oppressed populace.

I fervently hope that Iraqi regular-army conscripts decide to sit this one out. No one who watched them surrender, kissing the garments of American sergeants, could feel anything but compassion and pity for these men. I do believe that those that do chose to fight will be the hard core element of Saddam's blood-stained police state, the sadists and executioners who have tortured and murdered their own people on Saddam Hussein's orders for decades. Don't forget that. Don't forget the number that have disappeared in the night during his monstrous reign of terror. Don't forget well-documented, disgustingly common accounts of the children tortured to death in front of their parents, of girls raped in front of their fathers, not to mention the roll-calls of horror that will emerge when that evil is finally swept away.

And finally, don't forget *your* friends and family, the good people you work and play with, the innocent men, women and children of New York or Los Angeles or Atlanta, Chicago, Dallas, Boston, or whichever city we may condemn to radioactive vapor because we were too cowardly and indecisive to act on what we knew to be a threat.

We have thousands of nuclear weapons…it's hypocritical to say Iraq can not have them also.

We have had nuclear weapons for almost sixty years now. They have been used, twice, within the first days of that ownership to end the most horrible war in history and prevent many times the number of casualties, on both sides, that would have been lost had the war continued through the invasion of Japan. Despite many provocations, they have not been used since then. We have had chemical weapons for even longer.

Saddam, on the other hand, used his chemical weapons the instant he got his hands on them: first on the Iranians and then on his own Kurds – this after not once being used by *any* nation during all the desperate years of World War II. What does that tell you?

Many adults are given alcohol, credit cards, automobiles, guns and jet aircraft, once they have shown themselves worthy of the responsibility. We do not put these things in the hands of four year olds, and with very good reason. It may seem hypocritical to you; to me, the idea of keeping a drunken second-grader from waving around a loaded automatic while behind the controls of a hurtling 747 *just makes sense.*

This war is all about oil.

Demonstrably false for the reasons listed above. Nevertheless, let's grant the premise.

Oil is the only power source currently available to meet the needs of our post-industrial society. Not only our automobiles depend on this oil: it is also a primary source of electrical energy in this country, and is essential to the plastics we use in everything from MRI machines to CD players.

To say this war is all about oil is factually identical to saying that this war is all about maintaining our society and lifestyle. If that is not worth fighting for, what is? One may find that offensive ideologically, but as I see it, to be true to such a philosophy you must either drive a *solar-powered* electric car, ride a horse or a bicycle, or walk. You must remove your home from the city power grid. You must discard all plastic items. You must also abandon television, radios and movies, all of which rely on electricity generated by oil. You must forgo modern medicine, surgery and dentistry, likewise driven by oil-fired electricity at many stages. You must grow your own food.

Do all of these things, and you will have my frank admiration for your dedication to a moral cause. Do anything less and you are a hypocrite mouthing an easy lie in an attempt to strike a pose of moral superiority.

Furthermore, people who apply this argument are usually accusing us of stealing the oil. Now I suppose it's theoretically possible that everyone else at the gas station gets a wink, a nod and a *don't be silly* hand gesture when they try to pay for their gas -- me, I'm shelling out $1.83 a gallon for the privilege.

There has been a river, a *Mississippi* of our fives and tens and twenty-dollar bills flowing into the middle east for decades now. The idea that most of this has been squandered on scores of madly extravagant palaces, solid-gold toilets and leggy hookers should only further direct all fair-minded people toward the cause of Invasion. One of the many reasons I support this action in Iraq is because the people of that nation are sitting on a significant hunk of loose change. It is indeed being stolen from them – and I for one am convinced that once we deal with the thief that stole it, those revenues will be of enormous benefit to the people of Iraq, and aid them in the rebuilding of their country.

It is true we depend on oil for our lifestyle. However, if you look at it objectively, you might agree that oil does no one any good hundreds of feet below a barren desert. For us it helps power our society; for them it is a valuable commodity and a legitimate means of transferring a lot of our cash into their pockets. My car does not care where that oil comes from, but I do. And if my $1.83 / gallon can in the future go to the people of Iraq, I would find that both a blessing and a relief.

Still, the whole point is, as I mentioned, logically flawed – *fatally* flawed. Gas is cheaper now, in adjusted dollars, than it has ever been. Evil Oil KKKorporations don't need more oil on the market: it depresses the price. *More of something makes it cheaper; less of something makes it more expensive.* Although I do understand why this confuses some people – the whole supply / demand concept does seem to give the far left a great deal of trouble.

When gasoline is $13 dollars per gallon and lines stretch for miles around empty service stations, *then* will I begin to reasonably suspect this political decision has oil-based overtones.

We need a 'smoking gun' from the UN inspectors.

The problem with a smoking gun is *you can't find it until it's gone off.*

It is clear from documented reports of bribery attempts on UN Inspectors on the part of the Iraqis, to French inspectors tipping off Saddam about team destinations, that to accept this argument we *de facto* lose the game. This is why it is so popular. It ignores reams of testimony from defecting scientists, and all of the other evidence stated above. In fact, it raises the question that ignoring such a mountain of existing evidence requires such a willful burying of one's head in the sand as to make any proof insufficient. To such people, the smoking gun they require is a pile of radioactive rubble where Tel Aviv once stood, or legions of dead commuters in the London Underground, or the wildfire spread of smallpox through greater Chicago and beyond.

Scores of independent sources repeatedly and emphatically demonstrate that Iraq has massive quantities of biological and chemical weapons, and is working frantically to attain nuclear ones.

Those unconvinced by the existing evidence will be convinced by nothing less than their actual use against our military or civilians.

To hell with those people.

North Korea admits to having nuclear weapons and is threatening the region. They are a greater threat and must be dealt with first.

That a rogue nation can threaten the three most prosperous economies of Asia with nuclear blackmail (although, admittedly, China would not likely be as threatened as South Korea or Japan) does indeed raise a troubling question. And that question is, with such a clear example before our eyes, who can not believe that removing such a powerful lever from the hands of Saddam Hussein should not be job #1? North Korea already has these weapons. We cannot undo that. We can only prevent that from happening in the future.

Our options are dramatically reduced, and the consequences of miscalculation on either side *astronomically* raised, by such weapons in the hands of such an un-balanced, isolated and desperate regime. This is *precisely* why we must intervene in Iraq.

It is hypocritical and contradictory to negotiate with North Korea, which already has nuclear weapons, and advocate war on Iraq, which does not.

I will grant that it may appear so at first glance. But consider these two points: First, we relied on negotiations, diplomacy and signed agreements in order to prevent North Korea from obtaining these weapons. They developed them de-spite these negotiations and in direct violation of these international agreements. There are those who oppose this war, who say we should try this spectacularly unsuccessful strategy with Iraq. I would like to sell these people their next auto-mobile.

Second, North Korea thinks they can pressure us while we are preoccupied with Iraq. They are betting their empty, crop-free farm on this. They want us to become alarmed, right now. They hope to blackmail us before the last vestiges of their state collapses around them. That is a trap we have so far avoided.

There is a reason we treat Iraq in one fashion and North Korea in another. It is a very simple reason. In the case of North Korea, time is on our side; with Sad-dam, time works against us. This is not hypocrisy, it is sound and cogent strategic thinking.

And finally,

The United States has no right to launch a pre-emptive attack; we can only respond if we are attacked.

This is the most pernicious and dangerous argument of all, because it plays directly into our natural revulsion at being an aggressor and causing the deaths of innocent civilians.

As I mentioned, I see both Iraq's attack on Kuwait, and the Islamicist attacks on 9/11, as the pre-emptive attacks that started this pending conflict. But perhaps you do not buy that argument. Well, consider this:

We were attacked before, on December 7th, 1941, by a vast navy that had been assembling for years. We watched the Japanese build the fleet that attacked Pearl Harbor. We did nothing. We – the French and English especially – also did nothing as a bitter and vengeful Germany grew stronger and more daring. Appeasement was all the rage back then.

In the years following that naval sneak attack, and after a war in which unchecked militarism nearly brought civilization to ruin, it made sense to think that we could stay free by being strong enough to deter or repel any invasion. We would do – indeed, _we have done_ – whatever it took to create a defense so formidable that the mere idea of defeating it has become unthinkable, and to willingly provoke it becomes an act of state suicide.

Those days are gone.

We face an enemy willing – eager – to carry a suitcase into Times Square, press a button, and in one millisecond inflict more casualties on the United States than we have seen in all the wars of our history, _combined_.

It is an image so horrible that many simply refuse to believe it.

Believe it.

We ignore September 11th at our mortal peril. We no longer have the luxury of watching an enemy build military and naval strength over years or decades. We no longer face uniformed divisions massing at the borders. We face instead a group of depraved murderers to whom nothing is off-limits, who fear no earthly retribution, who love and glorify death for its own end and who hate not only all that we do, but _all that we are_ with a black bitterness that we cannot begin to imagine.

I believe we are standing at a doorway in history, squinting at forms we can barely make out in a dark room. We will, in the years to come, look at the confusion and doubt of the present hour as a turning point in the history, and indeed the *identity*, of our nation and ourselves.

For we are waking up to a simple reality. In a new millennium where a few diseased people can carry a suitcase with the power to kill millions, the lesson we must learn is simply this: *the only way we will be safe, prosperous and free is when **everyone** is safe, prosperous and free.*

Critics of this War on Terror call it 'eternal' and 'never-ending' as a means of discouraging us from fighting it at all.

But there can be an end to this war. It will end when *all* people are inside the bubble we have built for ourselves and our children – warm, well-fed, free to pursue their dreams and ambitions, their minds and bodies and women liberated, racial and tribal hatreds put aside, and so on.

The quiet idealist that resides deep inside in me, on a speak-when-spoken-to basis, actually believes such things are possible. After all, it works – pretty well – for *us*, and we Americans are children of all the world. We know what such a society looks like, and we have documents of such stunning clarity and hope as to show anyone the way.

The conservative I have become, however, is certain that if it happens, it will happen because of the actions and sacrifice of US Marines and not because of middle-aged naked hippies spelling PEACE on a golf course. It will take decades. It may take centuries.

Can we **force** freedom and democracy on people? It seems, from the example of Germany and Japan, that indeed we can. These societies once harbored fanatics no less dedicated to our destruction than the ones we face today. Now they are our trading partners, and often our friends and allies. The point at which it becomes necessary to force such a regime change will be determined by how ugly the swamp has become. And can anyone seriously argue that the people left after the defeat of the Nazis, Japanese Imperialists or American Confederates are not far better off today than they would have been *if they had won?*

I am not an ideologue in this regard, and I certainly don't want to send our sons and daughters out to fight and die for anything less than our safety and survival. But that, to me, is looking like what it might come to. Each success makes the next case easier, and each triumph further shames and silences our critics.

Sixty years ago, we were willing to sacrifice millions of American soldiers, sailors airmen and marines to keep our homeland safe. Such a task may be before us today. With our soldiers' skill, training and professionalism, and our unparalleled technical innovation and creative genius, we will not need anything like millions of soldiers. But it will not be without cost – it will only be necessary.

In this, I am guardedly optimistic due to our recent victory in Afghanistan. Not the military victory, magnificent though it was.

No, I am thinking of things like the reopening of their soccer stadium, the field where I have seen – thorough the *camera obscura* of the internet – women in burqas forced to kneel and then shot through the back of the head for the crime of adultery. Kids play *football* there again. *That's a* **win**, Noam Chomsky, you lying son of a bitch.

Little girls march to school in the morning, singing. *That's a win*, Robert Fisk. Old men wept as the Afghan national flag was carried by an actual Afghan army during their first free National Day in two generations. *That is a win for the Good Guys, too*, Harold Pinter. I hear of Special Forces sergeants organizing little league teams and I just smile like a little kid.

I'm smiling because, at last, we have dragged ourselves back from the mud and filth of the Cold War, from allying ourselves with what was only marginally the slightly lesser of two great evils in our proxy wars in Asia and South America and Africa. I'm smiling not just because of my bursting pride in the dedication and skill of our military, but in the essential kindness and compassion of these kids of ours who just want to do the right thing and come home. I'm smiling because I start to see before us an age where, in the words from the 1963 movie *The Ugly American*, we are no longer *"so busy telling people what we are* against *that we forget to tell them what we are* for."

We have a long and difficult road to travel in these coming years, and there will be ample opportunities for us to fall off the path. But I reflect on our own greatest peril, the dark days of our own Civil War, and I draw comfort from something not often remembered about that turning point in our history.

In the early days of that conflict, Abraham Lincoln saw one objective, and one only: *he* **must** *save the Union*. That was what marched the men in blue off to Bull Run: Save the Union. Lincoln said as much when contemplating the Emancipation Proclamation:

"My paramount object in this struggle is to save the Union. If I could save the Union without freeing any slave, I would do it; and if I could save it by freeing all the slaves, I would do it; and if I could save it by freeing some and leaving others alone, I would also do that."

But as the war dragged on and victory continued to recede, Lincoln found a new voice. Southerners could be counted upon to fight because it was their homes and institutions under attack. One poor captured Rebel, when asked why he was fighting on behalf of the rich plantation owners' right to keep slaves, replied, *"I'm fighting because you're down here."* Lincoln needed something with that emotional imperative, and he found it.

He found it after brave Negro soldiers – like the men of the 54th Massachusetts Regiment, immortalized in the movie *Glory* – showed to their northern skeptics that they were as gallant and effective soldiers as any in the Union Army.

He found it in the words of Frederick Douglass and Sojourner Truth. He found it by turning the dirge *"John Brown's Body"* into the inspirational *"Battle Hymn of the Republic."*

Lincoln turned the Northern cause into a crusade to set men free.

If we have the courage of our convictions, if we do indeed feel that life, liberty and the pursuit of happiness is worth fighting and dying for, then we may find that *freeing the world is in our national interest*, regardless of the cost.

So on the eve of this new tempest, let us remember, together, a final image – to me, the most hopeful of all.

Let us remember Afghanistan. Let us remember that the brutal Soviets we so sullied ourselves fighting during the Cold War had installed in their southern neighbor a puppet dictator, who ruled small enclaves at the point of a tank cannon and tore their nation into civil war that culminated in the atrocities of the Taliban. Let us remember the *million* Afghan civilians who died forcing off that yoke.

Let us remember an image from that ruin of a nation, in June of 2002, at a meeting hall in Kabul. Inside were all manners of warlords, refugees, opposition leaders, even their old king. Women demanding positions of power, wizened old tribal leaders opposing them at every turn, mullahs and warlords making veiled threats and all the rest of the unruly, loud, preposterous accoutrements of democracy that make up a Loya Jirga or a US Congress.

And let us remember the image of US soldiers, forming a cordon, a bubble of security around this howling, screaming catfight. Not inside. Not dictating terms. Not so much as laying a hand on a gavel. But rather outside, armed and powerful, seeing to it that the future of that tortured country rested in the hands of their own people, protecting this newborn, imperfect, and astonishingly fragile proto-democracy against the legions of Taliban, Al Qaeda and petty warlords who would like to see nothing so much as its failure. Remember them guarding the life and pure, undiluted courage of Hamid Karzai. And remember our soldiers giving them, day by painful day, another week, another month without torture and repression so that they in all their infinitely adaptable humanity have *the time* to come to find such things intolerable.

Remember that, and smile. Because *that* is America at war.

COURAGE

February 15, 2003

Sometimes, even when you are very young, something happens in your life that is so profound, so astonishing and so big that you just know everything has changed and you will never be who you were again. I had one such experience at age 5, and I was to have another eleven years later.

I grew up in Bermuda. My father was a hotel manager, so I grew up in the most perfect corner of Bermuda. I would go to Warwick Academy and sing *God Save the Queen* in my blazer and school tie. Usually we'd take the bus home, but when mom picked us up, we'd wriggle into bathing suits in the back seat and go snorkeling for a few hours. This was pretty much every day. And, like just about everyone else at that age, at that time, I had decided that my future would consist of being a railroad engineer, or a fireman, or a cowboy – that would be a Daniel Boone, coonskin cap, Winchester rifle and buckskin kind of cowboy, not the garden-variety pretty-boy kind with the chaps and the showy chrome six-shooters. I considered them a little too precious for real work, even at that age.

I didn't know it then, but I would have traded all of that for a father with a nine-to-five job selling insurance, because the price of such a life was a dad who lived his job. Most dads lived their jobs in those days. It's just that mine had a full day of work to do, and then a full night of entertaining as well.

So I was just happy to be spending time with my dad as we sat in the bleachers at Kindley Air Force Base, down at the other end of the island. A two hour wait in the sun is interminable at that age, but finally, six men in blue jumpsuits appeared, and walked down the flight line like robots. People applauded politely. I did too. Didn't seem worth a *two-hour* wait, though…

They climbed into their silver jets with the red, white and blue stripes and the numbers on the tails. I found out later that they were F-100 Super Sabers – really glorious airplanes, sleek and muscular. Down came the canopies in unison. Then they started the engines.

Better…

They taxied to the end of the runway, took off in a roar, and disappeared out over the turquoise and green reefs. Spectacular! Great show! Not sure it was worth two hours, and that one guy down there won't stop talking…

Launched on May 25th, 1953…powerful symbol of the American Indian…never missed a show due to maintenance problems, blah blah blah…

Hey, thought the five-year-old, the jets are gone, show's over, let's get out of the heat…

But behind my back were six of America's most powerful fighter aircraft and the best pilots on the planet, not a hundred feet above the water and racing toward the rear of our bleachers at nearly seven hundred miles an hour – just under the speed of sound. And I mean *just under*.

So when I looked down at this man in the blue jumpsuit, I couldn't hear them coming, because they were only a few feet behind their own roar. And when he said, *"Ladies and Gentlemen, the United States Air Force–"* something caught my eye at what seemed like a few feet above my head. I saw a blur of silver and red, white and blue, and that's about all I had time for, because the man shouted into his microphone the word *"–THUNDERBIRDS!"* and that's when the sound hit.

And that was about all she wrote for little Billy. I was pretty much done after that.

I've thought a lot about courage in the last few years. And what I've come to realize is that behind *courage* is a greater emotion still, and that emotion, not surprisingly, is *love*.

Think about it. Think of the infantryman who throws himself onto a hand grenade. Perhaps love of country brought him to that time and place. Certainly he loved his family, his wife and children. And more than that, even, he loved his own life, his chance to watch his sons grow into honorable manhood, to give his daughter away in a small church on a Sunday morning. All of this love may have given him the courage to come to the place where he would face that grenade, but it was *his love of his buddies* that overcame all of that in that one instant where the heart rules the mind and courage rises unbidden from its mysterious, deep harbor.

Actions like these, time and time again, leave me speechless and dumbfounded. And yet they are commonplace in times of great peril. I have sat in silent awe of the firemen that rushed into those buildings – and of *all* the firemen, everywhere, that do it every day. I think of passengers on an airliner who would, in that one moment of desperate courage, decide on the spot to fight hardened murderers who had spiritually and psychologically prepared themselves for years, to advance on their slashing box cutters, to break into the cockpit and push those controls forward, to stop the men from righting the plane, kicking and biting and punching as the ground filled the windows. I think of that kind of courage and am struck mute at the *love* those people bore for the rest of us. I gape in awe, like I did that day when I was a little boy, at the kind of society that can generate that common courage.

And in this imperfect, flawed nation of ours, perhaps more than anywhere else on earth, I think about the courage it takes to be poor, to face that sickening knot of worry and despair that comes with not having the money to pay your bills. For there is no more steady and enduring courage than that of a poor family, especially a single parent, who fights a never-ending battle of brutal hours at miserable pay, of perennially unrealized dreams, and of the desperate, numb agony of disappointed children. For people like that, who force themselves to work two jobs while we sleep, to avoid the temptations of crime and dependency while surrounded by luxury and wealth the likes of which man has never known…well, that is dogged courage of a sublime nature that passes all understanding.

If courage is *love coming to the rescue*, then what do we make of people who willingly put themselves in great danger? How are astronauts any different than bungee jumpers or other thrill seekers? Are men and women like that simply adrenaline junkies, people who do not feel really alive unless they face danger and death at point-blank range?

Do they indeed flirt with death? Because if they do, then that is not courage but rather a dark and filthy addiction. What kind of people do these things, and why?

———————————————

If we really want to get to the heart and truth of the matter, we must turn once again to Hollywood – for they, as usual, have gotten it absolutely, totally wrong.

For as is typical for so many who write about the military, Hollywood looks at courage and sees only *bravado*. Bravado is to real courage as a slick personality is to genuine character.

You do not earn the privilege of flying these amazing machines because of light-ning-fast reflexes or a cocky smile, or even a *best-who-ever-lived* belief in your own ability. *Everyone* who applies has these in spades. You get to fly jets, or Space Shuttles, because you have the **discipline** to study phone book after phone book of manuals and procedures. It is unglamorous, tedious, vexing work. There are armies of young men and women willing to do this, who fling themselves into jungles of facts and data for the chance to sit in that chair and face death on a daily basis.

I know this because I was one of them. And then, eleven years after six red, white and blue Super Sabers changed my life, after building every Mercury, Gemini and Apollo model in the known universe, after memorizing the details of every aircraft in the US and Soviet inventory, after getting a job at the Miami Space Transit Planetarium at age 13, after correcting the tour bus guides at the Kennedy Space Center (I wanted to be shot into space, and they wanted the same, only without the capsule), after leaving any hope of a social life at the altar of after-school physics classes, after lining up letters to Senators and enduring High School Counselors who told me 6'1" would make a pretty good basketball player, after all this and more than you can imagine, I walked out of the preliminary medical exam for the United States Air Force Academy with an optical prescription for the 20/25 vision in my left eye (20/10 in my right being irrelevant) and the inescapable reality that *someone else* was going to command the first Mars Mission.

That was a hard thing to do to a seventeen year old, and to this day I look at our military pilots and I am ashamed of myself. I know there's no reason or logic to it; it's just how I feel. Still. To this day.

The Space Shuttle is, without question, the most complex machine ever created. You look at her and see an airplane. Look deeper.

Look at her bones; her wing spars, her bulkheads and decks. Look at her delicate hydraulic blood vessels, her electrical nervous system, her computer brains and inner ear, her exquisite balancing organs. Look at the warm cocoon behind her nose, a little piece of Planet Earth set in a fortress against the vacuum and bitter cold of space. Think of her communications suite, her inertial guidance systems, her orbital maneuvering thrusters, her elevons and landing gear and rudder. Picture the slightest pressure on a man or woman's wrist sending her rolling or pitching to a fraction of a degree. Think of her eyes, her windows – windows that can hold back 2000 degree-hot plasma. Think of her revolutionary, reusable rocket motors. Think of her thermal tiles, so efficient at dissipating heat that you can hold a white-hot tile in the palm of your hand. Think of the thousands of them that make up her skin, each unique – every one.

We don't call industrial-sized air conditioning units "she." Well, most of us don't anyway. We don't refer to buildings this way very often, or to generators or dumpsters.

But vehicles... they are different somehow. If you do not believe it is possible to love an inanimate object, then you do not know too many teenage boys and their first cars. Ships have always been she. Airplanes, too. And I don't think this is so hard to figure out, because there is something about a machine that takes us places, something alive and magical.

Many foreign observers of America simply cannot comprehend our love of automobiles, but that is because they have never had to face crossing Texas. There is a rite of passage for everyone in the US, and that is your first teenage road trip. And no matter what kind of piece of crap you may be driving when you take that trip, that machine is serving you up pure, unrefined freedom and it's so delirious and liberating that it makes your head spin, and carves the songs you heard during those glorious hours into that part of your brain that makes you cry when you hear them again twenty and forty and sixty years later.

A guy on a Harley knows real freedom in the single, left and right direction of the highway. Sailors know it in two dimensions, the ability to point the bow anywhere on the compass and follow it, come what may.

And then there are those of us who have worked and studied and trained like hell so that we may know freedom in all three dimensions. Now a lot of people think this makes pilots a little arrogant and aloof. Not so.

The average pilot, despite the sometimes swaggering exterior, is very much capable of such feelings as love, affection, intimacy and caring. It's just that these feelings don't involve anyone else.

I knew, when I was sitting in those bleachers all those years ago, that those red, white and blue jets were *alive.* I always see airplanes that way. *They live.* They are here to set us free. And the most docile and sweet-natured of them can *only just barely* kill us.

Like most every pilot I know, I read everything I can about other people exactly like me who have managed to kill themselves in an airplane. Our crusty old flight instructors always said to us new pilots, *"Try to learn from the mistakes of others, son – you won't live long enough to make them all yourself."*

Again, like most every pilot I know, I have lost friends to the airplanes I so deeply love. No one very close yet, but that's just a matter of time. It's going to happen. *"When a friend dies, you lose a friend; when you die, you lose all your friends."* We say things like this when we start talking about our dead comrades. We say it to deflect the reality of it, of course, but what we really do is dig into the details of every fatal accident. *Ah, see – I wouldn't have done THAT.* You feel better.

Some of the things pilots do to get themselves killed are truly and staggeringly stupid, so much so you really do tend to look at it as natural selection. But if we're honest, we often see ourselves in the wreckage, catch a glimpse of something we almost did or might have done, or did, in fact, survive.

Like every pilot I know, I read these accident reports relentlessly, and for the same reason: to save myself from making that same mistake. And it works, too. And it does something more: it makes you face the possibility, the very idea of dying. Realistically and openly. You are making a trade with death – I'll deal with the horror in exchange for the wisdom.

I like to fly because it combines intelligence, ingenuity, passion, skill, discipline and guts. We do not flirt with danger. We try to get as far away from danger as we can. We look at the death of our friends and colleagues right in the eye so we know what it looks like when it comes for us. This is not a love or a fear of dying. This is confronting the fact that death is in fact real, and by doing so, by facing that, you do, indeed, develop **courage.**

Courage is not the absence of fear. It is taking action in the face of fear.

And I know courage is the stern face of love because I love to fly more than I fear being killed while flying. I do everything I possibly can to reduce the risks, knowing I can never eliminate them all. There comes a time when I can honestly tell myself I've been as careful as I know how to be, and then, *and only then,* is the time to strap in. I've made the risks and the fear as small as I can. The joy stays as large as it ever was.

One day, I was on a solo flight in a small, single-seat sailplane – a glider about the size of a bathtub, with long, thin, very efficient wings.

It's usually dry in the Mojave desert, but this was still early spring, and the San Gabriel Mountains were covered in snow. Wind hitting the mountains has nowhere to go but up, and so that's where I was – 80 knots, plenty of speed to get out of trouble – and perhaps two wingspans away from the trees. I was so close I could see squirrel tracks in the snow. Just thinking about a turn was all it took, and I ran the contours of those mountains certain that I would never have to come down.

And then I saw something I have never seen before or since. Off my left wing, between me and the mountains, moist air was being pushed up so fast that it was condensing, turning into cloud before my eyes. It was like an inverted waterfall of smoke, and there I was, dipping a wing into it. The power of all that lift, the force and the speed of it, all that free energy – and somehow, we hairless, gibbering, bickering monkeys managed to figure out a way to grab it and ride it. I remember thinking, *Four billion years of struggle and evolution put me in this seat right now. Billions of dead people spent their lives dreaming of what this must be like.*

And as I looked away from that upward rushing waterfall of air, I saw ahead of me another sight I had never seen before or since, for the sun was setting below a cloud layer, yet above a lower one, and there we were, just me and Apollo himself –– caught in an envelope of purple and gold glory that would make the most heavenly Hallmark card look like something done on an Etch-A-Sketch.

And I will *never* forget this feeling: I knew, right then, as if I had been hit between the eyes with a diamond bullet, that I no longer cared about dying. I had seen and done something that only the smallest handful of us have ever experienced, sailed a silent ship through a place that cannot be described or imagined. I didn't care if the wings came off. I didn't care if I got pushed through the grille of an oncoming truck on the way home down murderous highway 138. It just didn't matter to me anymore. I had done *this*. Anything that followed in this life was gravy, and I knew it as surely as if the thought had been with me all my life.

I wouldn't have traded that moment for the moon.

Of course, the risks we private pilots face pales in comparison to our military fliers, and is absolutely nothing compared to that met eye-to-eye by men and women like Rick Husband, Willie McCool, Dave Brown, Laurel Clark, Kalpana Chawla, Mike Anderson, and Ilan Ramon; nor does it require the courage and skill of Dick Scobee, Mike Smith, Ron McNair, El Onizuka, Christa McAuliffe, Greg Jarvis or Judy Resnik. These are the last crews of *Columbia*, and *Challenger* before her, buried with their ships in the skies over Florida and Texas. But many, many others have taken that walk in those spacesuits, smiling and waving as they pass the cameras on their way to their seats atop 2 million pounds of explosives, and they took exactly the same risks and bore them with the same courage.

It is fitting that we remember the names of those lost with their ships, but not fitting at all that most of us cannot name a single living crewmember, some of whom have taken that walk four or five times.

Story Musgrave was one of those people. He described the Space Shuttle as *"a beautiful butterfly that's bolted to a bullet."* Here's what he meant:

Your chairs are facing the sky as you crawl into the Orbiter. You can barely move anyway in your orange pressure suits – thank god for the technicians. They literally *ratchet* the five-point harness across your chest and legs. On a full flight, it's four on the flight deck: Pilot and Mission Commander on the controls up front. Two behind him, three on the deck below.

You sit for hours like this – minimum of three hours or so, often longer. There is a lot to think about, and I have no doubt that since *Challenger* rose and then fell on that cold January morning not one of them has been able to avoid seeing in their mind's eye that horrible forked smoke trail and raining, smoldering debris. No one talks about this. No one has to. There's a lot of smiling and nodding, but the chatter is kept to a minimum since the intercom is dominated by call-outs from launch control to the crew, most often the Mission Commander and Pilot.

There's a lot of built-in holds, chances to catch up and work minor, last minute problems. At the T-21 minute hold, the Flight Director polls the Launch Control Team to confirm we are go for launch. This is a solemn moment. It is, in essence, the passing of a cup of responsibility. Everybody takes a sip.

It's a little less dramatic than in the Apollo days (*Telemetry?* **GO!** *Cap COM?* **GO!** *Booster?* **GO FLIGHT!**), but it's still where we sign the check.

They pick up the countdown. There's another built-in hold at T-9 minutes. Any one of these can, and very often does, result in catching one or more of the one *million* components falling out of nominal status. That's either more delay strapped into your chair, or a trip home for the night, or the week, or the month.

T minus 31 seconds -- OBS takes over, with auto-sequence start at T-28. Software is running the countdown from this point forward, but anyone at any console can stop the launch if they are not happy.

Computers are checking each system twenty-five times a second. The crew hears everything. Pilot and Mission Commander are busy as hell, but the other five are essentially passengers, and now they are scared. Now they are calling on all of their courage, reasoning with themselves. Smiling at each other. That helps a lot. That and The Nod. The Nod is untranslatable. It means, very roughly, that *I know what you went through to sit in that chair, and you know the same about me.* It's not something you and I can do. This is something reserved for the very best people we have as a species.

That inner voice, the one we cultivate and nurture through untold hours of training and simulation, whispers to us, pushing out the fear: *Those controllers are the best there are. The engineers too. The technicians. All of them. We don't know if they can keep us safe but we know they've done their best, and that's as good as it gets.*

Ten, nine, eight...

Okay, head back. Here we go. On the flight deck, some orange gantry out the left window – everything else is blue sky. A butterfly bolted to a bullet.

At T-6 seconds, fire-hoses of fuel and liquid oxygen begin to flow to the three main engines at the back of the Shuttle. They only give us about a quarter of the thrust we'll need to get off the pad. But they're on fire now, pushing the Orbiter forward, giving the crew the sickening feeling that the ship is falling over. The vanes constrict and focus the thrust – we're going to need it all now. Everything she's got.

Come on, baby. Come on.

The entire shuttle assembly rocks back into place now, and even during these last five seconds, computers can catch a stray reading and shut it all down...

Three, two, one...

SRB ignition. The two flanking Solid Rocket Boosters ignite, pitching more than a million pounds more thrust onto the orange External Tank, the bullet that the butterfly rides into orbit.

And now you're headed for space, and there's nothing you can do to stop it.

The SRB's kick in, and that is what it is, a hammer to the back. You were scared before; you're *terrified* now. The SRB's are *horrible*, they're *pigs*, they scrape and hiss and rattle and they feel like they will shake that ship to pieces. Look at the cockpit cameras during launch, and you'll see the crew battered like they're taking speed bumps at two hundred miles an hour. Everyone hates and fears the SRB's; you'll never relax while they're burning.

15 seconds in and you're clear the tower. The Shuttle rolls 90 degrees left, fast. You're not only on your back now, you're tipping over upside-down and it's getting worse as you angle out over the Atlantic.

A few miles away stand the smartest men and women the human race has ever produced, and they are watching over you like a hawk. There's just so goddam little they can do for you now. They've already done everything they can and they're as much a passenger as you are.

You are probably too scared to think about it, and it is *certainly* too loud to hear, but further away, thousands and thousands more watched the glare as the SRB's lit. The Shuttle rolls off the pad in complete silence at that distance. It's surreal. There's nothing to compare it to. People are usually kind of quiet.

Then the sound hits you: you feel it in your chest more than hear it, the sound of millions of pieces of thick canvas being torn all at once. And then a funny thing happens, because you're surrounded by people but suddenly you're all alone out there – sunburn forgotten, mosquitoes a memory from a past life. You're ten or fifteen or twenty miles away, but it's just you and the white butterfly now, that's all there is. You're crying and you don't know it, you're screaming but you can't hear it, you're jumping up and down, and it's every time a Gator wide receiver ever beat a Florida State defensive end and he's just pulling away and ain't *nothin'* gonna stop him now – he's going all the way.

Go, baby! Go! GO! **Go you son of a bitch!** Yeah, they say she burns liquid hydrogen and LOX, but that's just camouflage. It's pure love that keeps that ship in the sky.

And she is going. She's going like a bat out of hell. And every traffic jam and dental appointment and blind date and income tax form is suddenly worth it to be able to see this with your own eyes, to live through a time like this…It's a pillar of fire and a pillar of smoke, but it's not God coming down to speak to us, it's us going up to have a word with Him. *Good* **GOD** *look at her go!*

40 seconds. The mains throttle back. Nothing stops the goddam solids: they keep roaring and hissing and knocking loose your fillings if you're dumb enough or human enough to keep your teeth clenched. We're at Max Q, and the Shuttle is experiencing the highest aerodynamic loads it can bear. We keep getting faster, but the air starts to thin. This is as hard as the air can push back, and if we do it at full power we'll be blown to pieces.

Fifty years ago it took all the Right Stuff we had in the box to push a tiny orange glider level through the sound barrier. Now we do it in less than a minute, straight up, from a standing start, with a spacecraft the size of a ten story building weighing a few million pounds. **Ka-BOOOM!** *Mach 1, baby, and you ain't seen **nothin'** yet!*

A little more than a minute and most of the atmosphere is behind us. Main engines back up to 104%

"Challenger *GO at throttle-up…*"

73 seconds.

"*Oh no—*"

That's as far as *Challenger* got that cold January morning. 73 seconds. End of story.

"Roger Columbia, we copy you go at throttle-up"

I know how they must have felt at 2:02 – a kick and a pop, and all of a sudden, the ride turns to pure velvet as the SRB's fall away. I know one of them must have looked at another and smiled. *We're safe now.*

Well, *safer*. Now a complete engine failure could result in a return glide to Kennedy. Forget all that nonsense about parachutes and escape poles. At mach 5 and climbing the air is as hard as concrete.

2:32 – we've been in the air for two and a half minutes, and we are high and fast enough now to *glide to Africa*.

4:20 – Two engine Abort to Orbit – if we lose a main engine now, the other two will get us to orbit. We can sort things out up there.

7:00 – One engine ATO. Even better. *We're gonna make it.*

7 minutes, 45 seconds. MECO. Main Engine Cut Off. Welcome to *by-God* outer space!

Everything is strapped down except your arms. They float in front of you like they do at the top of a roller coaster. Only this one is going to last for two weeks. You're weightless.

A few moments later the External Tank falls away, headed for the Indian Ocean. That funny dark spot is where some of the insulating foam came off during launch. It's happened before. Probably nothing to worry about…

———————————

Back during the Apollo days, before we forgot that we could accomplish anything we set our minds to, the Space Shuttle was going to be a different bird indeed. Not a butterfly strapped to a bullet at all, but more a hawk on the back of an eagle.

No SRB's, no O-rings, no foam insulation, no External Tank falling away into the ocean half a world away. No, the original plans for the Shuttle called for something that would have looked a bit like those pictures you've seen of the Orbiter riding on the back of a 747, as it's moved from Edwards Air Force Base back to Florida.

Almost all of the weight lifting off that pad is fuel. Why? Because it takes *insane* amounts of thrust to go straight up. The engines on a 747 don't lift us into the air – the wings do that.

All the engines do is keep the aircraft moving forward fast enough for lift to develop, and it takes a lot less energy to go *forward* than it does to go *up*.

In the original design, an orbiter sat on the back of a manned, winged transport. The shuttle would take off from a runway – any major airport would do – climb to about 100,000 feet using jet engines, and let aerodynamics do the heavy lifting just as it does on a jumbo jet today. Then, already moving at several times the speed of sound and with 95% of the atmosphere below it, the Orbiter would separate and using a scramjet – supersonic ramjet – claw for more speed and altitude until there was practically no air left at all. The front of the scramjet would close, making it into a rocket, and liquid oxygen would be added to the fuel. Although you wouldn't need too much – you were most of the way there already.

This was an elegant, reliable and very safe way to get to orbit. Once built, it would have gotten the cost of going into space down to rates that approached flying the Concorde. But to build it was expensive, and after Apollo 11, we had bigger fish to fry.

No one has been able to tell me what those fish were.

Anyway, never time or money to do things right, but always the time and money to do them over. And over.

Solid Rocket Boosters and foam-covered External Tanks were engineering sleight-of-hand tricks to get us to space on far less money than we needed to do it right. It was like making a lunar lander out of old boilers and playground equipment. To the extent that the Shuttle has flown 111 out 113 missions successfully is a testament to the skill and dedication of NASA's engineers and administrators, and not, I'm afraid, to the vision or commitment of the Congress, the President or the American People.

Look at the pictures of Columbia after a landing at Kennedy, and you are struck by just how *dirty* she was by the time of her last mission. Well, she was 22 years old – that's old for titanium and steel that's been shaken and burned and twisted and rattled, freezing on one side and boiling on the other during her weeks and weeks in the unforgiving vacuum a few miles above us. But it looks as though *Columbia* herself never failed her crew. *Challenger* certainly did not. It looks like components of the External Tank and SRB's did both Orbiters fatal harm. These ships were destroyed, and their crews perished, because of the various band-aids and cost-cutting work-arounds we applied to what was once a magnificent design. NASA was forced to do this to maintain our tenuous status as a spacefaring species, and I applaud and admire them for that ingenuity and courage. For all her design short-cuts, I would fly the Shuttle tomorrow. *Please* let me fly the Shuttle tomorrow.

———————————

The scales of Joy and Fear somehow balance. On its final mission, the *Challenger Seven* never got to space, and her crew died not long after she cleared the pad and climbed into memory.

But the crew of *Columbia* had a much larger helping of joy – sixteen days in orbit, almost a hundred sunrises and sunsets, playing weightless choo-choo trains through narrow tunnels and tweaking gravity's tail good and long and hard – and the *Columbia Seven* would be destined to pay for that by several minutes of knowing that they were about to die.

As they strapped themselves in for the long, quiet ride home, they had the satisfaction of a job so well done that NASA was calling it *the* textbook mission.

Rick Husband took his six crewmembers rock climbing during their years of training. He wanted to bond them into more than a crew. He did: he made them into a *family*. There's a picture of them in shorts and sunglasses, atop that mountain, admiring the view. They look like they'd known each other since grade school.

I'll bet they talked about that day as they pulled down their visors, and Willie McCool pitched the Orbiter on its back for the de-orbit burn. They talked about who was waiting for them, where they would go, what they would have for dinner.

As *Columbia* began to press against the first thin wisps of air, a little hint of gravity, a little push at the small of their backs must have felt strange after sixteen days of weightlessness. But it was time to go home. And like all coworkers facing the end of a close assignment and weeks and months of hard work together, I know they planned to get together over the years. I know Laurel and Mike were talking about their families, Dave and Kalpana already grinning about being the old salts next time and how much they would miss this team, this *family*, in all of their future rides on the bullet. Ilan Ramon must have invited them all to his house in Israel, perhaps a few years from now when things had settled down a little. It's beautiful there. I know that they meant it too, that these were not idle platitudes but real offers from people who knew they would be friends for the rest of their lives.

Perhaps ten minutes before eight am on Saturday morning, Rick Husband and Willie McCool started to pay attention to the data coming from the left wing sensors. It was 30 degrees warmer than normal in the left wheel well. Not much, considering the 2-3000 degrees on the leading edge of their wings and nose, but something to pay attention to. Anomalies are never good. There are no pleasant surprises in the flying business.

By 7:55 things were looking worse – a lot worse. Unbeknownst to the crew, telemetry beamed to the ground showed readings from the heat sensors in the left wing started to rise, and then drop to zero.

They were failing, in a pattern expanding away from the left wheel well. Tire pressures were way high on the left side, and then those sensors failed too. Sensors fail all the time. But this was different. This was a pattern, and it was spreading. And something was starting to pull the ship to the left.

I don't know the words he used, but I can hear the tone perfectly in my head, because it's exactly the same tone I've heard dozens of times on cockpit voice recorders. It's concern. Alarm, even. But it's cool. Disciplined.

All right, we've got a problem here...

The Pilot and Mission Commander probably never exchanged the knowing look that we'd see in the movie. They were too busy working the problem. But in the two seats behind them, and the three below, those five brave passengers looked at each other and now the smiles and the grins were gone.

Something was wrong with *Columbia's* left wing. The air that should be slipping over and under her like water off the back of a duck had found something to hold on to: almost certainly some missing tiles knocked loose by insulating foam coming off the External Tank. But 3000 degree ionized air was pushing into that wing, and heat sensors were winking out one by one because they were being burned through by gas far hotter and sharper than that at the end of a blowtorch.

Guys, we're in real trouble here.

The Commander would have told them. I have no doubt of this at all. You love and respect those people, people who have shown courage the likes of which we will never know. These are not babies, not shrieking, hysterical, self-centered celebrities either. These are astronauts. They *deserve* to know.

Air pushing backward and into that left wing continued to yaw the nose of the orbiter to the left. This **cannot** be allowed to happen – the ship will disintegrate if she doesn't come in at exactly the right angle. So the computers flying *Columbia* commanded the aircraft to roll right, to bring that left wing forward using the rudder and elevons, the controls on the wing and tail that made *Columbia* an airplane and not merely a space capsule.

It wasn't working. *Columbia* still pulled hard to the left, so hard that the computers fired the attitude control rockets on the nose to try and force it back into the relative wind. When that happened, when they heard the roar of those rockets firing in a last desperate effort to keep that ship intact, and when the rockets fired *again*, and *kept firing*, Rick Husband and Willie McCool must have known that they were not going home that day.

Guys, it's Rick. I don't think we're gonna make it.

And I know what courage did for these people. I know they looked at each other and nodded, and whether they actually said goodbye I know it was in their eyes. We know it. We *know*. We saw it on the deck of the *Titanic*, in the aisles on United Flight 93. On some level, they had all said goodbye to their families and their lives before they walked through that circular hatch, right below the word COLUMBIA.

When PSA Flight 182 collided with a small plane over San Diego in 1978, and dove straight into the ground trailing fire from the wing, the last words on the Cockpit Voice Recorder was a calm, level, *"Ma, I love you."*

And in that last second, there may just have been enough time, as that bulkhead wall opened into golden and purple light, to smile and think, *It was worth it. It was a great ride. I wouldn't have traded this for the m*

Buildings shook in Texas. *Columbia* was coming home.

CONFIDENCE

February 23, 2003

One night, I was sitting in a nightclub – maybe the first or second time I'd ever done so. I was just a puppy – eighteen, I think, for we could drink in those days. Anyway, it was a strange room: mostly concentric circles of dark tables arranged around a center, but the center wasn't a dance floor – that was off to the side. The middle of the room was just much better lit – almost like an auto showroom.

And right there in the center, in a small pool of light, sat a woman in a white dress, all alone. Calling her "beautiful" is like calling Yosemite "scenic." She was *stunning*. Grace Kelly beautiful. Catherine Deneuve beautiful. Plato wrote about how a chair was really just a dim shadow on the cave wall cast by the *ideal* of a chair. Well, this woman was the Real Deal. And there she sat, all alone, lighting up that room, maybe ten feet away from where my three buddies and I burrowed behind a dark table, nothing showing but our little red eyes darting back and forth like the terrified little weasels I thought we all were at the time.

I was about to learn a very powerful lesson. Wait, I want to rephrase that: I was about to be *given* a very powerful lesson. I didn't actually *learn* it for another ten or fifteen years. But the next ten minutes were nothing if not an education…

As I sat there, nursing my watery Screwdriver, I watched an absolutely endless progression of guys make that walk across that little patch of open space, sidle up next to her, and start talking. They never got past the first sentence. They didn't get shot down. They got *nuked*. **Vaporized.** One second they were there, the next there was nothing but a greasy stain on the floor where they had been.

And these guys were real smooth, too. Real *Rico Suave*. They had the wide lapels and the platform shoes and the quiana shirts (and may 1977 Miami burn in hell forever). These were not bumpkins like myself. These were *operators*.

Now most of you are old and wise enough to remember how the adolescent mind works, because the more she turned these guys down the more beautiful she became to me. It was like that old Twilight Zone shot where the corridor expands away from you as you run towards the door at the end. Remote. Unattainable. *Ahhhhhhhh.*

I could just barely hear her, too.

Would you like to Dance?

No, I wouldn't. Please go away, you're bothering me.

Sorry…

...often followed by a mumbled *what a bitch* as they slinked back in shame to face their friends. I thought, *she's just here to break hearts is all. She's not here to dance, or to have fun. She's just here to crush people.*

At that moment, I can say with confidence that I would rather have gone over the top at Gallipoli then walk across that ten foot expanse of lighted floor.

But I had a friend who was watching too, and he wasn't getting intimidated. He was getting angry. He was, like me, young, kinda dorky, and dressed, shall we say, more *conventionally* than the rest of the peacocks in the room. But as my eyes were glazing over in teenage awe, his were narrowing to slits as the Endless Parade of the Doomed walked into the meat grinder.

Finally, he had had enough. How did I divine this? Well, he shot to his feet, and muttered *"That's enough!"* through clenched teeth. That was my clue.

He threw down his napkin, took a belt of his drink, and worked his way around our table heading straight for fluffy wittle bunny wabbit with the *Sharp. Pointy. Teeth.* I remember I damn near grabbed at his legs, like a wounded Confederate begging a comrade not to advance on the withering fire coming down from Cemetery Ridge. *No Jim, don't do it!* I was thinking. *No one can take that hill. It's death to try!*

He walked up behind her, and so help me, he tapped her on the shoulder. I covered my face with my hand. She took a good long moment to turn around, too. She stared at him, the white wine in her hand just about the same color as her hair, and those cold blue eyes slowly looking up from his crappy shoes, past the rumpled pants to the okay shirt and finally right into Jim's eyes. She didn't say a word.

"Would you like to dance?"

Instantly: *"No, I would not like to dance. I* would *like for you to go away."* She turned back around without another word and took a sip of her wine. I heard a few people chuckle behind me.

Jim started walking, but instead of coming back to the Loser's Circle, he went around to the front of her small cocktail table. *No, Jim! Nooooooo!* And then he leaned forward, so he was a few inches from her face. And then he said something that burned itself so deep into my addled brain that I never forgot it, and never will. And he said it loud enough so that everyone could hear him, too. He said:

"Listen Princess, I just got off the phone. Turns out Prince Charming's horse just threw a shoe, so he's gonna be a little late tonight. Now why don't you stop showing everyone how miserable you are, put down that drink and come dance with me?"

She stared at him for a moment. And then she smiled. And then that's exactly what she did.

The three of us left about an hour later. Jim and The Vision had strolled out to-gether after about ten minutes on the dance floor. Nothing much to stay for after a show like that.

———————————

Next time you look at the moon, challenge yourself to think of something: there are footprints up there. Footprints, and tire tracks. Also three used cars, and one golf ball.

Why are they there? Because we *decided* to go to the moon, that's why. What a typically arrogant, unilateral, American conceit! But you know what? That footprint – you know the picture – will still be there, unchanged, a million years from now. In ten million years, it might begin to soften a little around the edges. But in a billion years – a thousand million summers from this one – it will still be there, next to glistening pyramids of gold and aluminum junk decaying under the steady cosmic drizzle of micrometeorite hits.

Eventually, in about five billion years, the sun will run out of hydrogen and start burning helium. When it does, it will begin to swell, consuming Mercury, then Venus as it enters its Red Giant phase. The forests will burn to ash, the oceans boil into steam and then be blown into deep space along with the rest of the atmosphere. Life will have been long gone.

But on the moon, there will remain six scraps of colored cloth. Red and white stripes peeking out from the dull grey lunar soil; perhaps a star or two on a faded blue field as the sun reaches out to reclaim her children. Very likely, they will be the last, best preserved monuments to our presence as a species on the face of the third planet now burning to a cinder below.

But eventually, they will burn too. The sun will contract to a white dwarf, the inner solar system nothing but black cinders, the outer planets shrunken and frozen corpses. Perhaps fifteen billion years from now, a time as far in the future as time goes into the past, there will be nothing here except a burnt-out and cold white dwarf.

But somewhere out there, *somewhere*, there will be four battered, unrecogniz-able hunks of aluminum and titanium and gold, spinning through deep space, their names recalling the spirit in which they were hurled into the abyss: *Pioneer*, and *Voyager*. And the day before the Universe dies, you'll still be able to dimly make out the stripes and star-spangled square, and read the words in the ancient language, from a dead race in the far distant past, when the stars were young and alive: UNITED STATES OF AMERICA.

There are at least five nations on the earth that had the technical skill, not to mention the money, to do something as grand and noble – as immortal – as this. Yet only one has done so. Why us? Why not them?

Confidence. That's why.

We are a strong nation. We'd damn well better be, because we carry the genes and mythologies of the most confident individuals on the planet, people unwilling to endure repression, persecution and enslavement by taking a chance on a place unknown to them, except perhaps in their dreams. We have come from every country in the world, from the free and prosperous to the hellish and horrific. Each individual immigration, from the native Indians crossing the Bering Straight, through Plymouth Rock, Ellis Island and LAX – each one an act of optimism and hope for something better.

And we are a confident nation. Indeed, the quality, more than any other, that is admired by friend and foe alike is our optimism, our sense of hope for the future. We may be condemned overseas for our many flaws, but it's hard to argue with an optimist who is willing to roll up his sleeves. And when we, as a nation, decide to do something…*it gets done.* We sometimes fail. We pay the price, fix the failures, and go on.

Footsteps on the moon.

Optimism and confidence colors everything we touch, from our movies and music to our skyscrapers and Space Telescopes. How else to explain the universal appeal of The American Dream, for that dream is indeed universal: freedom, safety, prosperity – and scores of other adjectives that can be summed up in that jaunty phrase, unheard of in a political document: *the Pursuit of Happiness.*

It is difficult for we Americans to fully grasp the effect we have on the world's psyche, to understand the depth to which American culture has permeated the globe. We dominate the political, economic, military, scientific and cultural spheres as no nation has done before us. This influence is quite invisible to the average American, because it is simply an extension of the institutions we are familiar with at home. We think nothing of seeing McDonald's or posters for *The Matrix* in Singapore, or Kiev, or Rio de Janeiro.

But imagine a landscape where, let us say, *France* had the same cultural impact on our shores: *La Baguette* restaurants on every corner, long lines around the multiplex to see *Jules et Jim 2000,* French troop transports idling down Interstate 10 in long convoys, French fighters flying to and from French air bases set out in the middle of former farmland, television filled with dubbed French sitcoms named *Mon Dieu!* and *Les Amis,* and everywhere on the news nothing but reports of what the French government was doing and how it was going to affect us.

Okay, stop imagining – this is like huffing paint; you can *feel* the brain cells dying. But this is the effect we have, and there are forces at work in the world, forces besides Islamic Terrorism who would like to see nothing so much as a confident, determined United States taken down a peg. Or two. Or twenty.

These are hard times, psychologically, to be a person who loves America. Hard because we do, indeed, wish to be liked by the rest of the world. Hard because we know in our hearts that we are good people, decent people who do not leap for joy at the chance to spill the blood of our own children and spend untold treasure just to have the hateful, pornographic thrill of seeing brown people blown to bits.

Yet we are accused of exactly this, and worse. We hear of polls saying that upwards of 75% of countries like England and France see the United States as the greatest danger to the world, and it knocks the wind out of us.
No, that can't be right. Can it? Can they really believe that?

Some do. *Many* do.

Some of this emotion is genuine, real fear and panic brought on by our unparalleled success, and our past miscalculations and blunders. Some of it is envy, pure and simple. Some is driven by pain, the pain of lost greatness and glory. Some is projection, a sense of how *tempting* it might be to hold such power, from countries with histories of *real* empires, real governors, and real subjugation.

And some of it – much of it – is intentionally aimed at our decency, our sense of restraint and isolation, our desire to get back to our own happy and safe lives and turn our back on the world lost in the delusion that we long to possess it.

The protestors we have seen recently know this very well. They accuse us of being Nazis. We hear people from Berkeley and Santa Monica railing that they live in a Police State, no better than the one in Iraq. They claim we want nothing but oil, filthy lucre – and ascribe to our determined action the most base motives they can devise: sheer profit. Diversion from economic woes. Racism. Paternal guilt. Bloodlust. The list goes on and on.

Like the terrorists we also face in these quietly desperate times, these people seek to attack us where we are the most vulnerable, and for the anti-American multitudes that means our **confidence.** They know as well as we do that if we were the cruel, bloodthirsty and vicious killers they claim us to be that they would all be dead in unmarked graves. Gandhi, after all, succeeded in freeing India because his non-violent strategy was aimed at the British – another fundamentally decent and humane people. Had he tried this against Hitler or Stalin we would never have heard of him, for he would be yet another of the nameless, faceless millions taken away in the night, never to be seen again.

Knowing we are a moral people, knowing that we want above all else to do the right thing, knowing that the idea of invasion and war is a hateful and desperate last resort for us, they target their message to our conscience and confidence, little decency-seeking missiles like BUSH = HITLER, NO BLOOD FOR OIL and GIVE PEACE A CHANCE. These people know that the only thing capable of stopping a determined America is America herself. That is why our confidence is under attack in so many ways, and from so many sides.

Is it working?

It is.

_____

There are many principled, patriotic Americans who are opposed to the Battle of Iraq. At least, I assume there are, for they are hard to pick out among some of the craven lunatics we have seen in the streets of the world these past few weeks and months.

I really shouldn't be so hard on these people, because many of them clearly mean well. They seem unable – or perhaps unwilling – to face the fact that history has passed them by. For today they are on the side of tyrants, rapists, torturers and mass murderers. Apparently, they'd rather be there than change their minds. But there is a different class of protestor that we have seen recently, and these are not well-meaning people who only seek to avoid bloodshed. They are people like International ANSWER, supported by the Workers World Party, backed by North Korea, and these people are, to use a somewhat overused, even *nostalgic* phrase, nothing but lousy, stinking Commies.

You'd think I would be ashamed to use such a jingoistic, hackneyed cliché as "lousy, stinking Commies." I am not. Here is a philosophy that has killed no less than sixty million people outright, through executions, forced starvation, Gulags and Great Leaps Forward. They have drawn us into the most filthy fights in Asia, Africa and South America, led us to sully and permanently stain our national honor fighting nasty, brutal wars in God knows how many places, and driven us to back local thugs and dictators whose only redeeming value was their promise to stop this disease from spreading.

Like Islamic Fundamentalists, they are deeply deluded people in love with a fantasy ideology that promises them revenge and the spoils of revolution, rewards that they are unwilling to work for and incapable of generating. Claiming the moral cloak of Robin Hood, these people want to rob from the rich – **and keep it.**

Those decent Americans who are doing a patriotic duty by protesting what they believe to be an unjust war do themselves and their cause incalculable harm by marching alongside these unreconstructed liars, nitwits and frauds. They are correct when they say that not all of them are anti-American, or Marxists, or both. But perhaps they can forgive us for getting this impression, as any look at these protests will reveal.

Look at the protest signs shrieking WELLSTONE WAS ASSASSINATED! and ONLY SOCIALIST REVOLUTION CAN END IMERIALIST WAR! These people are not protesting the war in Iraq. What they are interested in is crippling the US. They know they cannot confront us directly. They have no military assets now that the Soviet arsenal is rusting back into the ground. They certainly don't seem to have jobs, so they're not exactly an economic force. And everywhere their political views have been put into practice, the result has been spectacular: collapse and ruin in the best of cases, and repression, torture and mass murder in the worst.

These people are political, economic and cultural failures. They are *losers*. But they have a secret weapon. If they cannot attack us head on, in open daylight, then perhaps they can erode, decay, and rot our moral foundations slowly, imperceptibly. And they are doing this. And it is succeeding.

If large numbers of our own people can equate The President of the United States with Adolf Hitler, if we actually believe the US is the source of all the misery in the world, if we loathe and despise ourselves and our history and expect to be praised for it, if strength and morality and sureness of purpose can be openly mocked as ridiculous anachronisms, if our institutions can be spat upon, our flag burned and our ethics slandered – if all of this can happen, in public, and we simply accept it then something is indeed very wrong with our foundation and we had better start paying attention to it *right quick* while we can still save the building.

I'll tell you something. I'm glad they are marching. I'm delighted they are out in the open, on the street, waving signs like 9/11 WAS AN INSIDE JOB. Like the horrible attacks of September 11th, they have opened our eyes to a threat we have chosen to ignore for thirty years.

These people have launched a coordinated, full-frontal assault on our confidence, which is the reactor that powers all of our greatness, strength and success.

We **must** fight them. Our survival as a nation, as an *idea* of a nation, turns on this one battle. Because many of these people marching in the streets are simply shocked into silence when confronted with the evidence – that we did not put Saddam Hussein into power, that liberal college kids like me had bumper stickers saying BUY IRAQI WAR BONDS supporting Saddam in his fight against the Mad Mullahs of Iran, that we do not have a design on Iraqi oil, that we will not enter Baghdad as conquerors, but rather as liberators, and that all of the Chomskyite lies and deceptions and half-truths that they try to string into a paper-Mache worldview do not hold up to fact and history.

We can argue these points until we are blue in the face. But the easiest way to convince these people is to simply have them ask an Iraqi, or a Cuban, or a Pole what it is like living in this vile pit of corruption called America. They may want to ask these questions behind safety glass, for the reaction to this kind of question from people who have known *true* misery and oppression is usually quite explosive, an outburst of rage and fury at the insult being leveled at them.

Because it *is* an insult. These people have lost their freedom, their property and their family members to real tyranny, real murderers, and real repression. They have lived in *actual* Police States. There is nothing rhetorical about the beatings they have endured.

And to have a smug, clueless, morally blinded suburban American college student tell them that we live the same way is a **mortal** insult to their loss and suffering.

I used to wish that these gullible, pampered, anti-American Americans would go and live in a place like Iraq or Cuba or pre-liberation Poland -- and not as visiting American celebrities to be paraded around as Dictatorial propaganda pieces, but as common, nameless citizens. But that would be cruel of me, because likely we'd never see many of these people again. So I have modified my wish. I now only want them to spend a one-on-one evening with people who have risked their lives to escape such brutality, to see the depths of emotion and anger such bland and thoughtless lies engenders in them.

So for you people still against the Liberation of Iraq, you who claim that the People Spoke during the demonstrations, I have a single question for you:

During those protest marches, *where were the Iraqis?* There are many tens of thousands of these people living here and abroad. Seemingly to a person, they are passionately for intervention to free their countrymen and their relatives. If your theory is correct, they would be the loudest voices calling for peace and American withdrawal.

So I ask you again: ***Where are the Iraqis?***

A year or two after I learned about confidence that night in the bar, I found myself on the stage of the Gainesville Little Theatre. I went to the audition to baby-sit a girlfriend who wanted a part. There were not enough men auditioning, so they asked me to just come up and read opposite the women. Just read from the book.

I got the lead role, she didn't get anything, and that little affair ended a remarkably short time later.

Anyway, there I was, in my one-and-only appearance acting on a stage, playing Tony Kirby in *You Can't Take It With You*, which, coincidentally, was the first live stage play I ever saw and which is one of the great American comedies of all time.

It was an early evening in November, 1980, during my sophomore year at the University of Florida. As we were getting into costume and make-up, we were making the usual plans to head out for beers after the show, and maybe watch some of the early Presidential election returns.

Just before we went on, a woman burst into the dressing room, sobbing hysterically. I wish I were making this up.

"Reagan's won! He won! My God, we're all going to die!"

"Wait, hold on, that can't be right. The polls just closed a few minutes ago. And that's just the east coast--."

"He won, I tell you! Carter conceded! Oh my God, there's going to be a nuclear war!"

Even then, even at the height – sorry – the *depth* of my liberal thinking, I thought this was laying it on pretty thick. I didn't like Reagan, though. In fact, I couldn't stand him. I just thought he was old, wrinkled, feeble-minded and way, *way* out of touch with his retro patriotism and his idiotic smiling all the time.

See, I was twenty. I had it all sussed. We were a whole new generation, baby. The *laws of physics* do not apply to twenty year olds, let alone the lessons of history.

I knew *nothing*. What I learned about life under the Soviets I learned from *Sociology Professors* who had grown up in the same bland comfort and freedom I had. I was an idiot. They were idiots too. **But!** *They* should have known better! That's what we were paying them for.

Then, not long after, I met a friend who more than anyone, got me serious about writing. He was a Bulgarian poet and refugee, a man who risked his life sneaking across borders, hiding out in fields, eluding guards with orders to shoot him on sight. And this man was an intellectual, one of their best and brightest. He was a *privileged* victim, given access to good apartments, better shopping, even allowed access to western books and magazines.

And that was their fatal mistake, you see? He *knew* what life was like in the west. And he risked that life – the only life he had – to come *here*.

That is where I unlearned the doubts and suspicions I had about my country, thoughts placed in my head by my own egotistical sense of rebellion against my parents and by professors with agendas of personal failure and eyes blinded by bitterness and rejection. That is where I learned, second hand, what life in *real* Police States was like from someone who bore the fear and anger and frustration and contempt on his face every time he talked of home; home being a laboratory of misery where even the smallest human deeds – traveling, buying food – were turned into thousands of little lessons in brutality and humiliation.

We fought against that philosophy. Did we win?

Well, the Soviets have gone. And as we learned not long ago, the memories of the nations freed from their shackles have not faded as fast as those of some of our so-called "allies." These recently liberated Eastern European nations respect and admire America for standing up to tyranny – having the memory of tyranny fresh in your mind will do that to you.

On the other hand, those anti-American ideas, and their progenitors, have not gone away. They have prospered and multiplied in our colleges and universities, unbalanced by any effort to even the scales and let these competing ideas duke it out in the marketplace of free and vigorous debate. The tide of self-hatred, lies and slander has risen many, many times higher than I ever experienced in the early 1980's. That battle is still being fought. And we are not winning. In fact, we are in big trouble.

I have also noted that as these radical factions have gained traction in our universities, we have found our vision more and more hobbled, our ambitions more petty, and our hopes less noble and worthy of our effort. Back in the early '60's, during the run-up to the moon landing, NASA scientists were whispering the phrase *Saturn by '70!* Well, why not? Vision and confidence were the coin of the realm in those days. I remember watching *2001: A Space Odyssey* when it came out in 1968, and thinking, *Damn! Thirty years and that's all we can do? A 200 man revolving space station, regular Pan Am orbital service, and a single ship to Jupiter?*

As an Apollo kid caught up in the head rush of visions coming true, and the most outrageous dreams unfolding on television in living color, I actually thought *2001: A Space Odyssey* was way too *conservative.* Now here we are, a few years after that iconic date. It's been more than thirty years since we set foot on the moon. We have three men in a series of big boilers orbiting the earth. That's pretty much it.

But, we do have acid-washed jeans and reality TV.

What happened to the big dreams? In his famous Moon Message, President Kennedy said, "*We choose to go to the moon. We choose to go to the moon in this decade and do the other things; not because they are easy, but **because they are hard.**"*

Because they are *hard.* What happened to that loud, muscular, confident voice? What happened to that *vision*, that ability to see at our feet something invisible to others, far beyond the horizon? Where is our faith that a nation unlike any other can do great deeds, weld and rivet together the most daring and audacious dreams, and boldly go where no man has gone before?

Who else will do these things? If we take ourselves out of the vision business, when will we see the likes of the Moon Landing again, and by whom? The Chinese in 2016? Brazilians in 2054? Who? When?

Time sweeps all things back into the onrushing past. And we as a people have a decision to make: do we go forward, write new pages, and continue to swim upstream, or do we stop and dig in to our PlayStations and tailgate parties and 215 channels and let someone else do it? Maybe no one will do it. Maybe no one is confident enough to even try, let alone succeed. Maybe the peak of human ingenuity and vision was reached on July 20th, 1969, and that everything after that was the long, slow decline back into tribalism and superstition.

I, for one, refuse to believe it. I am *confident* that this will not happen. I know in my heart, as you do too, that our native genius is the ability to recreate and renew ourselves. These dangerous times will pass, and then, perhaps, we can afford to beat a few swords into spinning centrifuges and fuel tanks and plasma drives. *Saturn by ' 70* is a lost opportunity. *Saturn by '17* is not. And there are many, many other difficult, bold, audacious and magnificent things we can do when our confidence and vision are in full flower.

We can do them all. *We can.*

The bloom of American flags after September 11th shocked and horrified many of those who fervently wished such sentiments had gone the way of the Apollo program. We learned much on that awful day. I learned that our pride was waiting, just beneath the surface. It had been there the whole time.

Some people reading this were too young to remember what America was like in the late seventies. Moon landing? *Been there, done that.* We had just come off of a bitter, endless, pointless war. We had seen riots, assassinations, inflation, stagnation, and international impotence. The Office of the President had been tainted by scandal and treachery, lies and cover-ups, and frankly seemed never to recover. We were weak, we were scared, we were worried and we were timid. We were, in fact, much like I had been in that nightclub, immobilized by fear of failure. The idea that we could succeed at something great and noble had the saccharine taste of nostalgia. Our vision had left us. Our confidence was shot to pieces, lying in a rice paddy, below a Book Depository, in the kitchen of an LA hotel, and inside a DC condominium.

Then along came this man, this former lifeguard, and right off the bat, he had the brazen confidence to say something like this: "*The Democrats say that the United States has had its days in the sun, that our nation has passed its zenith. They expect you to tell your children that the American people no longer have the will to cope with their problems, that the future will be one of sacrifice and few opportunities. My fellow citizens, I utterly reject that view.*" And it was all uphill from there.

"*Millions of individuals making their own decisions in the marketplace will always allocate resources better than any centralized government planning process.*"

What does that mean? It means that a planning commission in Paris or Washington may *think* they know more about how to run a gas station *than the man who runs the gas station.*

But they don't. And this:

"*How do you tell a communist? Well, it's someone who reads Marx and Lenin. And how do you tell an anti-communist? It's someone who **understands** Marx and Lenin.*"

Brilliant. I honestly used to think this man was an idiot. If all I wrote in my entire life was a single line that pithy and on-target, I'd be deliriously happy. And this:

"Of the four wars in my lifetime, none came about because the U.S. was too strong."

I don't know about you, but I'm speechless.

Shelby Foote, writing in his immortal trilogy, *The Civil War*, describes Lincoln's power to write and communicate as music, as in, "And then the Lincoln music began to sound."

Ronald Reagan had that music. We hear in it again and again, that one pure note of confidence, the belief that what we are doing is right.

"Putting people first has always been America's secret weapon. It's the way we've kept the spirit of our revolution alive—a spirit that drives us to dream and dare, and take great risks for a greater good."

I'll fight for that. I'll fight for that idea of humanity. I will, so help me God. And for anyone who loves this nation and this ideal, what can we say about America that can compare to this image:

"I've spoken of the shining city all my political life, but I don't know if I ever quite communicated what I saw when I said it. But in my mind it was a tall, proud city built on rocks stronger than oceans, windswept, God-blessed, and teeming with people of all kinds living in harmony and peace; a city with free ports that hummed with commerce and creativity. And if there had to be city walls, the walls had doors and the doors were open to anyone with the will and the heart to get here...

"After 200 years, two centuries, she still stands strong and true on the granite ridge, and her glow has held steady no matter what storm. And she's still a beacon, still a magnet for all who must have freedom, for all the pilgrims from all the lost places who are hurtling through the darkness, toward home."

Note to the worried: Our music sings *"come here and prosper,"* not *"go out and pillage."*
I was one of those pilgrims, hurtling through the darkness of my own ignorance, towards this home we share and love so deeply. It's good to be home, at last.

Ronnie, forgive me. I'm sorry. I just had no idea at all.

And if that Lady in White is reading this: Drop me an e-mail. I'll knock you off your feet.

HISTORY

March 29, 2003

Life during wartime.

There's nothing I can say about the parade of still pictures, the faces on the television – except, perhaps, that they all seemed to share a fierce pride in their eyes, photographed for the first time in their Marine Dress Blues. Surely their families are proud of them. I certainly am, and I never got to know any of them. And now, I never will.

Names scroll in little yellow letters across the bottom of our glowing screens: Sergeants, and Captains, and Privates. These men have died for us. More will follow. We asked them to go, and they went.

All across this nation – here and there, sparkling across the map like fireflies on a summer night – sedans are slowly rolling to a stop outside of small, modest homes. Men in uniform emerge, straighten their tunics, and walk slowly up driveways. Doorbells are rung. Maybe here and there smiles will evaporate in shock and surprise as doors are opened, but more likely the face will be one full of stunned realization that the very worst thing in the whole world has happened. And children will be sent to their rooms. And the men will speak in somber, respectful tones. And sons and mothers and fathers and wives will be told that the one thing they love more than anything in this world has been taken away from them, that their sons and daughters will not be coming home, that their fathers or mothers have gone away and will never come back, not ever.

Why do we do this? What could possibly be worth *this?*

The war is an abject and utter failure. What everyone thought would be a quick, decisive victory has turned into an embarrassing series of reversals. The enemy, -- a ragtag, badly-fed collection of hotheads and fanatics – has failed to be shocked and awed by the most magnificent military machine ever fielded. Their dogged resistance has shown us the futility of the idea that a nation of millions could ever be subjugated and administered, no matter what obscene price we are willing to pay in blood and money.

The President of the United States is a buffoon, an idiot, a man barely able to speak the English language. His vice president is a little-seen, widely despised enigma and his chief military advisor a wild-eyed warmonger. Only his Secretary of State offers any hope of redemption, for he at least is a reasonable, well-educated man, a man most thought would have made a far, far better choice for Chief Executive.

We must face the fact that we had no business forcing this unjust war on a people who simply want to be left alone. It has damaged our international relationships beyond any measure, and has proven to be illegal, immoral and nothing less than a monumental mistake that will take generations to rectify.

We can never hope to subdue and remake an entire nation of millions. All we will do is alienate them further. So we must bring this war to an immediate end, and make a solemn promise to history that we will never launch another war of aggression and preemption again, so help us God.

———————————

This was the condensed opinion of the Copperhead press. The time was the summer of 1864.

Everyone thought the Rebels would be whipped at Bull Run, and that the Confederacy would collapse within a few days or hours of such a defeat. No one expected the common Southern man to fight so tenaciously, a man who owned no slaves and who in fact despised the rich fire-eaters who had taken them to war.

Lincoln was widely considered a bumpkin, a gorilla, an uncouth backwoods hick who by some miracle of political compromise had made it to the White House. Secretary of War Stanton had assumed near-dictatorial powers and was also roundly despised. Only Secretary of State William Seward, a well-spoken, intelligent Easterner and a former Presidential candidate, seemed fit to hold office.

After three interminable and unbelievably bloody years of conflict, many in the Northern press had long ago become convinced that there was no hope of winning the war, and far less of winning the peace that followed. After nearly forty months of battle and maneuver, after seeing endless hopes dashed in spectacular failure, after watching the magnificent Army of the Potomac again and again whipped and humiliated by a far smaller, under-fed, under-equipped force, the New York newspapers and many, many others were calling for an immediate end to this parade of failures.

It took them forty months and hundreds of thousands killed to reach that point. Today, many news outlets have reached a similar conclusion after ten days and less than fifty combat fatalities.

Ahhh. *Progress.*

———————————

A few years ago, I made up my mind to visit for the first time many of the places I had come to know so well. So before my 1996 Christmas trip to visit my father at his house adjacent to Valley Forge – another place rich with ghosts and history – I made a tour of as many Civil War battlefields as I could, driving northward through Virginia, seeking out the unremarkable hills and fields that I had followed with Shelby Foote through more than 2,300 pages of his magnificent *Civil War* trilogy.

It was bitterly cold the day I walked up the steep embankment where Hood's Texans broke the Union line at Gaines Mill, and then I thrust my hands into my pockets and walked a few hundred yards and three blood-soaked years away to the lines at Cold Harbor, where the remains of the opposing trenches lay almost comically close.

As I walked from the Confederate to the Union positions, the green pine forest was as peaceful and serene a place as is possible to imagine. And there I stopped, halfway between the lines, listening to the winter breeze swaying the trees, and looked around – at nothing. Just a glade like any other in the beautiful back woods of Virginia. And yet here lay seven thousand men – here, in this little clearing. *Seven thousand* men. The Union blue lay so thick on this ground that you could walk from the Confederate lines to the Union ones on the backs of the dead, your feet never touching the grass.

You can see them, you know. Not that I believe in ghosts, or the occult. But when you stand on a field like that, in a place like that, with a name like that – **Cold Harbor** – you *feel* it. You feel the reality of it. This *happened*, and it happened *right here*. The history of that ground rises like a vapor and grabs your imagination by the neck, and forces you to see what happened there.

The next day, I stood in a tiny rut, a small bend in a shallow, grassy berm, where for *sixteen hours* men cursed and killed each other at point-blank range, where musket balls flew so furiously that they cut down a foot-thick oak tree. Here, at the Bloody Angle of Spotsylvania, the fighting was hand-to-hand from the break of dawn to almost midnight; uninterrupted horror that to this day remains for me the most appalling single acre in human history. There, on that unassuming, peaceful, empty field – it might as well have been the back of a high school – men had become so agitated that they climbed the muddy, blood-slick trenches, clawed their way to the parapets to shoot at a man a foot or two away, then hurled their bayoneted muskets like a javelin into the crowd before being shot down and replaced by other half-mad, raving automatons.

What trick of time and memory, what charm or spell does history possess, that can turn such fields of unremitting violence and terror into places of religious awe and wonder?

Why are some people called to these places, in America and around the world, to stand in wonder – not only at the brutality of war, but at the transcendental, ennobling **power** of them? How does slaughter and death turn into nobility and sacrifice? Why can we recite the names of places like *Roanoke, Harrisburg, Phoenixville, Marseille, Kiev, Vanuatu* and *Johannesburg* with no more passion than we muster while reading the ingredients on the back of a cereal box, while names like *Antietam, Gettysburg, Valley Forge, Verdun, Stalingrad, Guadalcanal* and *Rorke's Drift* thunder through time as if the earth itself were being rung like a bell?

Today we are at War. The future is dark and filled with uncertainties. We are at a time of great peril and momentous decisions are being made by the hour. We know history is being written before our very eyes. No one knows how things will turn out – only history will know.

We can, however, step back from 24/7 embedded coverage. We can in fact gain what is most missing in these anxious days – **perspective.** Like all worthwhile journeys, this will take some time.

First, we need to go to the one place that could perhaps best make sense of all this blood and terror and waste and pain.

I found it, finally. As with all the other places I had visited, I had great difficulty realizing where I was because the reality was so much smaller than what I had imagined. Off in the distance stood Seminary Ridge, where Pickett and Armistead and the rest would march into history – but that was not what I wanted to see.

I had made my way over the boulders of The Devils' Den, caught my breath when I found myself in a small alcove where a dead Confederate had lain in one of the most famous photos from the war. And finally, I found the marker I was looking for, and walked – such a small distance – down and then up again that little stretch of hill.

This was it, all right. This was the place. I was standing on the exact spot where the very existence of the United States of America, where all of our lives and our history, all our subsequent glory and tragedy, turned on what lay in the heart of an unassuming professor of Rhetoric from a small college in Brunswick, Maine.

One of the most subtle distortions caused by history's telephoto lens is the sense of predetermination. We know the Allies won World War II, as decisively as any conflict in history. But in London, 1940, such an outcome would have seemed unthinkably optimistic. The fact is, it was a very, very near thing.

We look back on the Union victory in the Civil War with the same sense of it being a foregone conclusion. But it was not. By the second day of July in 1863, the mighty armies of the Union had been beaten in every major battle except Antietam – and that had been not much better than a tie. And they had not just been defeated. They had been *thrashed.* Whipped. Sent reeling again and again and again by a half-starved collection of scarecrows in homemade uniforms.

None of this was lost on the Union men that morning, not the least on that Professor of Rhetoric from Bowdoin College. He had seen, first hand, the disasters at Fredericksburg and Chancellorsville. For those men, as for us today, the future was dark and unknowable.

Yet history can often show where we are going by showing where we have been, in the same way that a ship's wake extending to the Southern horizon is a sure sign of a Northward course. And that course, for the Union, for the United States as we know it today, was bleak.

Were the South to win that July day, the first northern state capitol – Harrisburg – would fall to the Confederates. Nothing would stop them from reaching Baltimore, and Washington. If the Army of the Potomac lost yet again on this field, the South would very likely take Washington, the British would enter the war on the side of the Confederacy and the mighty Royal Navy would break the Union blockade. In the words of Shelby Foote, the war would be over – lost.

The Federal position was strong, but it had a fatal weakness. At the southern end of the Union line were two small hills. The smaller and nearer, called Little Round Top by the locals, overlooked the entire Union position. Artillery placed on that hill could fire down the Union line, wreaking carnage on the men below. The entire position would become untenable.

No one was on Little Round Top.

Across the ground that Pickett would cross the next day, this did not escape the eye of Confederate Lieutenant General Longstreet. He knew that if he could get some guns on that little hill the battle would be over. Indeed, the *war* would be over – won. He asked Lee if he could send his toughest men, John Bell Hood's Texans and Alabamans, to take that hill. Lee agreed.

Back on Cemetery Ridge, the Blue commanders realized, at long last and to their abject horror, the danger they were in. They immediately sent some regiments down the line to hold that hill, extending the left of their line up Little Round Top. And there, on the afternoon of July 2nd, 1863, history and the Professor of Rhetoric collided.

––––––––––––––––

Joshua Lawrence Chamberlain was an amateur. And everything he knew about tactics he had read, on his own, in a little book he carried with him in case it would come in handy. He knew that his 20th Maine Regiment was the extreme left of the entire Union army. In fact, he could look over to that man standing there, the one with the neatly trimmed beard: *that* fellow, right *there*, was the end of the line.

Chamberlain knew the significance of his position on the field. He knew if he failed the Union left would roll up and crumble the way the right had a few weeks before in the disaster at Chancellorsville. He knew the Union could not bear another defeat of that magnitude.

Up from the valley below came Hood's men: fierce, shrieking, caterwauling demons, the same set of wolves that had shattered the Union line at Gaines Mill and whipped and humiliated their opponents every time they had taken the field.

They came up through the thin forest yelling like furies.

Chamberlain casually walked the line, keeping his men cool, plugging holes and moving reserves while showing the utter disregard for his own life that commanders of both sides were expected to show during those horrible brawls.

Repeated and steady volleys drove the Southerners back, but not for long. They came again. Again they were driven back. Again they came with their weird and terrifying Rebel Yell, and again they were knocked back by withering volleys from the 20th Maine. The Northerners were holding on, but by sheer guts alone, for each charge and counter-volley knocked more men out of the line, heads and arms and torsos exploding under the impact of the heavy lead musket balls. Worse, they were by now almost out of ammunition.

The Confederates were skilled tacticians. When the men from Maine showed more determination than expected, they looked for a way around them, to hit the line from behind. Quickly they sent their men sideways, toward the Union left, trying to get around the corner and attack from the rear.

Chamberlain saw this. Armies could readjust themselves, but there was nothing in the little book about what to do with a single regiment. So he planted the flag, and on that spot, he sent men off at a right angle, like an open gate, to confront the flanking Confederates head on.

Again they came on, getting right to the lines this time. Again they were shot and clubbed back down the hill. Again they massed for another charge, their determination to take that hill as strong as the 20th's was to defend it. Only now, Chamberlain's men were completely out of ammunition. During this latest repulse the Rebel veterans had staggered back down the side of Little Round Top under a hail of rocks being thrown by the exhausted men in Blue.

And so we come to this exact time and place. It is the 2nd of July, 1863, just south of a small Pennsylvania town. You are on a small hill covered with thin pine trees. Your face is black with gunpowder: it burns your throat and eyes, it has cracked your lips, and you are more thirsty than you believed possible.

All around you are dead and dying men, some moaning, some screaming in agony as they clutch shattered arms or hold in their bowels. The field in front of you is covered with dead Rebels, and yet the ground looks alive, undulating, as the wounded Confederates try to crawl back to safety. In the woods below you can hear fresh enemy troops arrive, hear orders being issued in the soft accents of the deep South. You have no more musket rounds. There aren't even very many rocks left to throw. And you know that this time, they *will* succeed.

These men have never been beaten, least of all by you. You are a professor of Rhetoric at Bowdoin College in Brunswick, Maine. As you walk what is left of your line, you know you have fought bravely and well, done more than could ever be asked of you. You have no choice but to fall back in orderly retreat. Your men are out of ammunition. To stand here and take another charge is to die. It's that simple. These men are your responsibility. Their families depend on you to bring them home. Many have already died. To not retreat will likely condemn many more wives to being widows, not the least your own.

You look down past the dead and dying men to the bottom of the hill. Masses of determined Confederate men are emerging, coming for you. They are not beaten. They are determined to have this hill. Off to your left stands Old Glory, the hinge in your pathetic, small gate.

You know that this is a war to preserve a Union, a system of government four score and seven years old. Many said such a system of self rule could not possibly survive. If you retreat now, today will be the day they are proven right.

You cannot go back. You cannot stay here. Your men look at you. You utter two words:

"Fix Bayonets."

You can see the reaction on the faces of the men. *No, that can't be right. He couldn't possibly mean it.*

But you *do* mean it. You know history. In the middle of this shock and death and agony, amid the blood and stench and acrid smoke, you have the **perspective** even now to see what is really at stake here.

As Chamberlain walked his line one last time, he smiled, and shouted, *"Stand firm, ye boys of Maine, for not once in a century are men permitted to bear such responsibilities!"*

Today, the United States is at war with Iraq.

Before the Civil War, we would have said, "the United States are at War with Iraq." Before the Civil War, the United States was plural, a collection of relatively weak, sovereign states. After the Civil War, we were welded by fire and death into a single, indivisible *nation*. There is a marker, in a forest, on a hill, to mark that transition.

We are a nation because the Rhetoric professor did not retreat. He did not tire, he did not falter, and he did not fail. As the Confederates charged Little Round Top to take the hill, the battle, and the war, the schoolteacher from Maine drew his sword, and swung his gate around like a baseball bat, hitting the Rebels on the side as they leapt down upon the shocked and awed Confederates who promptly broke and ran.

There would, of course, be two more years of blood and carnage: Pickett's Charge was 24 hours in the future; the Bloody Angle and Cold Harbor further down that dark, unseen road. If you told the men of the 20th Maine that day they had saved the Union on Little Round Top, they would have looked at you as if you were mad. It was, after all, a relatively small engagement in the biggest, bloodiest battle in the history of the Western Hemisphere.

But you have to ask yourself if perhaps Joshua Lawrence Chamberlain might have had a glimpse of the future. *"Not once in a century are men permitted to bear such responsibilities!"* he had shouted. He knew, on some level, that this history being written large, that the actions of a small, battered regiment, indeed, the actions of a single man, would determine whether we would live in one country, or two.

In 1865 the issue of American Slavery, an issue dodged in 1783, an issue compromised in 1850, and an issue that tore us apart as a people was settled once and for all, by force of arms. By **War**. Secession was settled, too – settled most emphatically.

War settled whether the Mediterranean Sea would be a Carthaginian Lake or a Roman one. War settled whether Jerusalem would be Christian or Muslim. War determined whether a surrender document would be signed aboard the *Missouri* in Tokyo Bay or on the *Yamato* just off Alcatraz in San Francisco Bay. War determined whether France would be living through four years, or a millennia of darkness under Nazi supermen, and a weird, ghostly war determined whether or not there would be Englishmen and Scots and Americans living and dying in gulags in Siberia.

And four years of unimaginably brutal war determined whether or not the United States of America would in fact be a land where all men are created equal. War determined whether the fatal, poisonous stain of slavery would split the nation into two irreconcilable camps, or whether the blood and sacrifice of men at Little Round Top and The Angle and Cold Harbor would, in part, wash away that stain and put right that which was unable to be put right at the birth of this awesome experiment in self-rule.

We have markers on the fields at Gettysburg because there men died so that men and women like Colin Powell and Condoleeza Rice and Vincent Brooks and Shoshana Johnson and millions of other African-Americans would have a chance to experience the American promise as full and equal members. Having walked these fields of slaughter and murder, I now know that the marble and monuments are not glorifications of death, but reminders of the sacrifice of men determined to fight and die to do the right thing for people other than themselves.

Lincoln's purpose at the beginning of the war was to preserve the Union. *"My paramount object in this struggle is to save the Union. If I could save the Union without freeing any slave, I would do it; and if I could save it by freeing all the slaves, I would do it; and if I could save it by freeing some and leaving others alone, I would also do that."*

But if our Civil War was started for the most pragmatic of reasons, by the time it was over the motivation had changed. When Grant took overall command and swung the Union armies into the south like a sledgehammer, the war took on a brutality and carnage unbelievable even to those jaded by the previous horrors. And yet as the Union armies marched through the south singing *The Battle Hymn of the Republic*, the voices of the men would swell in choked emotion as they sang:

As he died to make men holy
Let us die to make men free
While God is marching on.

Sacrifice and death transformed that War, and remade the nation. Abolition, at the outset a position taken by a vocal minority in New England and the Midwest, became the great cause of liberation and freedom for all men.

Back in 1996, when I walked those fields, I did not know how such a thing could have happened. But now I do. For I see exactly the same thing happening today in Iraq.

No sane person wants to fight a war. But many sane people believe that there are times when they are necessary. I believe this is one of those times.

For it seems to me that if you are against *any* war – if you believe that peace is always the right choice – then you must believe at least one, if not both of the following:

1. People will always be able to come to a reasonable agreement, no matter how deep or contentious the issue, and that all people are rational, reasonable, honorable, decent and sane,

or,

2. It is more noble to live under slavery and oppression, to endure torture, institutionalized rape, theft and genocide than it is to fight it.

History, not to mention personal experience, shows me that the first proposition is clearly false. I believe, to put it plainly, that some people have been raised to become pathological murderers, liars, and first-rate bastards, and that these people will kill and brutalize the good meek people, and steal from and murder them whenever it is in their personal interest to do so. You are, of course, free to disagree about this element of humanity. I, however, can put a great many names on the table. History is littered with people and regimes just like this: entire nations ruled by murderers and thugs, savage and brutal men who could herd grandmothers and babies into gas chambers and march to battle with guns in the backs of old men and teenage girls for use as human shields. I believe these people are real, and that they cannot be reasoned with. I believe that there are entire societies where dominance and force are the norm, and where cooperation and compromise are despised and scorned. Again, history gives me quite a sizable list, and that list is evidence of the first order.

There are people – pacifists – who do not deny this, and these are the people who I really do find repulsive and deeply disturbing, for these are people who acknowledge the presence of evil men and evil regimes, and yet are unwilling to do anything about them. These are the people who cling to fantasies about containment and inspections and resolutions, people who acknowledge that barbarism and torture are rampant but who desperately cling to these niceties as long as nothing bad happens to *them*. When you point out to them that 9/11 showed that bad things can happen when you ignore such people, they simply point out that Hitler or Stalin or Mao is not as bad as all that, that they haven't done anything to us yet, that action against them is unconscionable and illegitimate.

There are also people who say *"better Red than dead,"* people who would rather face the possibility of slavery – for ourselves or others – than the certainty of a fight, with all it's attendant blood and misery.

I'm sorry to say it, but to me that is nothing but sheer cowardice and refined selfishness.

We fight wars not to have peace, but to have a peace *worth having*. Slavery is peace. Tyranny is peace. For that matter, genocide is peace when you get right down to it. The historical consequences of a philosophy predicated on the notion of *no war at any cost* are families flying to the Super Bowl accompanied by three or four trusted slaves and a Europe devoid of a single living Jew.

It would be nice if there were a way around this. History, not merely my opinion, shows us that there is not. If all you are willing to do is think happy thoughts, then those are the consequences. If you want justice, and freedom, and safety, and prosperity, then sometimes you have to fight for them.

I still don't know why so many people haven't figured this out.

Growing up a sci-fi nerd has a few – very few – advantages. One of the greatest was getting to read the *Time Guardians* series of novels by the late, and deeply gifted Poul Anderson.

These stories were the cream of a hoary old sci-fi genre, that being the idea of parallel universes, histories where interference or accidents caused the chips to fall in very different ways. Poul Anderson showed me worlds in which the Chinese discovered America, where Carthage defeated Rome. Other writers have taken us to worlds where desperate Americans vie for jobs as household servants to the occupying Japanese administrators after the American loss in World War 2, and to a 1960's Nazi Germany where all evidence of the Holocaust has been buried and destroyed. I've read accounts of Winston Churchill emerging from behind the barricades of 10 Downing Street, Tommy gun in hand, being cut down in a hail of bullets from the invading Nazis at the collapse of street-to-street fighting in London. There are many others.

All of these stories have a common thread: someone has gone back in time, tinkered ever so slightly, and produced a horrific world in which, for example, the Nazis and the Japanese divide their American possessions at the Mississippi. In them, something has gone horribly wrong.

But I have often wondered, what if *this* history, the one we know as reality, was the one gone horribly wrong? For example:

In the fall of 1999, the Clinton Administration took the hugely unpopular decision to invade Afghanistan to root out Islamic terrorists organized by a largely-unknown fanatic named Osama Bin Laden. Operation Homeland Security cost the lives of almost 300 servicemen, and did long-lasting damage to our relations with NATO, the UN, and especially Russia. President Clinton, at great political cost to himself and the Democratic Party, claimed to be acting on repeated intelligence that Bin Laden and his "phantom" organization – whose name escapes me – planned massive and sustained terrorist attacks against the United States. Peace protestors gathered between the towers of the World Trade Center in September, 2004 on the five-year anniversary of the illegal and immoral invasion, calling on President Gore to pay the UN –ordered reparations to the Taliban Government.

Or:

Today, April 20th, 2003 Germans again celebrate the birthday of Adolph Hitler with a parade down a stretch of the autobahn, one of his greatest achievements. Although forced from office in disgrace when a platoon of French soldiers contested his entry into the Rhineland in 1936, his rebuilding of Germany following the ruin of the Great War, and his subsequent lobbying for American economic support, culminating in the Lindbergh Plan and Germany's spectacular economic growth through the forties and fifties, so rehabilitated his reputation that he remains one of the greatest and most revered figures in German history.

And we can go on like this for a very long time.

I see history as an unimaginably huge and complicated railroad switching yard, where by moving a pair of steel rails a few inches one way or another, the great train of history can be diverted from Chicago to Atlanta. These switches may seem ridiculously small at the time, but the consequences are often immeasurable.

So when I stood on Little Round Top and walked down that little hill for the last time that day, I saw more than dead and dying men littering the ground. I saw two nations where today there is one. I saw a Second Civil War, perhaps in 1909, or 1913, for these two countries would never peacefully co-exist – not with people as proud and energetic as we. I saw not seven thousand dead at Cold Harbor, but 70,000 cut down in an hour by machine guns in the Battle of Tallahassee, saw the gas attacks along the Cleveland Trenches that left half a million dead and dying. I saw, perhaps, the dimmest outlines of a Third American War, fought perhaps in '34 or '37 with millions of civilians killed in great air raids over Washington and Richmond. Of course, these millions never died. They lived long and full lives, most of them – and had children, namely us. They didn't die, these millions, because the men at Cold Harbor and The Angle and Little Round Top *did*.

Now it seems fair to say that you can boil down the opinions of many of those opposed to the War in Iraq to a question uttered by leading anti-war activist Susan Sarandon, who asked, "*I want to know what Iraq has done to us.*"

There are two reasons to fight this war. One is so that History will never be able to answer that question. I don't ever want to read about the VX attacks that left 16,000 dead at Atlanta Hartsfield airport. I don't want to see the video of makeshift morgues inside the LA Coliseum as more anthrax victims are emptied from the hospitals. And I don't want to look at helicopter shots of a blackened, radioactive crater where Times Square used to be, or of millions of dead bodies burning in funeral pyres, like columns of failure, dead from starvation and disease in the worldwide depression that such an attack on New York would produce.

I'm sure Miss Sarandon, and others, would criticize this response as fantasy. I'm also sure that had President Clinton taken military action against Bin Laden in the 1990's, the idea that planes could be flown into skyscrapers, that thousands would die as the New York skyline collapsed upon them would be seen as equally fantastic and absurd. Preposterous. Paranoid. Impossible.

But the fact remains that History will be written one way or another. Saddam's crimes are well documented, as are his ambitions and his WMD programs. Are they worth stopping with force, before they have been used? I say yes, emphatically, and that anything less from the President is a dereliction of duty.

Many do not see it this way. I have to ask those people if they would have supported a military invasion of Afghanistan, with all the consequent upheavals, UN condemnation, and protest, in order to get Osama Bin Laden before he made 9/11 a symbol of disaster and death. The howls of protest that such people would have put up at such pre-emptive action are exceeded only by the shrieks *from these same people* that something wasn't done about 9/11 before it happened.

Here is what I personally believe:

I believe that after September 11th, 2001, the Bush Administration sat down and took a very cold and hard look at what was going on in the world. I believe that they came to the conclusion that the post-WWII policy of depending on a strongman, an Attaturk or even a Nasser, to lift the Middle East into the modern world was an abject failure. I believe that they saw a region so steeped in despair and failure and repression that it would continue to generate, through asymmetrical warfare and weapons of mass destruction, an intolerable threat to the United States.

I believe that they came to realize that even if we were to pay the price of living in a police state, we cannot stop terrorists with flyswatters. Despite our best efforts, sooner of later, some of them will succeed, either with jet-fueled airplanes, or smallpox aerosols, or Sarin-filled crop dusters, or a suitcase nuke in Times Square or the steps of the capitol. As long as the failure of Arab nations generates such rage and hatred, they will keep coming. There is no end to the numbers a swamp like that can generate.

I believe that the United States government has taken a very bold decision to take the first steps to drain that swamp, and that this War in Iraq is the throwing of a railway switch to divert us from a very terrible train wreck lying ahead in the dark tunnel of history yet unwritten. Surely they know full well that this action will, in the short term, cause even more hatred and anger to be directed to us. But I see this as a chance – perhaps our last chance – to eliminate one of the states capable of and committed to the development of such weapons, and in the bargain establish a foothold of freedom and democracy in a region notable for its resistance to this historic trend.

Furthermore, I see it as a means of averting such wars in the future, for it shows in the most stark terms available that we are **serious** about this issue, and more than anything, when we talk about the safety and security of the United States of America we *mean what we say.* Entire wars have been caused by miscalculations of an enemy's resolve. As Tony Blair made clear in his ringing speech before Parliament on the eve of the war, to back down now, to show ourselves incapable of action, would have made all subsequent diplomatic efforts essentially meaningless. Showing that we will fight – and fight all the way – will make it far less likely that our enemies will miscalculate the way we allowed Saddam and Bin Laden to miscalculate.

As national policy, it is risky, and it is extremely dangerous. It is also an act of astonishing courage and leadership, because the alternative is horrible beyond contemplation. We are in the very early stages of a great and difficult campaign, one fraught with many setbacks and much loss. Although chaotic and uncertain to us today, it is a campaign that makes sense only through the long lens of history, for despite the blood and destruction, and the faces of those brave men and women held up to us nightly, it is the course most likely to steer us through these reefs into the open waters of security and a peace worth living under – a peace based on real security, on a free and democratic and successful Middle East, not the petty and false peace of inaction and denial in the face of the threatening storm. The world faced this choice in the late 1930's, and chose an easy 'peace' – "Peace for our Time."

History records our reward.

Those who oppose this war may not be willing to face the pages of history that will forever remain unwritten by us taking this action in Iraq. But two things we can be assured of, and both of them are worth noting in these anxious times.

First, while we cannot say that Weapons of Mass Destruction will never be used against the United States, we *can* – because of this courageous action – say that they will not be *Iraqi* weapons. A swamp littered with chemical weapons shells, with anthrax-dispersing jet aircraft, and with a robust, stubborn and dedicated nuclear weapons program is being drained nightly before our eyes. That is a great victory.

Second, while the long-term outcome is hard to see through the fog of war, we are in fact sending our own children to die to set a people free. When Saddam's murdering henchmen are dead and gone, when he and his psychopathic regime lie burning and shattered like his posters and statues, we may – or may not – see people emerge from three decades of horror to greet us as liberators, once they truly realize that doing so will not cost them their lives.

But even if they don't, it does not matter. The Japanese and Germans saw us as conquerors and occupiers too, not to mention the people of Alabama and Georgia and South Carolina. All of these people fought, and fought hard, for regimes that had kept them in bondage. Nazism and Japanese Imperialism fell away relatively quickly and painlessly. American racism was a deeper problem; it has taken more than a century to remake this society, and while that war is not yet over it most certainly has been won.

We may or may not have prevented more attacks on the United States. We may or may not have generated a greater short-term threat from terror. I personally think that recent history has shown that resolute action, that taking the offensive, has been a great deterrent to terror, and that the operation in Iraq will do much more in that regard. I could be wrong. History will tell us, soon enough.

But of one thing I am absolutely certain. Despite all the switches in the rail yard, there is a flow and a direction to history that cannot and will not be denied.

It is the slow, uneven, grasping climb toward **freedom.** There are markers on Little Round Top, on the beaches at Normandy, and in the sands of Nasiriyah that show us where men have fought and laid down their lives, and willingly left their wives without husbands and their children without fathers, all for this idea. It is an idea bigger than they are, bigger than self-centered movie stars, bigger than cynical and bitter journalists, bigger than Presidents and Dictators, bigger, in fact than all human failure and miscalculation.

It is the idea that people – all people – deserve to live their lives in freedom. Free from fear. Free from want. Free from despair and hatred.

My country has, again, taken up that banner, and the behavior of our young men and women under unimaginable stress and provocation have filled me with fierce and unremitting pride. We fight, nearly alone, alongside old and true friends, British and Australian, themselves decent and honorable people, long champions of freedom who have their own Waterloos and Gallipolis and cemeteries marked with fields of red poppies, rolls of sacrifice and honor that should fill all American hearts with pride. For friends like this are worth having, and I will always prefer the company of one or two solid, dependable friends over legions of fashionable and trendy and unreliable ones.

And someday, centuries from now, in the world we all hope for but which only a few will fight for, all of this death and destruction will be gone. All that will be left will be small markers in green fields that were once deserts, places where Iraqi families may walk someday with the same taken-for-granted sense of happiness and security I had in Pennsylvania and Virginia.

And perhaps they will read the strange-sounding names, and try to imagine a time when it was all in doubt.

VICTORY
April 27, 2003

In January, 1979, I started as a Freshman at the University of Florida in Gaines-ville. I'd missed the fall registration, but not the fall football season, having driven the five hours up from my home Miami on several occasions to watch Gator home games. That had been the last of Doug Dickey's typical 6-5 or 5-6 years, and a new head coach, Charley Pell, was coming from Clemson to lead us into the Promised Land.

We were due. We were, in fact, long, long overdue. UF is a big school, and the state of Florida a gold mine of high school talent. But in nearly a hundred years, the Gators had never won so much as a conference championship. It was goddam *humiliating*, is what it was. Anyway, that was about to end with the '79 season. We had orange and blue bumper stickers shouting GIVE 'EM HELL, PELL! in anticipation of the Great Man's arrival. I bought ten of them, and I didn't even own a car.

Things were going to be different now. Our time had come at last.

I remember following the band into the stadium for the home opener on that cool, crisp, September afternoon. I was grinning like a lark, and why not? I was free, young, and truly independent for the first time in my life, walking a beauti-ful campus on a perfect fall day, surrounded by the most gorgeous women on planet earth.

Okay, so we lost. That happens. New coach.

Next was a night game against Georgia Tech. A tie. That tie was the high point of the season. We lost again. And again. And again.

But we kept playing. We lost again. Again. Again.

So there I sat at the end of the season, cold in my orange and blue sweatshirt, looking down at my soon to be 0-10-1 Gators facing the soon to be 12-0 National Championship Alabama Crimson Tide. Down 40-0 in the fourth quarter, we got an interception, then put in a third-string quarterback who made a **first down** – *on his first play!*

By God, there was still time to win this thing!

Actually, no. There wasn't. As we walked out into the parking lot, I looked around at the cars in the parking lot. Lots of folks had taken scissors to their GIVE 'EM HELL, PELL! bumper stickers. Most of the cars now had HELL, GIVE 'EM PELL! on the chrome.

I went back to Gainesville to do a sketch comedy show in 1992. This time things really had changed. While I had been in LA, a former Florida QB and Heisman Trophy winner named Steve Spurrier had come home, and, like Captain Kirk in the Genesis Cave, **he did not like to lose.** And so, they didn't. He took us from perennial losers, doormats, laughing stocks – to SEC champs four years in a row.

And then, one January night in 1997, 18 years to the day after I first landed in Gainesville, I was sitting in Ashley's Pub watching my Florida Gators play our arch-rivals from Florida State for the National Championship. They'd beaten us, by three points, earlier in the year – our only loss. They had beaten us time and time again. I *hated* them.

It was close at first. But by the end of the third quarter we started to pull away, and when Danny Wuerffel dove into the corner of the end zone in the 4th we knew we had it. I don't remember much about the rest of the night there, other than hugging everybody in sight and grinning like the Joker.

I drove up to University Avenue and parked the car. Traffic was completely stopped. Everyone in the city was on that street – everyone. People were dancing, hugging, weeping, and beeping their horns continuously.

Not this time, baby! Not this time! Not today!

I can't describe to you what that felt like that night. You really did have to be there, I guess. Not only did you have to be there, you had to know the history, the frustration, the humiliation and the almost unendurable, relentless disappointment that had been part of being a Gator fan for so many years.

You could have watched it on TV, but you'll never know what it was like to have that grin branded on your face, to walk up to homeless people and 85 year-old alumni and street thugs and kids and adults and everyone, *everyone* deliriously happy and dancing and hugging each other and just filled with such joy and elation and *community*. We had suffered together, lost together, come back year after year after year through endless defeats and dreams snatched away right under our noses, hoping together, and now, finally, this night had come. *Next Year* was here, at last.

I was honored to have done the video tribute to the team a few weeks later, in a celebration that drew 65,000 to the stadium just to say thank you. And when Steve Spurrier got on stage and said, *"This one's for all those Gator fans up in heaven,"* I remember thinking, *God, if that is not the corniest thing I've ever heard* before a giant sob *leapt* out of me and I looked up at 60,000 people crying like babies.

Just like me.

Now it is worse than folly to compare this to the feeling on the streets of Baghdad on April 9, 2003, when the statue came down and it began to dawn on Iraqis that the son of a bitch was really, truly *gone*. It is an insipid, indeed, an *insulting* comparison.

So why did I make it? *Well, because it's all I've got.* And that, in a strange and wonderful way, is exactly the point I want to make, for we have created a society so long immune from fear and repression, a safe and free and prosperous haven so encompassing that the deepest sense of liberation and victory that this American ever got to experience was when my college team won a stupid football game against the guys up the street.

We have been so safe, and so free, for so long, that it has warped our sense of history and human nature. It is, of course, a trade I am happy to make, but this isolation from the true horror and depravity that are everyday experiences in many parts of the world has imbedded in it, like a particularly lethal virus, the seeds of our own destruction. And it is this threat, much more than that from fundamentalist Islam and its organs of terror, that we must look at – closely, and deeply, and *often*.

I believe that many of those who opposed the war did so because they simply could not – or in many cases *would* not – imagine what life under **real** oppression is like. Remember, these are the people who say, and seem to believe, that we in the US live in a police state, under a murdering dictator, where propaganda is spoon-fed to us like willing idiots and political opposition is crushed mercilessly.

If you say such things long enough, and you spend all your time in the company of similarly tinfoil-hatted comrades, then you actually begin to *believe* that life in Baghdad under Saddam Hussein wasn't that much worse than life in Berkeley under the racist, election-stealing, Wellstone-murdering, Earth-destroying Republikkkan administration.

This nation has been for many decades under direct and coordinated attack by fanatics whose failure to gain respect and attention through the force of their arguments have turned their level of rhetoric to such a shrill and hysterical pitch that years of it have seemingly driven some of them quite insane – insane to the degree that they cannot see that acid baths, state rapists, children's prisons and daily torture and execution are not mere rhetorical flourishes – roughly equivalent to hanging chads and bulldozed *Dixie Chicks* CD's – but a desperate and ever-present **reality**. They did everything in their power to deny this reality, these Champions of Compassion, and Not In Their Name did these daily horrors come to an end. That is what six decades of freedom, security, tolerance and prosperity will do to some people: isolate them from the brutal reality of horror and torture to the degree that "evil" must be accompanied by sneer quotes and the motives of 300 million free and decent people are suspect while those of psychopathic mass murderers are not.

We can all agree that a campaign of unrestricted Islamicist terror poses a serious and immediate threat to this country. The fact is, given the means, these people could hurt us very, very badly, and that threat continues to be addressed.

But I am interested in a much deeper and more dangerous threat. This threat can not only hurt America; this threat can *kill* America. I don't say such things lightly. But this threat is so subtle, and so pernicious, that it is going to take us a while just to be able to fully identify it. Once we go to the trouble of doing so, however, I think you'll agree that much of what we have seen in the months since 9/11 will become much clearer.

We stand in direct opposition to forces who loathe and despise America because America offers a completely different theory not only of government, but of people, human beings. They have a theory, widely and loudly promoted, of who we are and what we represent. Many of these people – college professors, politicians, students, actors – are masters of rhetoric. They get paid to talk and lecture. It is a survival skill. It is what they do.

We see America one way; they see it completely differently. These ideas are at war, and the stakes are incalculably high for the future of America and the people of the world. *This* is the war we need to turn our eyes to.

As long as the true nature of America remained in the rhetorical realm, these people held an enormous advantage in the battle for our country's soul and its future. However, the crucible of war has put these two deeply conflicting theories of America and her people into a situation where one theory – ours or theirs – would be tested in the real world. It was, in fact, a sort of laboratory experiment on who is right and who is wrong. It transcended rhetoric, because it generates *evidence*.

Those who hate and oppose America, and what she represents to ourselves and to the world, feared this very, very greatly, and with good reason, as we shall see. They did everything in their combined power to prevent this challenge, this test of our conflicting visions. *Everything* in their power. *Reality* intruding into the living rooms of the world on a daily basis is a mortal threat to certain rhetorical positions that are at odds with reality, because a picture really **is** worth a thousand words, and at 30 frames, 30 pictures a second, live video can write entire encyclopedias in a very short time indeed.

What we have seen in Iraq is a Victory so large and so important that it dwarfs the spectacular military success in the sands of Mesopotamia. It is nothing less than the remaking of the political, moral and social landscape that will bear dividends for freedom deep into the coming century. It was a test, and a vindication, of a way of looking at this new and shadowy world we face, and perhaps greatest of all, it is a rebirth and restoration of American might on the side of the angels, where it has always belonged and which we have paid a terrible price for forgetting during these dark and desperate decades of twilight struggles around the margins of the world.

I have spent a lot of time thinking about this victory, and the magnitude of it has beaten me down time and again. We can perhaps only begin to get a handle on it when we step back. Way back. Way, *waaaaaaaaaay* back.

So come, let us reason a little…

If we look at human behavior through the long, sharp and cold lens of science, we have a limited number of data sets from which to choose. It would be nice if we could compare our experiences with those of other species, and perhaps some day we will. But for now, we are limited by our own history, and so there we must go.

We humans have existed in our modern form for roundabout a hundred thousand years or so…a thousand centuries, more or less, or roughly a hundred times the distance from the Norman Invasion of Britain in 1066 to the moon landing, the internet and the cell phone.

Throughout about ninety-three of those one hundred millennia, life was pretty much the same. You know the drill: *Hunt. Gather. Repeat.*

But about seven thousand years ago, in the fertile land between the Tigris and Euphrates rivers – *Mesopotamia* means *"the land between the rivers"* —people began to realize that certain grasses and crops could be planted and harvested every year; indeed, enough food was made available by this radical idea that people no longer had to roam from one place to another, hunting and gathering. What's more, there was now so much food that it no longer took everyone working pretty much full time just to stay fed. That meant free time, and that meant specialization: basket weavers, spear makers, architects, stone masons, artists, etc. And that, taken together, has come under the banner *Civilization*, and civilization started *right there*, where on modern maps you can find the word IRAQ.

So, to recap: for ninety-three millennia: nothing much new, although the whole *fire* thing made quite a splash at the time. After the invention of agriculture, writing, law and the wheel, however – all in Iraq – things began to pick up.

But with civilization came, for the first time, really large numbers of humans living in the same area, and something had to be done to keep order. And so these brilliant and creative Mesopotamians invented yet another of the wonders in the human toolbox: they invented government, and the state. It is to their great credit that these ancient Iraqis, even at the very dawn of civilization, recognized the danger in putting the power of so many harnessed lives into the hands of a chief. King Hammurabi, a just and wise ruler, developed a code of laws and held everyone, nobles and peasants alike, accountable to them, and for this he is revered as Hammurabi the Lawgiver.

And then everything went to hell.

Through division of labor the city-states grew more and more powerful, and when united under a particularly ruthless leader like Ramses or Alexander or Julius Caesar, the cities' great military and cultural power could be wielded into Empires, where for many periods in our noble and dismal history most of the people on the planet were ruled by a single individual, or dynasty. More of the millennia ticked slowly away, as empires rose and fell, and ages both Golden and Dark rose and set like centuries-long days and nights.

And our numbers grew. And the amount of **power** to be harnessed grew, too.

Then, after seven millennia of the Agricultural revolution, a new wave of fundamental change occurred, as European engineers – many of them Scotsmen – learned to harness power orders of magnitude more potent than human or animal muscle. And the amount of power the Industrial Revolution made available to heads of state grew exponentially.

Now we need to slow down for a moment, for now things start to get really interesting...

Up until a few centuries ago, humans and human culture have placed ever more power – military, cultural, economic, *raw* power – in the hands of the state. But then, all of a sudden, just as that power was really beginning to hum with the throb and hiss of heavy industry, a small, radical faction of humanity split off completely from this universal norm. They literally ran human experience right off the rails and into the unknown.

It was, and remains, an act so daring, so subversive and so **radical** that the most frothy-mouthed Berkeley student would drop their fist in wonder at it, had there been a Berkeley at the time.

Inspired largely by a spark, a strobe of similar thinking from a few long-gone city-states on the beautiful Aegean Sea twenty-five centuries before, a small group of these audacious and really mind-bogglingly confident humans decided, against all of human experience and historical precedent, to put a large wrench in the gears of the ever-growing state.

Those people are us.

For the first time in the seven millennia since Hammurabi, since people changed history by planting grass, a small, dedicated and brilliant group of humans decided that power would be taken away from the state, from the elite, from the bureaus and palaces of empire, and transferred to the most unlikely of places: back into the hands of the people planting the grass.

These humans had studied history. And philosophy. They spent all their waking hours, during every year of their lives, discussing the nature of mankind and the best way to govern and nurture this violent, noble, greedy and magnificent species we have become.

Using reason, they were able to define much of human nature, both the good and the bad. Poring endlessly through the alternately golden and bloody pages of our human experience in government, they sought to find a system of laws, a structure, that could harness ambition but limit greed, promote leadership but restrain tyranny, and free a people to make their own decisions and yet build in safeguards against mass hysteria and the dictatorship of the majority.

Their goal was nothing less than the liberation of the human spirit. Their success, though imperfect, was breathtaking.

Now we come forward the last two centuries, to this moment in time, through the Industrial Age and into the dawn of the third great revolution in human culture, the Information Age: which we are both experiencing, together, at this exact instant.

After two and a half centuries, how fare the descendents of this idea of removing power from an ever-growing state, shattering it, and returning it to the people? As an experiment, as a data set among seven thousand years of study, how well has this idea performed?

Reason will not give clear answers on such emotional and idiosyncratic concepts as taste and personal appeal, but some hard facts seem incontrovertible.

This experiment, this liberation of the individual from the state, has some qualities worth noting. This relatively small population has produced what is without question the world's largest and most robust economy – indeed, on economic grounds alone, the American economic miracle, puzzled out in large part by a Rationalist named Adam Smith has shattered all historical comparisons.

Listen to what this man had to say in the banner year of 1776, for he had found a way – for the first time in human history – to convert what had in other systems been considered a base yet universal impulse into a cultural and social virtue of the highest order:

Man has almost constant occasion for the help of his brethren, and it is in vain for him to expect it from their benevolence only. He will be more likely to prevail if he can interest their self-love in his favor, and show them that it is for their own advantage to do for him what he requires of them. Whoever offers to another a bargain of any kind, proposes to do this. Give me that which I want, and you shall have this which you want, is the meaning of every such offer…

It is not from the benevolence of the butcher, the brewer, or the baker that we expect our dinner, but from their regard to their own interest.

Now some committed idealists may find that a little gauche. But it is a sober look at the fundamental truth of who humans are and how we behave, and a system based on this insight… well, by God, it works. The insight, the genius of this system is not that people can make themselves wealthy.

It is that in order to make themselves wealthy through economics – through **trade** – *they make their trading partner wealthier too.*

The Mesopotamians figured this out seven thousand years ago. If I make a great basket, one that will hold just about anything, and a wobbly, bent spear that won't fly straight worth a damn, and you, on the other hand, make a mean, perfect, deadly javelin but your basket looks like a demented crow's nest and holds *nothing*...well then, guess what? If I give you one of my excellent baskets for one of your top-notch spears, when we walk away and go home we are *both* richer!

*It's a **miracle!***

Adam Smith is not finished. He says:

It *is the great multiplication of the productions of all the different arts, in consequence of the division of labor, which occasions, **in a well-governed society,** that **universal opulence** which extends itself **to the lowest ranks of the people.*** [Emphasis mine]

Now Adam Smith could be dead wrong. His theories about human nature could be just as flawed as those of another hominid I wish to discuss in a moment. So what does the historical data say?

It says that a new civilization, using a relatively small percentage of the world's population, so armed, can create prosperity and wealth of such magnitude as to boggle the mind.

Americans are often criticized – and perhaps with some justification – of wanting to quantify things in terms of money. Okay, fair enough. But it's tough to deny that in this well-governed society, the universal opulence has done a passably good job of extending itself to the lowest ranks of the people. Even the poorest Americans have electricity and clean, safe running water. That alone puts them in a relatively posh club, compared to the vast numbers who refuse to take up this philosophy. Almost all have telephones, and televisions. The number one health problem among Adam Smith's poor is that they eat too much.

I am not saying poverty is swell. I am saying that the poorest Americans live better than 80 or 90 percent of the rest of the world. I call that an endorsement of Mr. Smith's theory. You can call it whatever you want.

Money isn't everything, obviously. Many people opposed to this experiment in self-rule, faced with its undeniable economic success, would like to believe that it only produces a feral band of ravenous merchants: soulless, dim-witted rug-traders with no cultural achievements to speak of.

But hey, watch out for that -- *D'oh! Stupid evidence!*

Self-rule, freedom, openness to criticism and dissent, has produced not only an economic miracle but a musical, literary, cinematic, military, scientific and technological explosion the likes of which poor, dim history has never seen. Moonwalks – both Neil's and Michael's -- Spider-Man, J-DAMS, Eminem – all from the same human reactor. And we could go on and on and on…

So what the hell does all this have to do with the military victory in Iraq?

Patience, Grasshopper.

This unmatched leap in human productivity – intellectual, economic, artistic – requires a few essential ingredients.

It requires mutual trust. And it requires hard work.

That's about it. Not such a big deal, really.

Now here is where life goes to hell: there are large numbers of people, really vast oceans of them, who *despise*, in the core of their being, one or both of these essential ingredients for human success.

Look at the personal make-up of kings and potentates and dictators throughout history, and you will find that widespread trust of the common man and a willingness to work as hard as they do are not high on the list of their qualities. You will often find this among ministers and bureaucrats, and some college professors, too.

And yet these are the people who have benefited from – stolen, actually – the wealth generated by grass planting and basket weaving and spear making people throughout history. The wealth their hard work generated was promptly stolen by the state, and put into golden toilets in extravagant palaces – for the elites. It happened seven thousand years ago and it happened seven weeks ago. It has happened, continuously, through our shared human history. It continues, without any signs of fatigue, in many places to this very day.

As Mel Brooks says, *It's good to be the King.* Of course, if you happen *not* to be the king – not so good.

Now while concentrations of wealth in the hands of kings and dictators has become a little passé these last few decades, the state, and the *idea* of the state, is and remains very, very powerful. It appeals to all of our most infantile desires: *We will take care of you,* says the State. *We will feed and clothe and house you all. We will take care of your education, and when you are sick, we will provide a doctor.*

And all you have to do, is work for the rest of your lives, and give the wealth that hard work generates, to the State.

It follows that if one is willing to depend on the State for the very essence of life – food, housing, medical care – then the State assumes life and death power over the people that make up that society. Which brings us to another deep-thinking hominid, who wrote that the most perfect human society is one that takes *from each according to his ability*, and gives *to each according to his need*. And who collects and disseminates this largesse?

Guess.

Now, on the face of things, this theory of Karl Marx's is a damn sight more noble and refined than the *you do what's good for you, I do what's good for me, and we both are better off* pragmatism of Adam Smith. In theory, *Communism* is a moving and high-minded philosophy that is based on the highest human traits of compassion and sacrifice. This is why so many romantics and idealists are attracted to it. (*Pacifism* also recruits heavily from this pool, and for the same reason.)

Fortunately for our own personal enlightenment, history has put this idea – this theory of how people are made – into play as well. It is, for all intents and purposes, the direct opposite of the anti-state, radical experiment discussed earlier. How has it performed?

Not so well. During its trial in Russia, it managed to run the most resource-rich region of the earth into utter ruin and ecological devastation that will last for many decades, perhaps centuries. The State it produced killed no less than *forty million* of its own people, and it terrified and stunted, emotionally, intellectually and spiritually, the entire population to which it had attached itself. There is much noble and beautiful in Russian culture. Almost none of it came from this experiment.

Oh, and by the way, since it's easy to gloss over such things, let's say it again: *Forty Million* killed. Minimum.

Reason seems to tell us that if this system was as good as it sounds on paper, then it would be the Soviet economy dominating the world, Soviet movies playing in theatres around the world, Soviet songs on the planet's airwaves, and Soviet science and invention scattered across the earth like diamonds.

Oh, and uh, of course, there'd still be Soviets. Soviets winning the Cold War. Ronald Reagan dying of pneumonia in a Siberian Gulag rather than Mikhail Gorbachev making a Pizza Hut commercial.

Didn't pan out that way. **That's evidence.**

Okay, one data point doesn't make a line. Let's look at China, host to the world's largest population, one of its oldest cultures, and home to some of the hardest-working people on the planet.

Well, let's see: looks like at least thirty million killed by the State, the usual repression, torture and humiliation. No discernable cultural impact on the outside world. The number-one musical talent in communist China is…? I don't know. You probably don't either. The Chinese are making strides in manufacturing (they are also trying a new rulebook), but earth-shaking, history-altering inventions? Anyone? *Bueller?*

Russians and Chinese are smart people. Why such failure?

Despite the reams and rolls of evidence, there remains a committed, fanatical cadre of people who find the idea of a Benevolent State so compelling, so seductive, that they refuse to give it up in the face of any mountain of evidence to the contrary. They point to halfway states like Sweden, which, on the face of things, seem halfway awful by many standards. A lower GDP than Alabama or Mississippi – the poorest states in the opposing camp. But this isn't just about filthy lucre. The culture produces what? *Abba*, and Volvo. Loved the first, not a fan of the second. There is little invention, almost no outstanding contributions to science, technology, music or the arts -- although Bergman was terrific. It is a safe, decent place where everything is taken care of. It reminds me, in fact, of a very large retirement home.

This is exactly what many people want the world to become: a retirement home. Run by? *Guess who!* And they are doing everything in their power to see that it happens.

Okay, now to brass tacks. Enough history. Enough perspective. Back to the present. Back to the trenches. Back, indeed, to the point.

We have just fought and won a great victory against a very great threat to this Nation. I am *not* referring to our military victory in Iraq.

There are many people, here and abroad, who see the State – Communist, Socialist – as the end result for the world. They hunger and lust for the power that the levers of such a machine provides. They have failed, through laziness or defect of character, to amass any such prestige and influence on their own. They trust no one but their co-conspirators – and they don't trust *them* much, either. Many of them have not done a hard day's work in their lives.

But the State gives them power. It gives them the power to rule through committee and unseen, faceless bureaucracy. It is they who decide where all the stuff taken from each according to his ability actually *goes*. The ability to dispense food, jobs, housing and medical care provides genuine power, *real* power, life and death power.

Some of the people that pull these levers are benevolent. Some are not. If you get some that are not, who are seduced by this limitless, godlike power, then you and your society are in very deep yogurt.

The people who promote such a system constantly tinker with ever-changing theories that have in common only the fact that they fly in the face of all human nature and histor. They have convinced themselves, in the face of all evidence and experience to the contrary, that they know what is best for "the masses." They believe that *they*, without any practical experience in the world, know how to better run a grocery store or a factory than the people that *actually run* the grocery store and the factory.

They have Big Plans.

Nothing has stopped these people – **nothing** – from Hammurabi until today. With a single exception, they have ruled history.

That single exception, of course, is the United States of America.

And here is the fight I want to talk about: *here*. Because in order for these people to succeed, for the idea of a vast state run by elites to succeed, in order to start down this murderous dead-end road *again*, the United States as we know it must fail. It *must* fail, it *has to* fail, because the example of a free and prosperous United States, its vast power vested in its common citizens, acting as a force for liberation and freedom in the world and possessed of all the manifest rewards and glory its theory of humanity provides is an *intolerable* threat to those elites who see in the individual another faceless cog in the machinery of **power.**

America's unparalleled military might derives from a culture and a people so energetic, so hardworking and so ingenious that we can, frankly, *afford* to spend more than the rest of the world, combined, on defending that culture and people. We have had our Pearl Harbors and our Normandies. We have seen this experiment threatened by foreign militarism and we have made a collective decision to *never* put ourselves in that kind of danger again.

Because our theory of people works so much better than those who oppose us, America can afford to be unconquerable by force of arms. With many, many millions of well-armed and deeply patriotic citizens, it is essentially unbeatable even without a Defense Department. America's strength is broad and it is very, very deep.

You have one chance to defeat America today. You must shut down her reactor. You must kill the confidence, lie about the history, slander the Founders, undermine the morality, question the decency, mock the very ideas of self-sufficiency and self-defense, banish self-determination as a goal for individuals and the nation, destroy the intricate and delicately made checks and balances that inhibit state power, divide the people among racial and economic lines, and **under no circumstances** allow America be seen to actually do what it claims to do: be a force for liberation, creativity, prosperity and freedom to *all* people, everywhere.

America's strength must be must be seen as that of a greedy, blinded giant, a drunken bully stealing from the world. It must be endlessly, constantly described as *Imperial*, consigning it in a single word to a long line of repression and historical failure. Forget that we rule no other countries, forget we pay billions for our presence, rather than stealing billions at the point of a bayonet. Forget that we have **paid for** every single drop of oil we have ever burned, when we could in fact have easily done what we are accused of: stolen it at gunpoint. We do not, and did not, and *will* not – and they know it. We are, in fact, the anti-Empire. We have bucked history in every fundamental way. Wherever we sail is uncharted territory. No nation in history has done what we have done, and continue to do.

That is not allowed. People might go for something like that. *Imperialists. Bullies. Baby Killers. Infidels. Colonialists.*

We have, for the last fifty years, fought a terrible and dirty war against our mirror image. Our victory in the Cold War was so complete that the Soviet Union, the Superstate, was not only defeated and diminished, it just plain disappeared. And that is a terrible, terrible problem for America, because the departure of the Soviets from the collective memory has been so total and so abrupt that we are beginning to forget that they were ever here.

How else can people like Noam Chomsky and Michael Moore tally the sum of people killed in all the conflicts since the end of WWII and lay *all of them* at the feet of America? Why else could people blandly watch Bowling for Columbine total hundreds and thousands and millions dead, all hung around the neck of America, without so much as a *mention*, not a *hint*, not a peep of the words *Soviet Union?* Oh, and give it an Academy Award, and claim it is "the greatest documentary ever made."

How, in the name of God, is such a thing possible?

We have done some dirty, dishonorable deeds in the years since the end of World War II. They were done to fight a philosophy that has killed untold millions of people, brutalized and tortured countless more, and intimidated, humiliated and repressed *every* person that had the misfortune to be the guinea pigs in history's most horrible experiment in the power of the State.

But we did them. We overthrew popularly elected governments, backed some of the most loathsome and repressive regimes imaginable. In Vietnam we fought a war of attrition that was a decade-long root canal on our national soul. We ran interrogation schools that turned into universities for torture. They are stains on our nation, our history, and our honor, and like slavery, they will not go away, ever.

But let us never forget that they were the actions we took in response to the most pernicious evil the world has ever seen, and we did many evil things ourselves because that was the kind of war the communists chose to fight. It was, I suppose, better than a nuclear confrontation. But every charge of brutality and oppression leveled against this nation -- Allende, Vietnam, Nicaragua – was the direct result of a deadly serious war against a philosophy that has killed no less than *one hundred million* – a **thousand** Super Bowl stadiums filled with people -- and brought ruin and despair everywhere it has been applied.

But we have just won a great victory, a powerful and deep victory indeed.

The victory was not winning the war in Iraq. The victory was not even how we won. Not the daring, bold, and brilliantly executed strategy, although that will be studied for centuries. Not the technological and tactical virtuosity, which was unparalleled. Not even the destruction of the dangerous and pernicious fantasy that Americans have no stomach for a fight that involves taking casualties, or that American soldiers are a bunch of high-tech sissies who go home after you kill a few dozen. All of these are enormous victories in their own right, and they will expand like shockwaves for many years to come. But they pale in comparison to the one true test we have just come through.

I maintain that the ultimate victory we can claim was the fact that we were willing to fight the war at all.

America willing to stand up and fight for what it believes in is a force to be reckoned with – militarily, obviously – but *spiritually*, as well. America, armed with her principles, is a moral and transformational force of **awesome** proportions.

Our elitist opponents both at home and abroad – those with the Big Plans – recognized this very clearly. Because a full-blown shooting war would, in fact, be an experiment, in which their theory of America, their presentation of who and what we are, would be tested against reality.

This, too, could simply not be allowed – but they were done, defeated, whipped, when we committed the most courageous, audacious and confident military maneuver in U.S. history: we had the *genius* – the only word for it – to place reporters from several nations, and from every point on the political spectrum – among the troops, to not only see for themselves, but to show the entire planet, in real time, whether or not American servicemen are baby-killing murderers or the most tightly disciplined, courageous, humble, humane and morally magnificent army that has ever gone into battle in the storied history of this human species.

Just step back for a moment, and think about how monumentally confident that action was. Before it even started, without knowing how well or badly it would go, with dire warnings of street-to-street fighting that would echo the horrors of Stalingrad, and predictions from shrill and desperate cynics that hundreds of thousands of Iraqi civilians would die – *on camera* – we decided that we could trust our eighteen and nineteen year old grunts to do the right thing with bullets flying and the blood of their best friends on their uniforms.

Ah, but these were American kids, well-educated, highly motivated, decent and determined, and the most professional warriors, ambassadors and statesmen that ever walked this earth. Good God I am proud of every single one of them.

They changed military history in the sands of Iraq. That was a victory. They dispelled the terribly dangerous illusion that we would cut and run at the first sign of casualties. Another huge and vital win, one that strengthens our diplomatic hand immeasurably, and palpably raises our level of safety because a weak and impotent America, a hollow paper tiger, was the operating thesis of both Saddam and Bin Laden. Huge victory.

We and our allies, the magnificent British and Australian and even Polish troops we fought alongside of, have made it clear that we can and will fight, that we can and will win, and win big, and win big *quickly*. That means that we be far, far less likely to have to fight in the future. This is a very real victory indeed, and those poor, desolate families that lost loved ones might take some comfort from the certainty that their sacrifices not only won this war, but won many wars that we will not now have to fight, saved hundreds if not thousands of other American families from facing that shock and pain and grief in the future. That is a victory of monumental proportions. It should be celebrated. Those families have paid a very terrible and heavy price for it, in those hundred-odd poor and desolate households that will never be the same again.

All of these are important, but none of them begin to approach the real Victory, which was the American people showing that despite thirty years of the very worst that America-hating celebrities and professors and news anchors and politicians could hurl our way, we still have the ethical and moral integrity, the willingness to sacrifice, and the will – the **will** – to defend this nation and what she represents, both to ourselves and to suffering and oppressed people everywhere.

We fought despite a shrill and rising whine, like a jet engine about to explode, warning us, begging us, threatening us, mocking us, shaming us not to fight. But we did fight. And that is the Victory I want to celebrate. Not as a swaggering, macho attitude about kicking ass and taking names. But rather the sublime, astonishing and humbling realization that *everything* the enemies of America could throw at us – **failed**. We have listened to their lies since Marx took pen to paper, yet the vast, strong, and decent center of this Silent America did not buy into the idea that we are a nation of murderers, and simpletons, and 'sheeple.'

If we could withstand that assault on our integrity, on our values and our beliefs, coming out of the stains of dishonor we assumed to win the many proxy battles of the Cold War, then what will these America-haters be left with? That an action that prevented parents from watching their children being placed into industrial shredders should never have taken place because some clay pots went missing?

Who is left to believe these people now, except they themselves?

I never feared those losers, those cynics, those bitter, small, perpetually angry people. I only feared what they could do to the middle, to the center of the line, the people who get up and vote the way we will steer this ship of ours through the reefs and storms we sometimes face. They took their best shot. They took it at a time when their ammunition was piled as high as it will ever be in our lifetimes. They failed. They failed *miserably*. And in their failure they have shown what they are, and who they are, and what they really want.

International A.N.S.W.E.R, an offshoot of the Workers World Party, recipient of North Korean financial largesse and the driving force behind these rallies, does not care a whit about the Iraqi people. Nor does it want peace.

What it and many other sad little groups desperately want is the paralysis and destruction of the one force that stands in the way of their flawed and murderous ideals: **The United States of America.**

They didn't get it. Not this time. Not today.

"America bring democracy, whiskey and sexy!" said that unknown Iraqi man. This is not a trivial statement. He is saying that for the first time in thirty years, he will have his own chance for life, liberty and the pursuit of happiness. I thought his English was dead-on.

I hope these people stagger out into the sunlight of real freedom with a willing-ness to do those two simple things that seem to work so well: work hard, and trust each other. I think they will. They *started* civilization. They have earned, and well deserve, the chance to enjoy the fruits of it once again.

I hope they will resist the temptation to let oil revenues steer their future. It is not, in fact, a blessing. They are about to start to reap the benefits of the wealth of their nation. I hope they have the wisdom to channel that wealth into their people, into their education, their technical and artistic skill that was once so well represented in the cradle of law and good government. I hope for world-re-nowned universities in Baghdad and in Nasiriyah, producing respected scholars and scientists. I hope for productive farms in the Tigris-Euphrates valley, feeding the millions of the entire region, just as there were thousands of years ago. I hope for high-tech factories in Basra and Tikrit, textile mills in Kirkuk and cell-phone design firms in Mosul. And above all I hope they have the courage to read and study history, and to implement a system that looks something like the ones that allow these daily miracles in the West.

I hope that some day they might be able to forgive us the pain we had to cause them to get rid of that devil, that threat, and his evil toys. Many already do. I hope, and believe, that many more will do so in the years to come. We are still so very, very early in this long and difficult process. But perhaps, some day, they will be able to see that not only Iraqis died for a free Iraq. Americans died. Britons died. Australians and Poles and many others put their lives on the line as well. It would be arrogant and vile to expect gratitude, but I do hope, I deeply hope, that they will be able to understand why we did what we did and how much it cost us, in those poor, shattered homes across America and Great Britain.

And I have one final wish, which I know seems very unlikely, but which I will share anyway.

I fervently hope that someday, perhaps decades from now, Iraq will have a really top-notch soccer team. I hope that one day, they will get to the final round of the World Cup, and when they do, I hope it is Team USA they play for the championship.

I hope that the Americans play a tough, aggressive, masterful game, that they use all of the speed and skill and power at their command. And then I want to sit there watching TV as an old man, and watch the faces on the Iraqi people when the game is over, because I want to see that the most relieved and joyous they can conceive of being, is the day that tiny Iraq got out on that soccer field and *kicked our ass.*

MAGIC

June 07, 2003

When I was nine I saw a leprechaun!

I'm not kidding. I was in the back seat of our car driving up the hill from the hotel my dad managed, back in Bermuda. I'd ridden up that hill, in that seat, hundreds of times. I knew every rock and clump of grass by heart.

Anyway, there he sat, up against a familiar rock: little green pants, little green vest, little green top hat, small little bone-white pipe. Captain Ahab beard – white, no moustache. I screamed like we had just run over Lassie.

Stop the car!

What is it?

Stop the car! Stop the car!

Dad stopped the car, and I nearly broke mom's nose on the dashboard as I flew out of the backseat and ran for the rock.

Gone! The little bastard had ducked into one of his tunnels. This didn't surprise me much: it's tough enough to actually see a leprechaun, but to catch one – that was the real bitch. And by the way, I wasn't interested in Learning About His Little Customs or Making a Wee Friend for Life by letting him go. I wanted his pot of gold so I could buy a dolphin to go snorkeling with.

My parents had to restrain me with ropes to get me to leave. The second I got home I got on my bike and dashed directly back to the spot. I searched there every day for weeks. I never saw him again. If you had told me that having just seen *Finian's Rainbow* the week before might have influenced my nine-year-old imagination, I would have said, *Yeah, okay, but I SAW him!* And I did see him. I saw him with my own two eyes.

Fast forward six long, dry, magic-free years. Miami, 1975. It's Friday night and I'm on the roof of the Southern Cross Observatory at the Museum of Science and Space Transit Planetarium. I've just been made, as far as I know, the World's Youngest Planetarium Console Operator, an honor so monumental in the Great Halls of Geekdom so as to ensure that I would not get a date for at least three years.

So there I was, trying to convince a group of about twenty people that the image of Saturn they were looking at was not a slide taped to the eyepiece, when all of a sudden, someone screams: *My God! Look! UFO's!*

And sure enough, there they were: A V-shaped formation of dully glowing ovals flying pretty much right for us! People were screaming, crying, hugging each other. One of our Junior Birdmen ran for the phones to scramble the interceptors. And they kept coming: no running lights, no sound at all, just weird, slowly moving grey ovals.

I had waited for this moment since I saw the leprechaun six years before. I grabbed the binoculars, and--.

Dammit!

What?! Are they charging their Death Rays?

Nah. They're just birds.

How could they be *birds*? But they were. They were geese, with dark neck and wings, but white bellies. These white oval bellies were reflecting the city lights, but if you looked carefully as they got closer, even without the binoculars you could see the long necks and thin, flapping wings.

It was a flock of geese.

And then something happened that I will never forget: that crowd wasn't relieved; they weren't even disappointed. They were *angry*. They were angry at *me*. Not dogs and pitchforks and torches angry, but they were surly enough to burn the moment into my young brain.

I had taken away their **magic.**

There's a strange cloud that's settled over our modern society. It's a pervasive sort of bland contempt for an ingenious collection of lenses and mirrors that can reveal a giant ball of hydrogen, helium, methane and ammonia, billions of miles away, surrounded by untold millions of ice fragments in delicate orbit, yet one which will ascribe to the most banal unknown a life-changing, quit-your-insurance-job-and-live-in-a-tree status.

For our entire history, right up until a hundred years ago, the idea of flying carpets and magic lanterns held people's imaginations in thrall. Now that we have everyday miracles like jet aircraft and electric lights, all some people want is to return to a time when the *belief* in magic was common but the everyday blessings of magic – telephones, computers, antibiotics – didn't exist. Back in the anti-nuclear 80's lots of folks drove around with SPLIT WOOD NOT ATOMS bumper stickers, and I often asked myself, how much wood have these people *actually* split? I've done an hour in my 20's and I thought I was going to die.

It's sad, frankly – at least to people like me. I find it terribly, tragically sad that the more successful and comfortable we become, the more people pine for a time when none of these everyday miracles existed.

Outdoor bathrooms on January nights and miserable coal stoves that need to be tended hourly just to heat a pathetic half-gallon of tepid water need to be *experienced* to be believed – and not just in a 24 hour adventure, but *continuously*.

Death, hunger, cold, disease, infant mortality – we have fought them tooth and nail for millennia, for what? Apparently in order to so insulate people that they can long for "ancient wisdom", return to the "holistic tribal remedies" of the past, and hold up the most primitive and achingly poor cultures on earth as being the sole repository of "authenticity" while scorning every advance that they take completely for granted.

Magical thinking is everywhere today, and it is growing. It threatens the foundations of reason, individualism, science and objectivity that have delivered this success so well and for so long. It is **dangerous**. If we are to continue to thrive and progress, then we need to sharpen some sticks and drive a stake through the heart of this monster, and right quick.

I'll use the term *Magical Thinking* as a pretty big umbrella to cover a whole host of creeping intellectual chicanery: superstition, wishful thinking, pseudoscience, unsubstantiated claims, assertion, mysticism and anti-science.

Like so many of our other destructive tendencies, this whole mess really started in the latter part of the 1960's. It's a sad comment to make, because we were the first nation founded after the Enlightenment, and reason and clarity thunder so triumphantly throughout the Constitution that, in the immortal words of P.J. O'Rourke, the operating manual for an unruly nation of 300 million people is about one-quarter the length of the one for a Toyota Camry.

Of course, superstition and magical thinking have been with us since the dawn of time, but up until very recently we Americans have prided ourselves on our scientific bent, our Yankee ingenuity – which is nothing less than applying common sense, reason, and hard work to find new ways to solve age-old problems. For most of our history, our public schools were the envy of the world. The very *idea* that a whole nation could educate their entire population was so radical that scholars from around the world flocked to the United States in the nineteenth century to see such a bold miracle for themselves.

Even before the late 1950's, when *Sputnik* lit a fire under science and technical education, US public schools performed magnificently. Now I'm not a professional educator, but I suspect this might have had something to do with the fact that we were more interested in teaching history, science, writing, literature and math than we were about raising self-esteem, discussing birth control and indoctrinating political and environmental beliefs. There were specialized people who taught these things way back then, and they were called "parents." The only "soft science" taught in those days was "citizenship," a class that sounds so dated and quaint today that we can only lament how far we have fallen. The idea that we would teach people how the system works, rather than telling them what to think about it, has long gone. And we continue to pay the price for it.

Anyway, some time in the late 1960's Sauron gets the Ring and along comes the Hippie movement. Their entire philosophy was summed up succinctly in a slogan from the times: *if it feels good, do it.*

As a life philosophy, it simplistic and childlike. It is also extremely subtle and pervasive, and as a personal philosophy it has enormous seductive power. It frees you from the constraints of discipline, study, responsibility and ethics, not to mention relieving you of the burden of making choices based on evidence, reason, logic or fact.

Now those Hippies are college professors, and post-modernism is their Grail.

You know the drill: *No objective reality. All truth is relative.* You can believe whatever you want, when you want. You can be descended from *Atlantean Priests!* You can have *Mental Powers* to move objects, read the future, and speak to dead people! Even better, you can **save** six billion trillion tons of silicon, nickel and iron in the third orbit around the sun – a sphere that has endured 5 billion years of asteroid impacts, volcanoes, ice ages, and having its core knocked out and into orbit -- by holding up a piece of wood with some lettered cardboard on one end and by marching down the street chanting two-line political philosophies!

What's not to like!

Let's go kill some vampires…

Because it is so susceptible to fact and logic, the very best way to fight magical thinking is to simply grant the premise and look at the consequences. This is a silver-tipped, hardened oak stake dipped in garlic paste made from holy water when it comes to demolishing some of these ideas.

Lets' start with those geese bellies:

UFO's, proponents tell us, are physical vehicles from other solar systems carrying large-eyed, small bodied beings who are so technologically and spiritually advanced that they can wing through the light years at will, carry objects aloft on beams of light, move through walls, dispense advice for cultural survival and administer anal probes.

The constancy of the speed of light as a natural speed limit has been so thoroughly and completely tested and vindicated that these aliens must have learned to harness the power of entire galaxies to bore wormholes through spacetime, which would be necessary to have these infinitely fast, staggeringly maneuverable, gravity-defying, super-hardened space-metal saucers in the skies over our planet.

Sweet!

Well, turns out that in 1946 one of these antigravity, faster than light, space-metal disks…uh…ran into a hill. The ultra-classified alien voice date recorder yielded a single sound:*zzrrzzrrrD'oh!rrzzzrr!*)

Yes, in 1946 one of these ultra-advanced beings was arguing with the little pod-lings in the back seat, took his eye off the Iludium Q-36 Explosive Space Modula-tor, and then came the Earth-Shattering **Ka-Boom!** right outside of Roswell, New Mexico.

They – **The Government** – recovered a few strips of crumpled aluminum. UFOlogists point to the picture of the Air Force officer holding up a couple of Jiffy-Pop fragments as "hard evidence" – but as for me, I'd like my anti-gravity, faster-than-light intergalactic hyper-dimensional space-metal saucer to produce something more than one-twentieth the wreckage you'd expect from a Cessna 150 hitting the ground at 40 mph flown by some teenager experimenting with The Weed.

Apparently, Area 51 has at least one, if not several of these accident-prone ve-hicles. They are being 'reverse-engineered' by the CIA and other Black Organiza-tions.

I have on a cheap digital wristwatch. Don't ask why. Now presumably these mas-ters of gravity, wormholes and anal probes are far, far ahead of us in science and technology – hundreds, or more likely thousands of years more advanced. But let's take my cheapo, simple, everyday wristwatch back to a watchmaker of only 100 years ago – the finest Swiss watchmaker of 1903. What could he reasonably expect to reverse engineer?

Upon opening the back, he would find – what? No gears, no jeweled movements. No springs or hands. Completely silent, not a hint of ticking. The case – what is that? Not wood, not metal – more of that smooth, curved stuff. And what about that tiny green square wafer with the strange markings on it? Forget about mak-ing one that worked for himself – what the *hell* is that? What does it *do*? And the numerals – just a piece of clear plastic – only he has no idea what plastic is, let alone the liquid crystal matrix.

He pushes a button. The thing beeps. Where the hell did that come from! There are no visible bellows or acoustic horns to make such a sound. And the accuracy! And – my *god*! It lights up in the dark! No gas lines, no wicks, no flame of any kind!

Even the nylon strap and Velcro would be completely beyond him.

If the smartest man on earth of 100 years ago would be baffled and driven to madness by a $15 dollar watch, how are we expected to believe that NASA is reverse engineering a faster than light, anti-gravity Spaceship? The ancient Egyptians would have a far easier time reverse-engineering the Space Shuttle.

Why is it that every certified, approved, authorized and official UFO photo has been revealed by experts – or the perpetrators – to be a hoax? That can't be good. What does it say for the credulity of these people when you can see video reporting of three UFO's flying in rigid formation at night: a bright white light in the middle, and a red light on one side and a green one on the other? Startling footage shows a string of lights over Phoenix one evening, and thousands call the police reporting the alien armada. Looking at the video, it's clear that these are either a string of parachute flares or a sinister invasion battlefleet of slowly descending anti-gravity flying disks populated by super-intelligent alien creatures from another solar system. The military response was a deafening yawn. The news media, on the other hand, rushed to welcome our new Insect Overlords and began rounding up humans to work in their underground sugar caves.

But why bother with questions like this? If it feels good to believe that we are being watched over by advanced beings, then none of this will stop you. More likely, you believe that you are nothing more than an impotent, faceless cog in a vast conspiracy of silence and oppression, a victim of government cover-ups and hidden agendas, of dark metallic disks under canvas in subterranean hangars. If that's what makes you feel better about your failures and frustrations, then, hey – asking questions like this won't even slow you down.

But realize this: if your worldview requires all sorts of secret kingdoms, unknowable motives, and unseen forces moving behind the veil of normal human experience, then you have taken yourself from the realm of a free citizen responsible for his own destiny and that of his nation, to a frightened caveman quivering in fear of distant Thunder Gods: immobilized, helpless and in a state of abject surrender. You have thrown away the hard work of millions and millions of your fellow human beings who have worked and studied their entire lives to raise you from those very depths.

Shame on you.

There is a lake in Scotland inhabited by a giant, long-necked creature, a plesiosaur that we thought went extinct fifty million years before man came down from the trees. This gigantic, air-breathing reptile inhabits the cold, dark, murky depths of Loch Ness.

Got it. Granting the premise…

What have we got? Some stories from eyewitnesses. Like the one by the British naturalist who took the most famous picture of the Monster, the famed "surgeon photo." You've all seen it.

Only the son of the photographer has admitted that this single most compelling piece of evidence was a fake. He made a recreation of the model – it's about the size of a large rubber ducky (and if you look at the picture again, you realize just how small and out of scale it looks relative to the waves).

Divers and automated remote cameras have scoured the Loch. There's a picture of a fin – only the picture has been enhanced, rotated, and 'dodged' – the original shows an unremarkable – and *tiny* – bit of debris on the bottom. No sign of Nessie. What is much more damaging is that there is no sign of much of *anything* – especially fish. This ten-ton ancient dinosaur presumably does not order out for pizza. What the hell does it eat?

And this is most damning: plesiosaurs were *air-breathing*. Why is it that the best evidence for the Loch Ness Monster is a distant, grainy video of an 'unexplained' wake, shot in the far distance. This creature has to come up for air several times an hour. If we grant that there is a breeding population of aquatic dinosaurs surviving in Loch Ness, they should be sticking their heads out of the water like a giant whack-a-mole game, 24/7. If air-breathing dinosaurs really inhabited these lakes in Europe, and Africa and the US, then the best evidence would be the body hauled ashore by a shotgun-toting British Marine after Nessie ate a busload of tourists in full view of the world press.

Think about it. What if there really is an air-breathing dinosaur in this lake. How many HDTV recordings would there be in a single day. Fifty? A hundred?

Divers did find many sunken logs on the bottom of these peaty, dismal waters. Some of these will, on occasion, float to the surface as the gases from their decay increases their buoyancy. From a distance, they look like a dark, humped shape breaking the water. They eventually sink again.

So which is more likely? A log floats loose, maybe a boat wake propagates across a glassy lake for ten or twenty minutes? Or that a ten ton air-breathing dinosaur the size of a city bus, extinct for 50 million years, escapes detection in a fish-free lake scoured by dozens of cameras every day for the past fifty years?

But people swear they saw it! Same with the UFO's. Many of these people are lying – convincingly lying, as they did with Nessie's "surgeon photo." Some of them, though, are undoubtedly telling the truth. Like I said, I saw a Leprechaun when I was nine. Saw him clearly enough to stop the car. Saw him clearly enough to go back looking for him every day, for weeks, until my parents took such pity on me they put a few leprechaun dolls around the house in the middle of the night and swore up and down they had nothing to do with it – just so I could find *something*.

I saw it. That doesn't mean it was there.

The immediate, knee-jerk reaction to such hard-headed looks at magical events is to state that rationalists are shuffling grey automatons gloomily dissecting flowers and bunnies through thick lenses and tightly-pursed lips, relentlessly crushing wonder and awe.

What a bunch of crap.

I don't have a problem with UFO's, Bermuda Triangles, Sea Monsters, Ghosts, Crystals, Crop Circles and Atlantis because I think they are silly. Silly Things, like the *Ministry of Silly Walks*, are a prime ingredient of sanity.

I object to these things not because they are silly, but because they are *lazy*. They are just, in the final analysis, so incredibly boring, mundane and unimaginative, compared to the real wonders, the authentic magic. *Look! A Leprechaun! It's like a man! Only smaller than most men you normally see!*

We *ooh* and *ahh* at some circles stamped out in a wheat field, but completely ignore pillars of gas and dust so beautiful and so enormous that if you drove fast enough to cross the US in a second, your great–grandchildren would grow old before they reached the end of it. We, a species that can make things from individual atoms, who can decode the history of every living thing on earth, draw maps of the world of a billions years ago, take pictures of the far side of Neptune's moons, puzzle out virtual particles in a bubbling quantum soup, look into space and time back to the first .0000000000000001 second of the Big Bang and who can conceive of and live their lives by concepts such as honor and justice and freedom, can find enough REAL magic, enough authentic, verifiable wonders to keep us busy for as long as we live.

Yet this species stands in line to buy books about a face on Mars and how to keep razor blades sharp by storing them in a pyramid made from popsicle sticks.

We are failing our children if we let a two-dollar piece of particle board obscure the view of the redwood forest just beyond it. Give me half an hour in an observatory with *anyone* and I will introduce them to wonders they will think about for the rest of their lives.

They are more challenging than flying saucers, sea serpents, or wee people with their pots of gold. To understand them enough to be floored by their magnificence requires a little patience, a little imagination. It does, in fact, require some *work*.

But these wonders have one powerful advantage. They have the advantage of being **real.**

We all have people who have influenced our thinking – more, for in a very real sense they have made us into who we are. For me, one of the pillars of who I have become was the late Dr. Carl Sagan.

Sagan was not only a great writer, he was a scientist of the first order. When I first read *The Dragons of Eden* I could see, at last, some basis for why we act the way we do. And *Broca's Brain* is nothing less than a brilliant tour de force of how to weigh evidence and build a worldview based upon what is real. It is refined genius of the highest degree.

One of Carl's last works was *The Demon-Haunted World*. If you have any interest at all in learning how to tell what is real and what isn't then this book is indispensable. Carl Sagan fought a lifelong battle to teach people how to think critically, how to challenge assumptions, and how to marry the wonder and awe of an open mind with the tough, disciplined skepticism needed to stop your brains from falling out. In one chapter, called *The Dragon in My Garage*, he gives an example so eloquent I have to quote it in full here before we go on to slay bigger monsters:

'A fire-breathing dragon lives in my garage.'

Suppose I seriously make such an assertion to you. Surely you'd want to check it out, see for yourself. There have been innumerable stories of dragons over the centuries, but no real evidence. What an opportunity!

'Show me,' you say. I lead you to my garage. You look inside and see a ladder, some empty paint cans, an old tricycle – but no dragon.

'Where's the dragon?' you ask.

'Oh, she's right here,' I reply, waving vaguely. 'I neglected to mention that she's an invisible dragon.'

You propose spreading flour on the floor of the garage to capture the dragon's footprints.
'Good idea,' I say, 'but this dragon floats in the air.'

Then you'll use an infrared sensor to detect the invisible fire.
'Good idea, but the invisible fire is also heatless.'

You'll spray paint the dragon to make her visible.

'Good idea, except she's an incorporeal dragon and the paint won't stick.'

And so on. I counter every physical test you propose with a special explanation of why it won't work.

*Now, what's the difference between an invisible, incorporeal, floating dragon who spits heatless fire and **no dragon at all**? If there's no way to disprove my contention, no conceivable experiment that would count against it, what does it mean to say that my dragon exists?*

*Claims that cannot be tested, assertions immune to disproof are veridically worthless, whatever value they may have in inspiring our sense of wonder. What I'm asking you to do comes down to believing, in the absence of evidence, **on my say-so.***

[Emphasis mine -- BW]

When a person wants to believe something, no amount of skeptical questioning, logical contradictions or contrary evidence will move them. Couple that with the example of the dragon – the constant moving of the goalposts of proof and verification, and you have the basis for modern magical thinking. And if UFO's, Loch Ness Monsters and Bermuda Triangles can draw so many believers, how many more can we recruit with more nuanced sleight of hand?

Look around. In the months leading up to the Iraq war, how many people were saying we should hold out and let diplomacy work to remove Saddam? Had diplomacy worked in the previous 12 years? No. Had anything changed since then? It had not. So how will it work this time? **Magic!** That's how.

And so to believe that diplomacy, and not force, would remove Saddam from power was a case of *deeply magical thinking.* Plus, you get to come out against killing people! That feels good! *Let's do it!*

If you claim that capitalism is evil, and that a better society can be built from common ownership of everything, administered by a benevolent state – well, this is identical to saying that you have a dragon in your garage. Now I'm an open-minded fellow. Let's take a look at your claim. Haven't they tried this before, in Russia. Wasn't it a disaster? *They didn't do it right.* Okay. What's different this time?

Hello?

But see, *sharing is nice.* Being nice feels good! *It's a twofer!* Everybody works together. Everybody gets along. The community cow is sick at 3:30 in the morning in February in Minnesota, and *all* the communal farmers fight each other to be the first out of bed to attend to the livestock that no one owns and no one is responsible for! Could work! *Mnnnnn...sharing...*

There are still many people who cling to the magical notion that George W. Bush did not legally win the Presidency in 2000. Challenge their contention with evidence and watch them move the goalpost:

Bush stole the 2000 election. No, he had the majority of electoral votes. *Yeah, but Gore won the popular vote.* The President is not elected by popular votes. He's elected by **electoral** votes. *The electoral college is outdated.* Well, maybe it is and maybe it isn't, but you don't get to change the rules after you lost the game. *Gore really won Florida.* Not according to three recounts he didn't. *The recounts don't matter because the Supreme Court selected him.*

The Supreme Court only told the Florida Court to play by the rules. *Bush stole the election **because I say so!** Ahhh.* At last. Now we get down to brass tacks.

People believe that adapting the Kyoto treaty will *save the earth.* If you only do one thing today that will raise your self-esteem and promote diversity, then saving the planet and all of its species cannot be oversold. If you think building the perfect society feels good, just wait till you get a taste for saving an entire planet and everything on it! What a rush *that* is!

Think of the arrogance of that statement, the sheer magic involved in a belief such as that. The earth will be here for five billion more years regardless of what you or I do. What are these people really saying? The Earth's environment has been far hotter, and far colder, than it is today. Which environment are we to save? Human industry may – in fact, likely *does* have some impact on global temperatures. How significant is this relative to massive factors like solar output? We don't know. The one thing we do know, with certainty, is that the more technologically advanced and wealthy the society, the cleaner all of its industries become. Want a clean planet? *Fill it with rich people.*

Even the proponents of Kyoto admit that if fully ratified, it would only delay *their own* worst-case model's warming by two or three years over the next century. And all we have to do is wreck the world's economy. Then we can all go back to that magical time when a few million humans lived in villages and drank herbal teas and sang songs around the campfire and poet-kings ruled lands without warfare and sacred crystals kept everybody healthy just as they did in Atlantis.

Now, ask any professional magician how they pull off their illusions and every last one will tell you it's all about *misdirection.* Sadly, those boring, insensitive, dead-white-male laws of physics don't allow for quarters to disappear into thin air.

So to make someone believe that precisely this has happened, we need to physically make that coin go someplace where it is not expected. And the way to do *that* is to make everyone look *somewhere else* for a moment.

Humans have retained several reflexes, and for good reason too – they keep us alive. All of today's animals are reflexively attracted to fast motion in their field of vision. There were undoubtedly many animals that did not have this brain wiring, and these extinct animals are known by the scientific name, *breakfast.* If you're a two-ounce tree shrew or a one-ton wildebeest, something moves fast in the bushes it would behoove you to give it your undivided attention.

This is hard-wired, and there's not a damn thing we can do about it. So watch a magician carefully next time he makes a coin disappear. You'll see one hand move quickly – and that is the hand you will watch. *Coin's in the other hand.*

Misdirection.

Now to show you how this works in the real world, I need to tell you a story about a real man named Robert Wayne Jernigan. I guarantee you this story will make you very angry, but this is the kind of world we live in today.

Robert Wayne Jernigan is now 28 years old. People who knew him said he was quiet, somewhat stand-offish. He was not widely liked in high school.

Four years ago, a witness reported seeing Jernigan enter a building in a remote suburb of Dallas *with an axe*. Four people were found dead at the scene, including a nine year old girl. No charges were filed. Less than two days later, Jernigan turned up again, this time at the scene of a suspicious fire in a day care center. Miraculously, no one was injured. But it was just a matter of time.

During the next several weeks, it is possible to place Jernigan at the scene of no less than thirteen suspicious fires. Eleven people died. Eyewitnesses were unshakable in their determination that Jernigan had been on the scene. And yet the police did nothing.

Jernigan had long been fascinated with fire. A search of his apartment revealed fireman-related magazines, posters and memorabilia. Despite the deaths of fifteen people, despite repeated eyewitness accounts and photographic evidence placing Jernigan at these fires, no criminal charges were ever filed against Robert Wayne Jernigan. He remains a free man to this day.

And rightfully so. Because Robert Wayne Jernigan is an ordinary fireman for the Dallas Fire Department.* He is not a serial arsonist at all.

Now re-read the previous paragraphs and tell me where I lied.

Everything I told you was factually true. But the spin, the context, the *misdirection*… The press always reports serial killers with all three names – Robert Wayne Jernigan sounds a hell of a lot more ominous than Bobby Jernigan.

Quiet, stand-offish, not widely liked – instant psychopath, if you read the papers. Entered the building with an *axe* – oooh! *That* ought to get the blood boiling. That the people had died from smoke inhalation I decided was irrelevant to the story…

And so on. And so on.

This is how you lie by telling the truth. You tell the big lie by carefully selecting only the small, isolated truths, linking them in such a way that they advance the bigger lie by painting a picture inside the viewer's head. The Ascended High Master of this Dark Art is Noam Chomsky.

I have long admired Noam Chomsky. It must be absolutely intoxicating to be able to write so free of any ethical constraints. Chomsky flitters and darts through the vast expanse of human experience, unerringly searching out those few, isolated data points that run contrary to the unimaginably vast ocean of facts crashing ashore in the opposite direction.

Here's a Noam Chomsky moment for those of you without enough duct tape to wrap around your heads to keep your brains from exploding while you actually read his works:

Let's say we stand overlooking the ocean along Pacific Coast Highway. From high atop the cliffs, we look down to the waves and the sand below. I ask you what color the beach is. You reply, reasonably enough, that it is sandy white. And you are exactly right.

However, there are people who cannot see the beach for themselves because they are not standing with us on this very spot. This is where Noam earns his liberal sainthood. Noam takes a small pail to the beach and sits down in the sand.

If you've ever run sand through your fingers, you know that for all of the thousands upon thousands of white or clear grains, there are a few dark ones here and there, falling through your fingers. With a jewelers loupe and an *exceedingly* fine pair of tweezers, you carefully and methodically pluck all of the dark grains you can find – *and only the dark grains* – and carefully place them, one by one, into your trusty bucket.

It will take you a long time – it has taken Chomsky decades – to fill this bucket, but with enough sand and enough time, you will eventually do so. And then, when you do, you can make a career touring colleges through the world, giving speeches about the ebony-black beaches of Malibu, and you can pour your black sand onto the lectern and state, without fear of contradiction, that this sand was taken from those very beaches.

And what you say will be accurate, it will be factually based, and you will be lying like the most pernicious son of a bitch that ever lived.

Why do so many people take this hocus-pocus at face value? Because, like any audience at a Magic show, they want to believe.

Do this long enough, and you will become an Icon– no more hours spent sorting sand for you! No sir! And finally, after a few decades as Icon, you may manufacture whatever data you need to make your case, and not one of your followers will call you on it.

Shortly after 9/11, and somewhat before the *"Taliban forces did finally succumb, after astonishing endurance"* St. Noam thundered that America's "Silent Genocide" in Afghanistan would kill – *pick a number, any number* -- somewhere between 3 to 4 million civilians. At one point, he intimated that up to 10 million could die.

The real number was around 500.

Being Noam Chomsky means you get a pass for being wrong not by a factor of ten to one, or even a hundred to one. In Afghanistan, Chomsky was wrong by a factor of **20,000 to one.** Being that wrong on a regular basis means going for a $2.99 Happy meal at McDonald's and paying $59,800 for it. It means frugally walking out of a *Nothing Over 99 Cents!* store with the seven most expensive items, having just put $138,600 on your credit card. That's how wrong Noam Chomsky is.

Misdirection. Unsubstantiated allegations. Undocumented assertions. Counting a few scattered hits and ignoring millions of misses. You can prove anything in this manner, if your audience is a willing accomplice and refuses to challenge you.

Michael Moore used exactly this technique to make people believe that America is a land of terrified, racist murderers who are armed to the teeth solely because of their fear of black people. For this he was given an Academy Award, and *Bowling for Columbine* has been called "the best documentary film ever made."

I told you this story would make you angry.

I saw *Bowling for Columbine* in a small art house in Santa Monica, attended by what I think was a small knot of NPR movie club pass holders. This is like watching *Triumph of the Will* in Nuremburg stadium seated between Goebbels and Himmler. You know before the lights go down that *they're gonna **love** it.*

We're used to the willing suspension of disbelief when the theater goes dark. This agreement between the audience and the filmmaker, the magician, is what allows us to watch a kid get bitten by a 'radioactive spider' and believe that this will give him the power to climb the side of a skyscraper and shoot webs from his wrists. This is good magic. This is what art is all about.

It takes a particularly badly-made and clumsy film to become so unbelievable that you find yourself muttering, *Oh, come on!* at the screen, and *Bowling for Columbine* is nothing like that badly made. It is a lie so carefully and meticulously crafted that you find yourself sitting there in the dark thinking, *I have to admit, he's got a point there.*

It's only later, when the magic is over and you're walking to your car, only when the narrative flow has released you to swim to the shore of reason, that some people begin to ask some questions. Let me take a few examples from the movie to show you how this lie is constructed on a brick-by-brick basis.

Moore's thesis – near as I can follow it – is that America commits vastly more handgun murders than the rest of the world. Well, there's no disputing that. You would think Moore would make the point that it's because we have such easy access to handguns. He does not. He claims that there are plenty of guns in Canada, but they don't have our murder rate.

The movie's premise is that we kill people with guns because we Americans are terrified all the time, and the one thing we are most terrified of is Black people. But cross 10 feet over the border into Canada and that terror instantly – you might say *magically* – disappears.

Hope I didn't wreck the movie for you.

The title comes from Moore's assertion that Harris and Klebold, the Columbine murderers, were so immune to violence that they went bowling in the morning before they shot up the school. It is a chilling thought. Didn't happen. But that shouldn't get in the way of a chilling thought, especially when it's your opening thesis.

The opening scene features Michael Moore in the North Country Bank & Trust in Traverse City, Michigan, which was running a promotion saying that for every account opened, they would give away not a toaster or a walkman, but a *gun*. We see Moore filling out the paperwork to open a new account. This done, the teller hands him a rifle. Moore exits the bank, thrusts the rifle into the air like some well-fed Sandinista, and over the freeze-frame says *"maybe it's not such a good idea to give people a gun…in a bank!"* Oh, how the NPR film club tittered at *that* line!

This isn't just misdirection. This is, pure and simple, a goddam lie. The bank did offer this promotion, and when Moore heard about it, he found out that when you open the new account, they give you a certificate. You then have to **go to a gun shop** to **pick up the gun.**

This wasn't damning enough. So Moore convinced the poor, decent, gullible people who ran that bank that it would be much better publicity for them if they could hand him the gun right there in the bank. *Uh, well, um…okay. If it will help you with your movie.* But the bank did not hand out guns on the premises. Moore created this scene to advance his premise. It's a funny scene. It is most emphatically *not* a **documentary** scene.

Moving on.

Not wanting to appear one-sided, Moore interviews a few randomly selected gun owners. And who could be a more random handgun owner than John Nichols, brother of Terry Nichols, co-conspirator of Oklahoma City lunatic Timothy McVeigh?

In the interview, John Nichols seems on the verge of total emotional collapse. He makes off-color comments and has a spooky, lithium-deficient smirk that appears at awkward and inappropriate times. After a few moments, this completely random and therefore totally typical American gun owner takes Moore into the back room to 'show him something.' He does not allow the camera to enter. A subtitle tells us that John Nichols has put a gun barrel in his mouth. We can hear Michael Moore gently begging him to stop, to put the gun down.

Not only a fair man, but gentle, too. When it comes to misdirection, Master Moore has the strongest kung-fu.

Littleton, Colorado is a nice, safe, upper-middle class neighborhood. It's the kind of place you'd want to raise your kids. It is also home to a Lockheed plant, and Moore goes on the make the assertion that this 'climate of death' from these 'weapons of mass destruction' is responsible for the Columbine killing spree. Presumably the school shooters in other communities had to settle for magazines and websites of missiles to work up their Death Culture madness.

This would be a stretch – a *real* stretch – if the 'entire community' was indeed wrapped up in 'America's Defense Industry Culture of Death.' But the Lockheed plant in Littleton, the one using ominous missiles as a backdrop for an interview in the film, builds launch vehicles for *communications satellites* – you know, the ones used by HBO to broadcast *Bowling for Columbine* across the nation. This little detail was left out of the movie. Keep your eye on the flick of the wrist; pay no attention to the slow palming of the coin.

One of the most widely-quoted sequences, one that drew squeals and applause for the Santa Monica Art House Crowd, was a cartoon series showing Moore's history of the United States. Terrified white people in England get on a ship, sail to the New World, meet dark, friendly, all-around swell dark-skinned people, and kill them all out of paralyzing, abject fear. Slaves are imported to maintain an excuse for us to stay armed. The black people are then summarily killed to the last man. And so on, with the screaming, yelping, frozen with fear white people shooting everything in sight.

Oh, how true. When the box office attendant, who was black, handed me back my change a little too quickly for comfort I had to drop him with 23 rounds from my trusty 9mm. The snack bar attendant – *a mulatto if ever there was one* – asked me if I wanted butter on my popcorn in a really threatening way, so it was a shotgun blast to the head for him. And the usher, who was Mexican, took a hostile step towards me as he opened the theater door. Not being *completely* dark-skinned, I decided it was safe to just stab him in the eyes with my ballpoint pen.

This is what he wants you to believe. His European audience, generally salivating at the chance to hear an American describe his country as a bunch of idiotic, murdering, terrified racists, howls with approval.

Moore then recounts the story of a 6 year old boy who went to school with a handgun and murdered a little girl. We meet his mother, a young African American woman, in the courtroom, crying and terrified, handcuffed, orange jumpsuit, the whole nine yards. This woman, says Moore, was forced by *welfare cuts* by those *evil bastard Republicans*, to leave her child with relatives, get up *before dawn*, and *ride a bus*, for *hours*, so that she could go to *a shopping mall* and serve biscuits to *rich white people*.

Moore rides the bus in the pre-dawn hours. It's depressing. I was watching this, and I thought to myself, *you know, maybe we have gone too far.*

But when I got to the car, I realized, hey, wait a second. *I've had to get up in the predawn hours and take a bus to go to work.* Millions of people do this every day in America. It's society's fault that this woman has to get up and take a bus to work? And the relatives she left her kids with? It was a *crack house.* Guns and drugs were everywhere. And the fact that she is a black woman standing hand-cuffed in a courtroom has precisely *nothing* to do with this. It is much more likely that this would have happened to an equally unskilled white mother.

And furthermore, if you had a six year old child, and you absolutely had to leave him in a place like that, would your kid take a gun to school and shoot someone? Or do you think that *maybe, perhaps,* just *possibly,* this tragedy had more to do with this individual's parenting skills than the fact that she has to take a bus to go to work in the morning? Is this an indictment of a heartless society, or an insult to the millions and millions and millions of Americans, black and white, rich and poor, who get up every morning and go to work without their children murdering a classmate during the course of the day?

Bowling for Columbine is not a documentary. It is propaganda, created in many cases from whole cloth, and in others by selective interviewing, biased editing and false assumptions.

Much of it is, in fact, downright lies. That it was awarded an Oscar only reveals that the Academy Awards have suffered as much ethical rot as the Nobel Peace Prize, in that it was awarded by faceless voters who wanted nothing more than to take a swipe at the Bush administration.

As for his assertion that Americans kill because they are nothing but terrified white people, a quick look at the murder statistics will show any dispassionate reader that this is, in fact, nearly the exact opposite of the truth. Black-on-Black violence is many, many times greater than White-on-Black violence.

Michael Moore claims to be the Conscience of America and the Champion of the Common Man. He is **neither.**

If Michael Moore was only interested in saving innocent lives, he would have done better to have tackled a subject that kills many hundreds of times the number taken by handguns, namely, obesity-related diseases. Is that a cheap shot? It is. It is a *factually-based* cheap shot, which is more than can be said about *Bowling for Columbine.*

We find ourselves living in a time when people grow increasingly unwilling or unable to determine fact from assertion. In a society ruled by the people, this is a fatal condition.

Where magical claims go unchallenged, where feeling good about something is the measure of its truth, public policy plummets into the same disconnect from reality that has doomed entire civilizations.

As always, we face a choice: we can live our lives by fantasy ideologies and wait for the train wreck called reality, or we can learn not what to think, but *how* to think. How to test and compare the barrage of information and statements we receive on a daily basis.

Howard Zinn has a theory of American History. Victor Davis Hanson has another. Which one is right? How do we know?

A few nights ago, during my one of my regular visits to the main sensor screen at **USS Clueless** (*www.denbeste.nu*), I read something that absolutely bored a hole in my brain. You always have to pay attention when you read Steven Den Beste, but this was something else again. I could feel the veins in my temples throbbing like I was a Talosian trying to keep Captain Pike from seeing that the top of the mountain had been blown off. My hands and feet went cold, then numb, as the blood rushed to my head. I staggered into the kitchen, ripped open a five-pound bag of sugar, and washed it down with Hershey's syrup: *brain needs more glucose!* **Brain must have more glucose!**

Steven was talking about how people think – no, more than that. He was talking about what thought is. He talked about thought as a series of *heuristics*.

I liked the American Heritage Dictionary entry best: *Relating to or using a problem-solving technique in which the most appropriate solution of several found by alternative methods is selected at successive stages of a program for use in the next step of the program.*

Now remember, I'm fresh from the Krell Mind Machine myself, but as I understand it, what we know and what we believe are a series of heuristics, which basically means we use models – little index cards – when we deal with problems. A simple heuristic might be *touching a red-hot stove burns*. We don't have to keep touching the stove every time to find this out. All we have to do is touch it once – I remember doing it and so do you – and now we emphatically know *red hot burners* **bad.**

This is a simple heuristic, and a damn good one. But as Steven points out, a heuristic doesn't have to be true all the time – just enough of the time for it to be a useful mental shortcut.

Now I'll be the first to admit that the right-wing raving lunatics meet the left-wing barking moonbats somewhere off the map where There Be Dragons. So how useful is a complex heuristic like *Democrats can't be trusted with national security?*

Hot stove burns is right pretty much every time: it is an effective heuristic, certainly useful, but pretty damn narrow and limited. That is, its predictive power is good, but the things it accurately predicts are pretty limited. *Democrats can't be trusted with national security* is far more complex, open to infinitely more variables and exceptions, and therefore will be less accurate. It will be proven wrong more often. Roosevelt and Truman were Democrats, and they could hardly be improved upon.

But if you think about *how* you think, you may realize that everything we see in the world is colored by our enormous pyramid of ever-more-complex heuristics, our personalized set of index cards on how the world works.

When we have discussions, like this one, what we are essentially doing is trading cards; I'll try to give you a *Democrats can't be trusted with national security*, but you may respond with *Republicans don't care about anything beyond their own wallet.*

We nod when we read or hear something new that makes sense to us, but that's only because, while new, it is a conclusion that makes sense *based on the heuristics we already hold.* It is a new assumption based upon less complex assumptions, based on still less complex assumptions, all the way down.

Big fleas have little fleas
Upon their backs to bite 'em
And little fleas have lesser fleas
And so ad infinitum

(and these small fleas
of course, in turn
have larger fleas to go on
and larger still, and larger still,
and larger still, and so on)

Now…

Post-modernists will look at this and come to the conclusion that because we all have these internal clichés, all truth is relative, there is no objective reality, and a nineteen-year-old English Lit student knows the true meaning of Hamlet better than Shakespeare does.

Here, in my experience, is a very reliable heuristic: *All Post-modernists are idiots.* Of course, your mileage may vary.

As usual, they have gotten it exactly wrong. It is true that no one can re-learn every lesson they have learned throughout their entire lives every day. To build on knowledge, to grow smarter, to become educated, is to add layers based on the existing foundations.

Science works because each layer is inspected – by science itself – and checked for accuracy. Entire theories, entire skyscrapers of ideas, have been demolished because new experiments proved that a single, simple piece of foundation data was in error. As new experiments provide new information – repeatedly, reliably, independently and in the expected quantities – these then become the steel and concrete that we build newer, taller and stronger theories, stronger heuristics.

And the end result is cell phones, antibiotics, MRI scanners, 747's, weather satellites and the internet.

This process is the exact opposite of magical thinking. It is disciplined. It is rigorous. It is determined to follow the evidence that reality provides when we question it through experiment. It does not have a destination in mind – it follows the path wherever it may lead. Its results are not always comforting, which means it requires courage to walk that path.

And wherever it has been applied, the results have been absolutely **magical.** Miraculous. Astonishing. Awe-inspiring.

It is also a way of thinking that we Americans formerly tried to apply to politics with pride. *Show me. I'm listening.* We abandon it at our mortal peril.

Because of this rational, disciplined, skeptical, hopeful and ultimately joyous way of looking at the world, we have been able to behold wonders that no poor human imagination could begin to predict. It is the mirror-image of seeing the world as the drab, lifeless, mechanical thing that mystics accuse rationalists of. Rather, it is driven by the elation that we can do difficult things well, see layers upon layers of the infinitely large or infinitesimally small being peeled back, generation after generation, to reveal an entirely new stage and cast of wonders and miracles. Big fleas have little fleas…and so, ad infinitum.

If someone chooses to run their lives by the horoscope printed next to the comics, that is their business. They certainly have the freedom to do so. But when magical ideologies are put forward as political positions of equal weight and value, as a chart to sail the ship of state, when *assertion* carries the same weight as *proof*, we will surely lose our way. And then we will have nothing left to save us but all the luck we can wring from whatever leprechauns we can get our hands on.

*I made up Robert Wayne Jernigan only because I do not have, at hand, a real fireman with real stories to tell. If I had, I could have sold the story even better by adding the real-world details such an interview would have provided. The more data points I have to choose from, the better I can build the lie.

TRINITY

Happy Birthday, America.

A few days ago, I was sorting out stuff in my OLD PERSONAL CRAP box. And there, below my HUNTINGTON LIMOUSINE commemorative wristwatch, beside the putty-encrusted Vulcan ear tip extensions, and right there on top of all of my 80's pins (I'M NEARLY FAMOUS, UGLINESS STRIKES 1 OUT OF 4, WHY CAN'T I BE RICH INSTEAD OF GOOD LOOKING?) was something I hadn't seen in a long while. It was a business card – and when I flipped it over, it said MINDFIRE FILMS, INCORPORATED. It had a cool logo designed by my personal design studio, my too-talented friend Steve Stipp: an oval head with glowing eyes and fire for hair – too much like those damn skulls in DOOM that I would encounter years later. But the best part was beneath the logo:

BILL WHITTLE
PRESIDENT

How old was I when I had these printed? Nineteen? Twenty, maybe? I remember incorporating very well, because it cost about $150 and all you got for it was that cool thing you used to emboss your Seal on all the Important Financial Documents you would be Signing. I remember thinking $150 seemed like a lot of money, too – you could get some 16mm stock for that kind of cash.

But there we were: Incorporated American Teenagers. I was the president of a motion picture company. Why? Because I didn't want spend four years trying to get a crummy $500 grant. I wanted *real* money to make a movie. I wanted **investors**.

And I got a few, too…the poor bastards.

Today, on her 227th birthday, the United States stands astride the world as the most economically, militarily and culturally powerful force history has yet revealed.

Why?

Well, one reason is because here in America, a practically broke 19 year old kid can be the President of a Corporation, that's why. *Of course* some of these fail. Most of them fail, *spectacularly* fail, flaming wreckage, *oh-the-humanity* failures. I've had many of these, personally. More will no doubt come. It's easy to succeed in a country that lets you fail this often and this easily.

The ingredients for greatness, goodness, success, happiness and prosperity are not hard to find, and yet so much of the world is a political and economic disaster.

Again: *why?*

Because folks, *it ain't the ingredients.* **It's the recipe.**

So we're off on a little all-American road trip, this time to figure out why our economy, when sick, is stronger than anyone else's, when healthy. To see if we can figure out how 300 million strangers, all the troublemakers and upstarts from every nation in the world can come to one vast continent, be given more freedom than any people before or since, and manage to become the most prosperous, powerful, tightly-knit nation in history. And how come we invent everything, too? Must be something in the water out there.

We're gonna go find out. Let's just hop in the car and see if we can't chase down that American Dream. You know the one: Think of a better way. Take a chance. Start a business. Put in the extra time. Work hard. Buy a house. Live a better life than your parents and a poorer one than your kids. And do it all in a place where you can be free and happy and safe.

America is a success machine. Yes, it's easy to fail in America. It is also the easiest place in the world to succeed, to do the big things – become wealthy or famous – or just carve out a comfortable little patch of ground to spend an afternoon barbequing or watch your teenage kid drive off in their brand new used car.

It's a siren song for many people, this idea of freedom, this dream of making your own life according to a script you wrote in your head. But it's not for everybody. It requires some courage, at times. It demands hard work. It can challenge your bland security. It's not *cheap*, this American Dream – nor should it be. And it lives and breathes *optimism*. Without that you're sunk.

So y'all hop in the back and I'll roll down the top. It's a gorgeous day, we've got the Beach Boys on the stereo turned up to eleven and we're hitting the road looking for the three things that make America hum. And no crybabies! We don't have the time or the energy to waste on mean-spirited, bitter complainers – people who are so filled with gloom and doom that *It'll never work* is stitched into the slack elastic of their unchanged underwear.

Whiners. Defeatists. Pessimists. *Losers.* Big "L" on their forehead. Can you think of another word for gloomy, reality-challenged crybaby that begins with the letter "L"?

I can.

To hell with those people! It's our birthday, dammit. This one is for *us*. **Americans.** This includes all you Americans living in foreign lands with foreign passports, speaking foreign languages and holding foreign citizenships. *You know who you are.* If you're an optimist, if untrammeled freedom makes you giddy, if you think you know of a better way to do something and just want a chance to try, if you can tell right from wrong and still care about the difference, if you're soft hearted and tough minded, if you think we could all get along just great if we'd all just leave each other alone, if you don't like to fight but know sometimes you just have to, and most especially, if the idea of leaving the huddled masses and joining the pursuit of happiness has a mystical appeal for you, then you are already an American in your heart. Welcome home. Get here any way you can. We need people like you.

Hop in the back and let's get outta here. But before we shove off, three quick things:

One: this is a big country. Go to the bathroom NOW. We're heading out to the desert – that means doing 80, *minimum* – and were not stopping 'till we get below ¼ tank, so figure three hours. And that's 80 mph, not eighty of those crappy little kilometers. Remember, US minimum wage is about 3 gallons of regular an hour. Even when we start out working at McDonalds, American teenagers have a pretty long leash – 'bout a half-continent per paycheck. *Part time.*

Two: Keep an eye out for **Jackalopes.**

Three: Rest Areas are For Emergency Use *only*. There is nothing scenic and interesting about them. Stopping *anywhere* other than to get gasoline and food is to admit failure and defeat. Real Americans judge their progress by the number of Rest Areas they can pass in one shot. That sign we just blew past – *Next Service Station 96 Miles* – means that you can go to the bathroom in a little under an hour. I told you to go before you got in.

Oh, and bring your favorite CD's or cassettes: Fleetwood Mac's *Second Hand News*, *One Week* by Bare Naked Ladies, *Ballroom Blitz* by The Sweet: anything that *moves*, 'cause that's what we're doin'. We've got the top down, the shades are *on*, I'm knocking out the beat on the steering wheel and where we're going, there ain't no NPR...

I used to live in the desert. I spent about a year and a half out here among the scrub grass and the Joshua trees – long enough so that when I went back to Florida the mere sight of a puddle of standing water would make me gape in amazement. I was working at a glider port, which meant flying gliders, launching gliders, and when I wasn't flying or launching – most of the time – it meant standing out in the 114 degree heat and raking rocks. For rock gardens. Know what's underneath a layer of desert rocks? *More rocks.*

The place was run by a former Navy test pilot. In the Navy, enlisted men with free time are only capable of doing one of two things: painting the grey deck grey – *again* – or planning the hideous murder and ritual cannibalism of the Commanding Officer. So rocks it was.

I'll venture a guess that most Europeans – most easterners, for that matter – aren't really emotionally ready for just how open and remote things are out here. The sky is a deep blue bowl from horizon to horizon. *Big Sky.* It leans down on you. You spend an hour or two out under that sky and you can feel yourself *decompress.* It's a bit like your first scuba moment: disorienting, not exactly comfortable, but cool.

It seems an odd sort of place to look for the key to America's greatness. We're a long way from any city. A *long* way. Well, you'll see when we get there. Not far now.

The desert is a great place to hide things. It's a great place to *test* things. And that's where I'm taking us: a test site. One of my readers was kind enough to invite us way the hell out here and give us a tour of a place I've wanted to see for a long, long time. There's a lot of history out here, see? Right at the end of this windy little road…

That giant molehill over there, is, in fact, a bunker. Steel blast doors, reinforced concrete buried under a huge mound of earth. Of course, it's starting to rust and show some age now. That makes it even more ominous. Seeing it reminds me of something – what is it? Oh. Got it. The old historic sites at the Kennedy Space Center – *was that the blue tour or the red?* – where you could stand in the Mercury blockhouse a few feet from where they lit the candle under Alan Shepard on May 5th, 1961. Same look and smell of old steel and concrete, ancient, Paleolithic electronics, the sound of frantic slide rulers decaying off the walls.

The wind is whipping like a --.

Well, the wind is whipping *hard,* so hard that as we climb to the top of the bunker we have to lean steeply into it. And surprisingly, it's damn cold, too – I'm glad I brought the jacket. It's snapping loudly in the gale, and the wind is kicking up dust and small pebbles that sting the back of our ears as we turn and look down and out at the test site.

We're here because this is what American power, American *might* is all about. Right there in front of us, out there, in the middle of nowhere.

That's the place.

I believe that there are three elements – just three – that we mix in just the right ratio to perform our national alchemy. Look around you at the rest of the world.

Those who use none of these ingredients are disasters, basket cases, failed states where misery and poverty crush the life out of what is almost an indomitable human drive to create, to nurture, and to prosper.

Almost indomitable. There are governments, theories, and people that have managed it after many years of hard and dedicated work.

We together have wasted enough time talking about these failed ideas, these various and sundry kleptocracies, these stinking, wretched **failures.** We know what they are and we know what they look like. Today we are hunting *success.*

One of the three, *any one,* buys you a respite. Not a huge one, perhaps, but a glimmer of hope. Two, and life begins to become livable. Grey, perhaps. Uninspired. But livable.

Pull all three together and you have a society worth living in. Pull all three together in just the right way, and you have a *reactor,* a fire-breathing creativity engine that unlocks in each of us the very best people we can become.

Stop guessing. Sorry, but it's not God, Guts and Guns. The Arabs have God, the Russians have Guts and the Colombians have Guns – you want to live *there?*

We're going to take a moment to look at each one of the three, each element in this national Trinity of success and prosperity.

These three pillars have several things in common. Their first and greatest strength is that they are self-correcting. They require *optimism* – remember that: that's *critical.* They are beyond flexible: they are supple. No, even more – they are *fluid.* And yet each has strict rules that must be rigidly obeyed for the reactor to produce full power. This combination of a rigid internal structure, coupled with astonishing flexibility, is what gives them mind-boggling capabilities that leave us gaping in awe at the results.

Two are pretty easy to understand. One isn't. So let's be sensible and do the hard work first.

———————————

The first of these three pillars has several names: private property, the free market, enlightened self-interest…but the first essential element of the American Trinity, and the hardest to come to grips with, is **Capitalism.**

Capitalism just galls some people. *They just. Can't. Stand it.*

Now I have thought about this one long and hard, and no matter how I look at it, I come to the same striking conclusion, and that is this:

Where you stand on the political spectrum, what you think of rich and poor people, and what you think about rich and poor *nations* and how they should act in the world, comes down, in my mind, to one single issue, and one only: **Can wealth be created, or can it only be redistributed?**

If you believe, as I do, that wealth can be manufactured out of thin air, then there is no limit to the amount of wealth you can amass. And since you are creating it out of thin air, there is no moral onus on making money – you work hard to create it and have stolen from no one. There is an expression for this: you *earned* it.

Indeed, since charity depends on excess wealth, excess capacity, the more you make for yourself the better off everyone else is. You can even throw charity out the window if you are so hard-hearted; the fact remains that you will spend that money to get the things you want, and the more you have the more you can spend. That money goes to other people. This interchange is called "the economy," and rich societies are rich because they understand in their bones the centerpiece of Capitalist thinking: *Wealth can be created from thin air by human ingenuity and hard work.*

Now people on the left have, in their guts, a revulsion towards the rich and the wealthy, because when ever they see wealth they naturally assume that it was stolen from people without any – the poor. That rich man in the private jet has taken the wealth from all the poor people and is therefore a criminal.

If you think about all of the protestors you see on TV, whether they be against US "imperialism", or globalization, or corporations, or claim to be champions of the Poor, both here at home and for poor nations in the world – all of this anger and seething resentment, all of this bitterness and invective, can be attributed, when all is said and done, to having chosen to believe that there is only so much wealth in the world, and that rich people and rich nations gain and maintain wealth by stealing prosperity from the weak.

This is so idiotic, so demonstrably false, that you really have to wonder why we are having this discussion. All of the money owed to rich nations by the poor – money that was lent to them to lift them from poverty, and then squandered on palaces for dictators and Socialist prestige projects like International Airports in the middle of nowhere – all this money totaled together, is a small percentage of the wealth generated by rich countries in a single year. The idea that the United States can steal 10 trillion dollars a year from dirt-poor nations that don't produce anything of value is absolutely **insane**, and yet, *and yet,* we hear it again and again and again from the professionally outraged who must be dim and obtuse beyond human imagining to keep making such an absurd and ludicrous lie the basis of their entire philosophy.

If we can prove that our core tenet is correct, that wealth is limited only by imagination and the desire to work hard, then not only does the left's economic theory come crashing down like a Statue of Lenin…their entire view of US power has to be fatally flawed, as well. Because if we make enough wealth to be able to buy our oil *at prices set by the seller* – consult reality for confirmation of this annoying fact – then perhaps we are not in places like Iraq and Afghanistan to steal oil from poor Arabs. There must be some other reason for it. Something completely unintelligible and unknowable: national security, perhaps, or simple disgust with torture and repression and terrorism. Things like that.

Get this through your heads, you socialist ninnies! There is not a big, limited pot of wealth that is filled with the Magic Sweat of Authentic Third World Laborers, that America uses its military to steal from when we run out of wealth here at home.

Here's something even the dimmest hippy protester / poet should be able to wrap his mind around:

You buy a legal pad: **$1.29**
You steal a Bic pen from the counter at Kinko's: **free.**
You write the script for *Weekend at Bernies 3: Bernie's Revenge!*: **free.**
You hire someone to type it: **$30.00**
You have Kinko's print 5 copies: **$62.20**
You mail the 5 copies: **$7.82**
5 idiots in Hollywood love the idea: **free.**
They enter a bidding war: **free.**
You get a check for: **one…million…dollars!**

So let's see…that $1,000,000, minus the $101.30 in expenses…uh…that means… You, the village idiot, have just raised the Gross Domestic Product by, uh, *one million freaking dollars*, and have made a personal profit of $999,898 dollars and 69 cents.

Where did the $999,898.69 come from? **It came from thin air!** You created it, out of nothing. You added value to the stock of paper and ink you started with. From the monumental talent you posses, the gift of intellect, the pen that made Shakespeare weep with envy, you have created WB3. You've given millions of people two hours of side-splitting hilarity, for which they will part with $8.00…and you have *created wealth*. What's more, when you go and blow it all on the pointless material crap that makes life so much fun, you'll be bringing in a little extra for the Sea-Doo distributor, the BMW dealer, the girls at *Cheetahs* in Las Vegas, and all the others. Not to mention putting – I dunno – maybe *half a million freaking dollars* into welfare, Social Security, Medicare, the National Endowment for the Arts and the world's first fusion-powered, laser-armed, flying stealth submarine, the *USS George W. Bush*.

You did not have to steal $999,898.69 from a farmer in Angola.

And in just the same way as your finished screenplay is worth more than the total cost of the paper and ink you needed to write it, so too is my 2000 Ford Escort ZX2 worth more than the hunk of iron ore, the silica for the glass, the chemi cals for the plastic and tires, and the cost of the factory, the electricity to run the factory, and the salary of the people who build the car. That car, like that screenplay, has greater value than the raw materials that comprise it. Through human ingenuity, value is added. Wealth is created *from thin air*.

More relative wealth is created from building a Learjet than making a pencil, but then again, there are a lot more pencils than Learjets. Any time we make either, or any of the millions of things in between, we create wealth. **From thin air.** We did not go and take the money at bayonet point from some *campesino* trying to scratch out a living somewhere, and if I hear that lie again from those *magnificently* dense, blind and smug idiots, well, from now on I'm just going to haul off and kick 'em in the nuts. We should not have to keep going over something so simple, so basic, and so completely and totally **obvious**.

That capitalism generates wealth is beyond debate. This capitalist reactor of ours easily invents more, learns more, and produces more benefits in a year than mankind did under a millennia of rule by Kings and Barons and Caliphs and Emperors. It's just amazing what people can do when you just get the hell out of their way.

As an economic system for increasing prosperity, you just can't beat it. And those who hate and despise capitalism can't argue with this – they just can't. What they can do, perpetually and loudly, is talk about how *unfair* Capitalism is. Because it allows the hard-working and ambitious to keep the rewards of their hard work and ambition, Capitalism does indeed produce some pretty uneven results.

But does *uneven* mean *unfair*? Depends on how you measure fair.

Now far be it for me to split linguistic hairs and argue over what the definition of "is" is. But if we're going to get to the heart of this unfair business, we have to ask ourselves, unfair to whom? Because if we are to talk intelligently about this, we're going to have to understand something right out of the gate: life is unfair. If life were fair, we'd all be the same – same intelligence, same drive, same capabilities. But we're not. It is a hallmark of our species that we vary wildly in these and many other categories. That's what makes us so *diverse*, and we sure want to celebrate *that*, don't we?

So, when we talk about making things *fair*, making them *equal*, we find ourselves in the same impossible conundrum as we do when we discuss *The Irresistible Force* meeting *The Immovable Object*.

Cool! Which would win?

Neither. It's an oxymoron. The definition of Irresistible Force means that there cannot be an Immovable Object, and vice versa. You have to pick one or the other. They are mutually exclusive.

Likewise, when we try to measure fair and equal, we have to face the hard reality that people are different. So, do we want to measure an equal front end: **equality of opportunity** – or an equal back end: **equality of results?** Can't have both.

Here's why:

When the Declaration of Independence thundered that *All Men are Created Equal,* it meant equal in those essential elements: equal under the law. Equal in terms of basic human rights. Equal in dignity. Equal in the sense that if someone with a lot of money thinks they can cut in front of me at an ATM line, just because they're rich, then *they can just kiss my Royal Irish Ass!* – that kind of equal.

But to believe that all people are equally *capable* is to…well…not be paying attention, as a quick game of one-on-one half-court between Michael Jordan and Michael Moore will quickly reveal. *(Note to Don King: There are millions, and I mean* millions *to be made off this idea. Call me.)*

There will always be people smarter than you, and people more stupid; people more and less motivated, ruthless, connected, ambitious, frugal, hardworking than you are. Nothing can change that. Nothing *should* change that – because there lies the Gulag. People are different. Leave them alone. Encourage the down-hearted, by all means. Help those in need when they ask for help. But otherwise *mind your own business, bub.*

Society is as fair as it can get when all people have equal opportunity to make what they will of themselves. We are not there yet. We are close. We are much, much closer than many would have us believe.

But people are different. They will always be different. They will succeed and fail differently. There's no two ways around it.

Like so many flawed ideas beloved by the far left, equality seems like a noble enough goal. *Until you think about it.* People have different capabilities. So do you want *equality of opportunity* – as I do – where people can make of themselves what they will? Or do you want *equality of results,* where society steps in to make sure that everyone comes out the same?

If society had a magical way of raising the bottom up, of speeding up, buffing up, and tidying up Michael Moore, thereby giving him the means to beat Michael Jordan in our (sadly) mythical game of half-court, well we'd all be the winners and life would be just dandy. But, alas, this wonderful, brilliant idea is marred only by the annoying fact that it is demonstrably impossible. Michael Moore can never play as well as Michael Jordan. *Never.* If you want that game to come out a tie – equal! – then you are going to have to hobble Michael Jordon.

You're going to have to remove a foot or two from his femurs, stitch him into a clumsy, bulky, ugly suit adding a few hundred pounds, heavily sedate him to slow down his mental powers, fill him full of cheap booze to degrade his aim and coordination – oh, and really mess up his face surgically. No fair if people are rooting for him disproportionately! That might hurt Michael Moore's self-esteem and limit his ability to compete.

Do all these things, and more, and you will have two equal players. You will have a really stupid, incompetent, pointless game. You will have removed all the grace, power, style, finesse and genius from a gifted and noble man, and added nothing whatsoever to his opponent. You just made Michael Moore equal to Michael Jordan. Is that fair to Michael Jordan?

And after you've done all these things, Michael Jordan will still hand Michael Moore his ass because he thinks and acts like a winner and not a victim.

Equality under the law: *good*. **Essential.**

Forcing people of differing skills, motivation and capability to be "equal:" *ruinous*. **Suicidal.** And deeply, deeply unfair. But, for the Berkeley crowd, there's no reason why a fatally flawed, disgusting, historically-demolished idea can't be retried – and retried – *and retried…* So long as it will fit on a 2x4 foot piece of cardboard that you can hold on the end of a stick while dancing in a public fountain wearing a star-spangled diaper.

Does Capitalism, and its equality of opportunity, produce cruel results? It does. Does Socialism, and it's equality of outcome, produce a fair and happy society? Ask the Russian farmers under Stalin. Ask the Chinese under Mao during the Cultural Revolution. Ask the Cambodians under the Khmer Rouge.

Oh, wait – you can't. They've all been murdered.

Our opponents across the Great Reason Divide care not a whit about the logic of this. Their house is built on compassion, and that's basically all they've got. So, *What about the poor?!*

Well, that's a serious question, a legitimate question, and there is in fact an absolutely compelling answer to that question.

But---!

The satisfaction you derive from the answer will be dependent on a very simple emotional equation that you already have stored in your head, namely: *do you love the poor more than you hate the rich?*

I can see by the way you are staring at your Birkenstocks that you are disoriented and confused. Let me rephrase the question: would you rather see the poor live better, or would you rather see the rich torn down? I know some people think you need to do the latter to get the former, and in this they are quite completely raving mad, not to mention provably wrong, as we shall see in a moment.

Just think about it for a second. What means more to you? Seeing poor people live better, or seeing rich people taken down?

If you said the former, then we are in complete agreement, and congratulations on your high moral character. If you said the latter, then you're just a mean-spirited, bitter failure with nothing better to do with your endless supply of free time than steal from and bitch about those more hardworking, industrious, motivated and socially worthwhile people than yourself. In fact, why are you still here? Don't you have some signs or giant puppets to make or something?

Now I can see a few honest souls who don't really see how cut-throat capitalism helps the poor. Well, that's fair, because capitalism is a study in contrasts. In fact, this would be as good a time as any to admit that I've spent much of my life worrying myself sick about making enough money to pay the bills. You'll just have to take my word for this. I know what it's like to have your phone and electricity cut off. I know what it's like to avoid the telephone and the mailbox – in fact, I know what it's like to avoid a stern knock on the door.

It *sucks*.

But even during the many times I've been out of work, flat broke, worried sick and living off the kindness of my life-saving friends – you guys know who you are – even then, when I was practically throwing up from fear, even *then* – I have never, *ever* considered myself a poor person. I have always thought of myself as a rich person experiencing **severe** cash flow problems.

Attitude.

That is a distinctly American attitude. Optimism. Hope. Ambition. You break these chains in your head *first* – everything else will follow.

Now in order to fully appreciate why Capitalism is such a blessing – including being a blessing *for the poor* – we have to understand what poverty is. We have to have a definition of poverty. And we have to understand what it really means to be poor in a rich country, and to be rich in a poor one.

We keep hearing certain professional (as in paid) complainers bleating about how the rich get richer and the poor get poorer. That's just wrong. That's demonstrably, provably false. *It's a lie.*

The rich get richer, and the poor get richer too. At least here they do.

American poverty is defined by a certain income. These people are poor by definition. I'm not trying to be sarcastic, and I'm not trying to minimize the pain of it – I'm just stating a fact.

Now, what does it mean when we learn that the poorest Americans have incomes higher than 90-some percent of the rest of the world? What does that *mean*?

Poor people in America have electrically powered homes. They have the same clean running water the rest of the city residents have. Almost all have telephones and television. Many have a third-hand piece of crap automobile like my last three cars. (My current ride has had one previous owner and 12,000 miles and it feels new. I've never owned a new car.)

Does it suck to be poor in America? *It depends on who you talk to.* If you spend your life calculating what Bill Gates made while you were sleeping, chances are you'll be pretty ornery. But if you look out into the rest of the world, and even a few decades back into history – American history, a rich country's history – then you just might begin to realize that you, a poor American, are living better than just about any other humans in history, and I am including the richest people of just sixty or seventy years ago – a single human lifespan for a poor American. A hundred years ago, if the Crown Prince caught the flu, that richest, most powerful person on the earth, likely as not, **died**. At this hour, at this instant, people of all incomes are being saved from certain death in clinics and hospitals by treatments unimaginable a few short decades ago.

Some facts are undeniable – that's why we call them "facts." Lifespan and infant mortality are scientific data sets that pay no attention to ideology. They have been rising all across the globe, and rising *spectacularly* where capitalism has taken hold. Rich, capitalists countries – the ones with those evil kkkorporations, are also far cleaner – *Greener*, you might say – than poor, socialist ones. That's got to stick a little, thinking about that, up there in that tree night after night, for years.

Where monumentally thick governments, like that of China, are finally *forced* to get out of the way and let people work to improve their own lives – we call this process *"making money"* – the results are simply dumbfounding, given the amount of poverty that has been foisted on that industrious and hard-working nation for a few millennia of raw tyranny. Ask your solid, upper-middle-class in Egypt, or Vietnam, or Belarus, if they'd like to get a chance to start a new life as a poor American. Then get the hell out of their way, if you don't feel like tasting the sidewalk.

One of the few places where longevity is falling drastically is in the ruin of Russia and her poor, literate, long-suffering people. Communism is still killing those poor bastards. It's like a disease that stalks you even after it's been eradicated.

What a filthy legacy.

Now I told you this one would be tough, but we're almost done with it. In order to show how Capitalism helps the rich, the poor, and the middle, we have to look at income.

Unfortunately for the grey-ponytail crowd, this will require *just a smidgeon* of math and a little tiny bit of other stuff they didn't study for when they were out getting high behind the dumpsters.

It involves a graph. If you are one of those people who are now reaching for a pencil and paper, then you already pass and spend the rest of study period at the library. The rest of you pay attention, especially you kids way in the back whose every other word is **Nazi!** The rest of us are getting a little tired of having to keep explaining this to you. *So pay attention!*

In your mind, draw a vertical line down the left side of a piece of paper, and a horizontal one across the bottom. Yes, it makes an "L" Moonflower...

The left-hand, vertical line represents the number of people. The higher we go, the more people there are. The horizontal line is income: the further to the right, the more silk you get to wear.

Now place a bell-curve along the bottom line. Okay? A Bell Curve. Simple.

Now, down on the bottom left are the poorest Americans. There are relatively few really desperately poor people. As we move to the right, into higher incomes, we see more and more people – the line goes higher. We're still on the left side of the curve – the cheap seats. Most of the people – the bulge in the bell -- make an average salary: that's why we call it "average" (You statisticians leave means and medians and that stuff out of it. *Just play along.*)

Okay, now as we move to ever higher incomes, we see fewer and fewer people making the big bucks. Numbers go down. And then all the way at the end sit Bill Gates and Sam Walton all by their stinking rich selves. Okay?

Let's call that a snapshot of America today.

Now, if we rob from the rich, and give to the poor, then what happens?

The rich people get poorer, the poor people get richer...the ends contract...the bell curve gets *narrower*. The right side, the rich side, moves left – poorer. The left side, the poor half of the curve, moves right – richer. In a socialist utopia, there is no curve; there's just a single vertical line in the middle called *The Salary*. Collect all the revenues, add 'em up, divide by the total number of people and pay them all the same exact amount.

Everybody makes the same: *the Salary.* Let's say it's fifty grand a year. Brain surgeons, the guy who cleans the toilet at the 7-11 – everyone makes fifty grand.

Fifty grand! **Woo-hoo!**

Now let's set aside for a moment the non-trivial issue of whether or not such a society -- which rewards 12 years of intense medical study and endless hours doing breathtakingly difficult and essential work *exactly the same* as the guy who spent his teen years stealing stereos, getting high and listening to White Snake –is more "just" and "compassionate." Look at the bell curve --- or what's left of it.

There it sits. It will start to slide left as motivation and industry and ambition and just plain dreaming of a better life goes out the window. What's the point? Fall asleep behind the glass at a service station, you make The Salary. Put in overtime, start a business, get an extra degree, invent the telephone – you get The Salary. Only we're not producing as much. The Brain Surgeon decides it pays just as well to take tickets at the movieplex, and he's got a lot more free time, plus the movie. Productivity goes down. We produce less, so now the average of what we make goes from fifty grand to forty-three nine. Then thirty-six grand. Then Twenty-One. Then eleven. But everybody's equal! Equally destitute and equally hopeless.

But I'll even throw this *essential* argument away for a minute.

Let's just agree that everybody makes fifty grand. Forever.

If we went perfectly communist a hundred years ago, when the Big Idea started, that "average salary" would have been closer to five grand a year.

D'oh!

What the hell can you buy today with five grand? Well, quite a lot of hay, some dry goods, perhaps a corset for the missus. But it doesn't buy anything of value today. What will fifty grand buy in a century? Some crappy new Volvo, perhaps a PlayStation? What about a personal transporter, or a NeuralBoy? You'll need to make *500 grand* to afford those puppies.

Now if you'd just been smart and listened to Adam Smith, he'd tell you: you don't improve peoples lives by narrowing the bell curve. You improve people's lives **by moving it to the right.**

Is this so hard to figure out?

I guess so. For some people this is like learning calculus – in Greek.

If your goal is to pull the money from those goddam rich people, then realize all you can do is raise the poor to the middle. On the other hand, if you don't give a damn about people richer than you, and everyone does the best they can, then *there is no limit to how far right a wealth-creating engine can move the curve.* Poor people today make more money than average people did a hundred years ago, and they can buy much cooler stuff with what they make – like televisions.

So write this on your palm, because there will be a test in the afterlife: if you want to help the poor by taking from the rich, *all you can do is take all that they have.* Take from the industrious, the ambitious, the clever and the hardworking long enough, and they will go somewhere else and get rich – again.

And then where are you? Your bell curve gets narrower, and as the gap between rich and poor shrinks, you have a few years, maybe a few decades of smug satisfaction as the whole edifice topples slowly to the left and collapses. The rich get poorer – *good for you* – and the poor? Well, simple. They starve to death.

Behold Africa. What an egalitarian paradise! All starve equally.

On the other hand, there is no limit – again – **no limit,** to how far to the right, how rich, capitalism can make even the poor. Some people will do better than others, because some people worker harder, or smarter, or longer than others, and some are just plain luckier. That's life. And if that's the case, then some people, by definition, will be the rich half, and some will be the poor half. And at the far end of the poor half will be the people we call The Poor. It doesn't matter how much money they make, or don't make. The bottom ten or fifteen percent we will define as The Poor. Seventy-five years ago, these poor Americans lived in shacks with dirt floors. Today they live better. Not as well as the rest of us. But better. The rich get richer, and the poor get richer, too.

We can narrow that bell curve, reduce the gap, if we so chose. We can have bland, benign socialism of, say, Scandinavia. When we reign in the industrious and the inventive, we can narrow the difference between them and the unfortunate. And we will give to the rest of the world…what, exactly? Electric lights? Airplanes? Weather satellites? The non-existent laser in your non-existent DVD player? Computers? Miracle drugs? Carbon-fiber structures? MRI scanners? Where have the vast majority of earth-shaking inventions come from?

Uh-huh.

These socialists point an accusing, bony finger at America's huge gap in outcome. They have a point. I point a perfectly toned, buff finger back and ask, *where is your genius?* Where is your creativity? Where are your movies? Where is your music? Where are your breakthroughs? Where, in fact, is your *contribution?*

And where is your passion, you poor, passive, grey people? Here we are, working like hell to move the world's bell curve to the right, and you're just tagging along for the ride! Unfair! *Unfair!*

Look, I am all for every reasonable, proven method to help the poor. Job training, educational grants – I'll pay for that. And I'm all for a safety net. It's the safety hammock I have a problem with.

And if each and every one of us lifted ourselves up by our bootstraps, if every American was a millionaire, then someone will *still* have to sit at the left side of that curve. In a country club of billionaires, the guy with 900 million is a schmuck. In the richest country in the world, its poorest citizens live better than the vast ocean of human history. And yet there are poor Americans. That's *reality*. It's not fair. History – recent history – shows it can't be made fair, unless you can make human capability, human creativity, all the same. This is indeed possible. You can crush people's creativity and intelligence, and steal their hard work. There is the socialist laboratory of Africa, Cuba and the former Soviet Union as models. Go live there for a year before you throw your next Molotov cocktail at a G7 meeting.

I want to be rich. I'm tired of being broke. I'm doing something about it, too. I am working like *an animal*. I am putting in 12-14 hour days, and weekends, for weeks on end, and no end in sight.

I don't have to do this. I could get by on a lot less. But see, I have a burning desire. I want to own my own airplane and see the world at 200 knots. That is my dream. And so I *make the choice,* daily, to work harder than I have to because there are things that I could never, ever have in a socialist society. There are more licensed pilots in Los Angeles county than there are in all of Europe – and that's just an example I am familiar with. America is an economic dynamo not because of the big corporations like Boeing, GM and GE. It is productive out of all proportion because there are so many people with so many small businesses trying to make a better life for themselves. LA county, alone, has what I believe would be the 22nd largest economy **in the world.** People work hard – and *smart* -- in America.

I'm one of them. Chances are, you are too. Many places in the world won't let you work harder to get further. The State throws you a crappy apartment, a crappy car, a crappy job – so enjoy your crappy, hopeless life.

How fair, how compassionate, is *that?*

I'm doing something else, too. I'm giving up what's left of my free time, because the fact of the matter is, I'm writing a goddam book, and all you rich folks nodding a few paragraphs back – well, you get those checkbooks ready.

If you think chasing filthy lucre makes you venal and reptilian, just wait till you meet the kind of person who would rather legislate themselves into money than work for it.

Now if the subject of money was the endless plain upon which vast herds of nonsensical ideas flourished and thrived, then government is the watering hole around which all species of dim-witted theories naturally gravitate to.

It's like a trip through *Lion Country Safari:* we've got our faces pressed to the glass in amazement as the Idiotarian ideas thunder by. *Look, a Hildebeest! It's attacking it's mate!* So let's just keep the windows rolled all the way up, and move on. This one will be a lot easier.

The second item in the American Trinity is far easier to understand and agree upon, so let's just all have a moment of silence for all of those men and women who gave their lives, and continue to give their lives, for **Freedom.**

This, surely, is the single most astonishing American invention: a government whose rights are limited by the people. And as with the first pillar of our Trinity, the idea of limited government causes thin tendrils of smoke to rise from the ears of those on the Far Left. Really give then a healthy dose of this concept and they start to shake and vibrate like Fembots before their heads explode in a shower of sparks.

Now it's not fair to be too hard on these people. After all, we as modern humans go back for several hundred thousand years, and we have always had chieftains and barons and kings to tell us what to do.

A few days ago, I was spending a few moments reading an online poll taken on why the rest of the world hates America. Many people had posted comments, and while all of the answers were entertaining, this one was priceless:

What behaviour can you expect of a country who sought independence because it didn't wanted to pay taxes?
Gonzalo Arriaga, Finland

Citizens, behold the soul of a slave! Gonzalo *loves* paying taxes, thinks it is sub-lime ecstasy to walk down that golden hall, pathetic handful of shriveled potatoes and a scrawny chicken in hand, and lay them – *eyes averted!* – at the feet of the master. *The more we smile the less he will beat us.*

If you want a quick rule of thumb about what kind of person you are dealing with, ask one of these folks lined up at the government feed trough a simple question: *whose money is this?*

Money is a work token, remember. We get money in exchange for our work, our creativity, our inventiveness, our sweat.

Whose money is this? Whose sweat is this? Whose missed family time is this? Whose inventiveness is this? Whose *genius* is this? *Whose work is this?*

You want to know whose money it is? *It's your money,* that's whose money this is. **Your** money. Not the King's money. The King never worked a goddam day in his life. Not the State's money. Your money. *Your* sweat. *Your* hopes. *Your* ingenuity.

Yours.

When we talk about Freedom, that central, mystical pillar of the Trinity, we are not talking about *government*. We are talking about *Freedom*, and they are not the same. Democracy is a tool. A republic is a tool. The US Constitution is the greatest tool to unlock human creativity in the history of the world, and I no longer give a flying damn if some people recognize that fact or not.

To date, the Founders have accomplished the unthinkable: they have made freedom idiot-proof.

Democracy, The US Republic, and the Constitution of the United States of America are stainless-steel, lifetime-guaranteed tools to **limit government** and **preserve freedom.** Because government is nothing more and nothing less than other people telling you what to do.

Can we all hold hands and say that together?

Government…is *other people*…telling *you*…what to *do.*
Government…is *other people*…telling *you*…what to *do.*
Government…is *other people*…telling *you*…what to *do.*

And let's be clear on one point: many people, perhaps most people in this world, *fear* freedom. They will never admit it, but it is true. When the lights go out and they look at the ceiling before they go to sleep, the idea of being responsible for themselves, for feeding and clothing and defending and ordering their lives, scares the *hell* out of most people out there.

Poor, servile Gonzalo, Ward of the State, is not the aberration; he is the *norm.* We ignore that fact at our own peril, fellow citizens. Everybody wants a little freedom, little bite-sized pieces of freedom, like a cheap toy handed out in the state-sponsored Happy Meal. But *real* freedom, untrammeled, unrefined, raw self-determination: that requires more than a vague desire. That requires some *guts.*

Now while some limited government is a necessary evil and can, on rare occasions, do some good, let us never forget that deeply moving scene at the end of *Braveheart*, when Mel Gibson looks down at his disemboweled intestines, then out to the Baleful Crowd of Oppressed Peasants, and with his dying breath utters his last word on earth:

Bureaucracy!!

If Capitalism is a litmus for optimism, then the idea of State is one for independence. And it really comes down to whether or not you conceive of yourself as a child who needs to be taken care of, or as an adult who can make his own way. Freedom isn't free. If you want the State to feed and clothe you, to provide you a job and health care and housing, don't think that comes without a price.

It comes with a hefty price, unbearable in my mind, and I'm not talking about what gets taken out of my wallet, either.

It makes us dependent, and dependence makes us stupid. It makes us stupid and willing Gonzalos, the same money fodder that have fed those in control for millennia. Happy Dependence day, everyone!

There's a scene in *Bowling For Columbine* where Michael Moore interviews a typically decent and friendly Canadian as he emerges from a health clinic. The poor fellow had, as I recall, some serious injury, and Mssr. Moore wanted to know what it had cost him for treatment.

The man couldn't reply. They hadn't charged him. This took Michael Moore's carefully rehearsed breath away! No charge? You mean, you got that medical attention *for free?*

That's right, eh.

Cut to beatific look on directors face, as if he had just been handed a clean plate at a Shoney's Breakfast Bar.

Folks, Canadians are great people. They are not a stupid people. So can we not, please, not ever again, call this Free Health Care? It is **Pre-paid** Health Care. That Canadian fellow paid for that treatment every week, for the past twenty years. It was taken out of every paycheck he made. He paid for that medical care, and much, much more. He paid for it whether he needed it or not. And he not only paid for the doctor, he paid for the bureaucrats and administrators in the National Health Service or whatever it is called. It was not free. It was paid for. Whether he needed it or not. When he has fully recovered, years from now, he will still be paying for it. Every week, from every check. That car or vacation he couldn't afford, got eaten up by health care he paid for but did not need.

So the question is, who better decides what kind of health care you and your family need: you, or Hillary Clinton? I understand that not all poor people can afford health insurance. Again, being a decent sort of fellow beneath my strikingly handsome exterior, I don't mind paying a little extra for Medicare for people who need help. I can even live with my insurance rates being higher to cover the cost of caring for the uninsured at the Emergency Room.

But! What I most assuredly do *not* need is for someone taking my money to give me a health care system I do not need or want. As my all-time idol P.J. O'Rourke once said, *if you think health care is expensive now, just wait till you see what it costs when it's free.*

This is a great example of the seduction of the state, because "Free Health Care" sounds like a great deal. It's Caring! It's Healthy! And it's Free!

It's *not* free. And not only do I object to being told what I need and don't need, I also object to the idea that some dim-witted Student Council dork thinks he knows what's better for me than I do.

P.J. Again: if you think that Public is an altar to worship at, put the word "public" in front of these words and tell me how you feel: *Restroom. Swimming pool. Transportation.* Here's another: Take the words *Decision, Officer, Appointment,* and then add the word "political" to the front end and watch them drop in value.

So, look around. Look at how people feel about government, and ask yourselves, does this or that person think of themselves as an adult or as a helpless child? Freedom is not for children. Freedom means responsibility. It means making tough decisions yourself. Freedom is not government. Almost all government is the enemy of freedom; the bigger the government, the more powerful the enemy.

The things government does well, the things government *should* be for, are few and simple. If you want to know what these things are, you will never do better than this:

We the People of the United States, in Order to form a more perfect Union, establish Justice, insure domestic Tranquility, provide for the common defense, promote the general Welfare, and secure the Blessings of Liberty to ourselves and our Posterity, do ordain and establish this Constitution for the United States of America.

Simple. Direct. Perfect. The most wondrous sentence ever written.

P.J. – last time, I promise – once wrote something to the effect that the US Constitution has kept 300 million unruly people united for two centuries using an operators manual ¼ the length of the one for a Toyota Camry.

So as far as I am concerned, I say: *Government, you can do this, this, this and that – that's it, that's **all**, shut up and go away. Build us some Interstate Highways and some aircraft carriers and stop hanging around looking eager.*

Compare this to the recently unveiled European Union constitution, weighing in at a modest 225 pages (down from the 97,000 pages of accumulated laws and regulations known as the *acquis communautaire*. *"Acquis Communautaire",* by the way, is French for *"we're f---ed."*) The main "author" of this abomination, which reads like a refrigerator repair manual written by a guy who really digs refrigerators, was Valéry Giscard d'Estaing of France, who in the spirit of restoring Franco-American relations compared himself to Thomas Jefferson. This is completely unfair to Mr. Giscard d'Estaing; Jefferson would have had to have written for decades, if not centuries, to produce a document this lifeless, meaningless and dense. Oh, and that's if he had, uh, actually been the author of the *Constitution,* rather than the *Declaration of Independence.*

As I say, I'm not an unreasonable fellow. Some government, some restrictions and regulations are good. The FAA actually does a very effective job at giving us the most safe and extensive transportation system in the world. In cases like that, even though the government doesn't actually produce anything, it does add value in terms of safety and user confidence.

And that's how we should look at every regulation and law. Does it add value, or is it just one of those plastic pancake alien amoebas on Deneva that lands on Spock's back, or yours, it's tendrils working their way into your nervous system until you are finally driven mad with pain and commit suicide?

My friend, the irrepressible Kim Du Toit, once asked me what I thought would happen if every government agency had to cut 25% of their regulations – they get to decide which ones, of course. I think that would be A Good Idea Generally – certainly worth trying on a test basis. How many of these regulations are there to protect you from yourself?

Children need to be protected from themselves. Adults don't need to child-proof the pool. They already know how to swim.

And after all this, after all these creeping intrusions and regulations, we're still the most free people, with the least intrusive government, on the planet. Go figure.

Freedom. We've still got more of it than they do. Reason number two why *we rock.*

And behind door number three, the easiest of all to get a grip on, that perennial favorite, father of good old Yankee Ingenuity: **Science.**

We work hard. Lots of nations work hard. But we work hard *ahead of the curve.* Hey man, we *define* the curve. That curve belongs to *us.*

We are the fast adaptors. If European technology is cutting-edge, ours is bleeding-edge. Whatever it is, it was almost certainly invented here, and even if it wasn't, it still will live or die on how it does in America.

America has horrible, appalling public schools -- they used to be the envy of the world. But our universities are the envy of the world. The sheer amount of money and mental freedom we have – starting to see how this Trinity works? – means that the science done at US universities is the best science on the planet, and it is produced in mammoth quantities. Those pictures taken of Triton, that distant moon of Neptune on the outer edge of the solar system? They were not snapped by the European Space Agency. Or the vaunted Japanese. Or even the Russians. No sir. Those pictures of Jupiter, and Saturn, and the surface of Mars and Venus and Mercury, we brought to you by some long-haired, badly-dressed geniuses at Cal Tech's Jet Propulsion Laboratory. Some of these guys barely have their driver's licenses.

They're the smartest people on the planet, and I stop the car and get out to Kow-Tow every time I go past them on the 210 Freeway. Geniuses. American college kids.

(Capitalism + Freedom) x Science = Voyager.

Trinity.

Not only are we great scientists, we are great tinkerers. How many ideas – airplanes, light bulbs, personal computers, a thousand others – had been floating around for decades, or centuries, or millennia, until American ingenuity, that practical, hard-headed garage engineering, got a hold of them and made them actually *happen?*

I live in two worlds. On one side, the hard side, is aviation. I cannot think offhand of another field that is as technology and engineering intensive. And with a smattering of exceptions, all of the innovation in experimental aircraft is homegrown. Almost all of the new avionics, the new materials and the breakthrough designs: homegrown.

But the other world I inhabit is that of entertainment, a soft field. And even there, I am surrounded by twenty-first century, cutting-edge, American technological mastery. Every time I fire up my *Avid Media Composer,* I can count the sixty-odd patents listed on the start-up screen. Those of you unfamiliar with non-linear, computer-based editing may find this hard to believe, but I assure you that we can now do in an hour or two what would have remained impossibly complex twenty years ago with a month of work on tape and film. *Avid, Pro Tools, Photoshop* – all American inventions. Invented by tinkerers. Kids, mostly. You know, those idiot Americans you hear so much about.

One last story about this American Trinity before we go back out to that bunker in the desert and then home.

Waaaaaaayy back at the top of this journey, I told you about looking for investors, and finding some. So let me tell you about a man who I would love to name, but won't. He is a scientist. A *real* scientist: a geologist.

While he was a University professor, he and his (*business!*) partner found a more efficient and more accurate procedure to get some data they, and other geologists, needed frequently. So they formed a company. They went private. They hired Grad students, paid them a fortune relative to any other jobs they could possibly get, and gave them a piece of the company. Brilliant.

So now, this new procedure harnessed all of the work, ingenuity and ambition of a bunch of very bright young men and women whose intellectual passion and economic rewards were pulling in the same direction. Stampede!

They began to become ten, then twenty times more efficient. Accuracy and quality remained superb, because accuracy was in fact their product. And since this was what they had all wanted to do with their lives in the first place, they worked nights, weekends, whatever it took to make this company a success.

And it was a success, a spectacular success, and remains so to this day. The former grad students are set for life, and my friend's father, the scientist, is now a millionaire many times over. I admired and respected him from the very first, back when they were drinking powdered milk to save money. He is a brilliant, hysterically funny, generous and good man. He now owns three houses, and a mountain. He worked for, he *earned*, every handful of dirt on that mountain. He has made scientific data more accessible, more accurate and more inexpensive than it would have been without him.

And I will say this about him, and about the many other millionaires I have known: he was the first in, and the last out of his office every day, for decades. The boss never leaves work. The Money Fairy did not accidentally stagger into him after a night of heavy drinking. He worked *hard*, and *smart*, and deserves every dime.

And he has bailed me out – twice – and kept my dreams alive. Twice. Without this man, without his genius, his ambition, his hard work and his generosity, you would not be reading this, for I would not be here today. I have taken his investments and failed him. Twice. And he still talks to me.

I guess because when it's all said and done, it's only money. There's more, in the air, where that came from.

––––––––––––––––––––

Okay, back to the beginning of this Road Trip: The Desert. The Test Site. The Blast Doors. The Bunker.

Trinity. American Power.

But see, you're undoubtedly thinking about Los Alamos, New Mexico. About Atomic bombs. About July 16th, 1945. About *Trinity*.

But we're nowhere near Los Alamos. We're in California. See, that's what you get for sleeping in the car.

There are people out there who maintain that we are a strong nation only because of our military might.

That's exactly wrong.

Our military might does not make us strong. We have military might *because* we are strong. It is a by-product of our strength, not the source of it.

Any idiot can build bombs. Our Trinity sits not on some desert sand seared into glass at an abandoned, sad pillar of stones. It's in our heads and our hearts, it's in our *genes*, this beautiful, gorgeous marriage of money, freedom and ingenuity.

We're not here to look at some dark sigil, some monument to destruction. We're builders, we're dreamers. We're in the *Mojave* desert, under cloudless skies split by man-made thunder, a place where people strap themselves into bullets and dare sonic booms to get out of their way.

We're going to space, dammit! And best of all, we're going *on our own dime*.

The test stand looks exactly like the Viking Lander would if you'd built it at Home Depot. Get a little closer though, and the finesse, the genius is in the details. Anodized gold, remote-controlled, cryogenic valves. Stacks and stacks of huge horizontal gas tanks, like the big babies they fill balloons from, all plumbed together to push enough liquid oxygen to get to where it needs to go.

The bunker at the distant corner of Mojave airport used to store ammunition back in the day. Now it stores TV monitors, a home-made control console, lots of chairs, boxes, pipes, pumps, and an old, battered Jet Ski. Oh, and it stores Rocket Scientists. About a dozen or so.

I'm not in there with them, though. I see enough of the world on television monitors. I'm crouching down on the top of the bunker, perhaps thirty yards away. If this thing explodes, I won't be able to duck in time, but I can make myself as small a target as possible and still see this with my own eyes.

Foam "ears" are handed out. I pretend to screw mine in. I'm already half-deaf from years working in a Miami night club. I want to hear this thing, but that's because I am an idiot.

Fifteen seconds!

The Home Depot Viking … farts. White cryogenic gas spurts from valves on top, sending a white frozen plume across the desert. It's a disappointing sound. Okay, so you have to purge the LOX system, but--.

Five seconds!

Another noise, throatier this time. Wisps of super-cooled gas emerge from the back of the combustion chamber, which looks like nothing more than a plain silver coffee can – no cool bell-shape, no piping, no sign of any---.

BBBBBAAAAARRRRRRRRAAAAAAAAAAAPPPPPPPPPPP!!

Holy God!!

A thirty-foot tongue of white hot flame *lights up the midday desert floor* – did you get that? This is the sound that God makes after polishing off a case of Old Milwaukee and a jumbo sized bag of Cool Ranch Doritos.

It lasts exactly 1.3 seconds. And no, now that I think about it, it's not "a tongue of white-hot flame." It looks nothing like white-hot flame. White-hot flame would be friendly, compared to this. This is a supersonic plasma spike, that's what it is, the shock diamonds backed up into the chamber like…well, like shock diamonds. A photograph was taken in broad desert daylight and *stopped down* to catch the brightness of the exhaust plume!

When you actually see something like *this* this close, you have one thought, and one thought only, and that is: **DO IT AGAIN!!**

And they do. Several more times. I watch a few from inside. (And I screw in my ears from now on.) The same procedure, again and again. Test. Inspect. Discuss. Restart.

Every now and then, some distant shriek of tearing canvas causes us all to run outside like little kids following the ice cream truck, as a different company is trying a different rocket engine, about a quarter of a mile away. It's not even close to full power out there, and it's kicking up a huge brown dust plume.

Down on the Home Depot rocket, that little coffee can goes from room temperature to 420 degrees Celsius in a fraction of a second. We peek inside, trying to divine the signs from the burn patterns – the data will take days to decode. They are kind enough to let me inspect it. I nod like I know what I'm looking at.

These are great people, too, the nicest bunch of men and women you'd ever want to meet. Once they manned the halls of Lockheed and North American and Northrop and Grumman. Now they're out there, working for peanuts, building rocket motors for themselves, just a little garage-based, mom-and-pop aerospace company called **XCOR** *(www.xcor.com.)* They built the EZ-Rocket, flown by Dick Rutan, the man who piloted the Voyager around the world, nonstop, unrefuelled. Dick stepped out of the phone-booth sized airplane after 9 days; his first words on the ground were "see what free men can do?"

If I hear another soul talk about the death of American ingenuity, I will bring them out here to meet those normal, smiling, somewhat scruffy, every-day rocket scientists at XCOR. I will introduce them to test pilot Dick Rutan, and his brother Burt. Burt Rutan is one of those people whose work you cannot look at without the word *genius* escaping your lips in a hushed whisper, unconsciously. His company, Scaled Composites, a few doors down, has a working, flying spacecraft.

No, that's not fair. They've got a working, flying *space launch system*. And they are going, by God! They are flying into Space. The whole lot of them: XCOR, Scaled, a few others.

This is the Trinity I wanted to show you. It's not just aerospace – it's all through the very fiber of this magnificent, brilliant country of ours.

These people are using their own money, their own freedom and their own ingenuity to do what governments won't give them the means to do: follow that ultimate dream, into and through that deep, delirious, burning blue and out into by-God outer space! Well, if you want to be an astronaut, here in America you can build your own spaceship and you can go.

These people, these private citizens, are the best people there are. Smart, dedicated, disciplined dreamers who have the guts and the savvy to do what all of Europe, or all of China, or Japan, have yet to do: fly in space. XCOR needs about $10 million to build a working space plane: that's about the promotional budget for *Legally Blonde 2*. No one knows what Burt has spent at Scaled. We only know it wasn't tax money and no one has ever been killed working for him over the past quarter century of tearing out the foundations of what we thought we could do.

I have one thing to say to these people:

ME!! PICK ME!!

So how stands this magnificent experiment, this monument to ambition, hope, freedom and ingenuity on her 227th birthday? How's the old girl holding up after all these years?

Militarily, she is unmatched, unrivaled. The men and women who serve and defend her today are not only the most capable, disciplined, and effective soldiers in her storied and glorious history; they are the most motivated, decent, flexible, daring and victory-prone troops deployed by any nation at any time. The all-volunteer, citizen soldiers arrayed in the defense of this experiment in self-government have placed the United States in a position that I cannot find a precedent for in history, for they now comprise a force so powerful and effective that the idea of a direct armed attack upon us has become actually unthinkable. To that extent, we can stand on this Fourth of July and think of a promise we have kept to those young men trapped in the sinking hulls at Pearl Harbor, to those airmen flying through fire and blood to hit their targets at Midway or Frankfurt, to the Marines in the jungles of Tarawa and Guadalcanal, the kids who never came home from beaches at Normandy, and all the others who have fought and died to preserve and strengthen this union and who through whose sacrifice we stand here free and alive and happy today.

The stain of racism, the dagger that nearly pierced our heart, continues to fade, its practitioners in a full-scale rout from a battle that may not yet be over but which has certainly been won. We can look out upon the most ethnically diverse nation on the planet and see not the looming disaster that darkens the horizons of much of Europe, with vast, furious, and growing populations of unassimilated radicals, but rather the serious beginnings of a society where people are indeed judged not by the color of their skin, but by the content of their character. The office floor on which I work is a kaleidoscope of racial, national and sexual identities. They are not only my colleagues, they are my **friends**. The fact that much remains to be done should not blind us to the really remarkable battles won in the hearts of each of us since Dr. King looked out from the shadow of Lincoln and shared a dream that becomes more real every day. *Good for us.* That, too, is something to stand proud of; something worth celebrating with fireworks.

Our economy, even when hung over, continues to show a broad and unshakable strength, the envy of the earth. American productivity leads the world, as we do in scientific breakthroughs and world-changing inventions. The fact is, fierce competition does indeed keep us honest. Science and freedom eats superstition and tribalism for breakfast every morning. We don't have time for that nonsense.

Our water and air are far cleaner than they were a generation ago, and what comes out the back of a modern automobile is practically cleaner than what goes in. The black streaks behind departing jetliners, rivers that catch fire, belching brown smokestacks and the little blue-grey puffs of poison floating up in their millions from sputtering tailpipes are a fading memory. We can do even better, and we will.

Of course, our times are defined by a new enemy: a brutal, ruthless, utterly inhuman scourge that targets little girls' birthday parties and office workers and commuters on a bus home from work.

I stand in mute amazement at some of the angry voices I have heard from Europe, who claim as a virtue having put up with terrorism for decades, and who emerge through some sick moral wormhole into a position where fighting back is looked upon with scorn and derision. *Get used to it,* they say.

Well, here's an Independence Day thought for you cowards and defeatists out there in your millions: *to hell with **that**.* Since that horrible morning I have had the consolation of knowing that thousands of those murdering bastards have had, as their last thought on earth, the realization that maybe 9/11 wasn't such a good idea after all.

And I have also watched in total admiration as a genuine leader stood up to pressure the likes of which I have never seen, and committed this nation to the removal of two of the most odious regimes on earth. With them have gone all sorts of future mischief, and likely, certainly *hopefully,* we will continue to trample this snake until our enemies realize that resorting to Terror will bring them nothing but the swift and total end to their regimes and ambitions, not to mention their personal death and ruin. The jury is certainly still out, and will remain so for many years to come.

But I, for one, feel like a man who has watched history's great projector rewound, with Churchill at Munich standing in for Chamberlain, with Fascism crushed in the cradle and a horrible, brutal lesson learned – by a few, at least – at long last.

So Happy 227th Birthday, America. Thank you for all you have done for me and my family. You have asked so little of me, and given me so much, that words seem absolutely inadequate. *Thank you.*

And where ends this Trinity of capitalism, freedom and ingenuity?

Far be it from me to be one of those mindless ideologues who wish to see the United States triumphant for the next century, or 500 years, or a thousand. No, I'm not that kind of person.

I want to see her triumphant **forever**. I want that shining city on the granite cliffs to keep that beacon of freedom and hope and optimism alive for as long as we are human, to continue her painful, never-ending, beautiful growth towards a more perfect Union, to be the ideal that we all struggle and fight for each in our own way and according to our own inner lights. I want that lamp to light the way down through history, the scourge of tyrants and torturers in ages yet to come. I want her to remain the polar star of those whose hope, optimism, genius and hard work have lifted, and continue to raise, all of us from the darkness of our animal selves.

And someday, somewhere, I hope and believe those Stars and Stripes will snap and flutter in unimaginably distant skies. I hope and believe that proud parents will sit on bleachers and watch their kids playing little league baseball on brave new worlds we can barely dream of. Right now, at this moment in time, it looks like a great, big, magnificent, empty universe. One day, a day closer to us than July 4th, 1776, I think those wagons will roll again, out to new frontiers, carrying painful lessons learned and yet filled with the identical hope and optimism and confidence that alone define us as a people and a nation.

Some species, somewhere, is going to do it.

It might as well be us.

RESPONSIBILITY

August 20, 2003

Every now and then, I get a letter from someone who has temporarily lost their cable TV and, desperate for something – anything – to fill the void, they write me asking what my pre-*Eject!* life was like.

Well, kind of run-of-the-mill, really. Like pretty much every other American Teen, I took a sharp interest in Astronomy, hung out at the local planetarium, got my first-ever job taking tickets, and was soon running the multi-media star shows. Who among us can't look back to those crazy summer nights in high school, hiding up in the catwalks behind the inner aluminum dome, or trying to catch a Frisbee in the strobe lights used to suggest a rocket launch, or blasting Pink Floyd at 380 decibels at 2:00 am while flying through space in a million-dollar installation before we were old enough to get our driver's license?

Hello?

Hello?

Anyway, there was this exhibit out in the lobby – they're actually fairly common – that was very simply a hard plastic funnel, like a 6 foot diameter solid tornado. You took a steel ball bearing and gave it a push, and looking down from above, it looked like it was 'orbiting' the hole at the center. It would drop down into the gravity well, accelerate, then loop up and out to the flatter region further away – a perfect elliptical orbit.

It's a great exhibit, because it simply and accurately displays a concept that changed the way we look at the entire universe. Einstein realized that Newton's mysterious attractive force – Gravity – could be explained as a warp in spacetime, like this funnel. It was a new way to see things, a much better way. Science today is hot on the heels of a theory to unify all of the forces in nature: the Grand Unification Theory.

I believe I have come up with such a theory for politics.

Sometimes it seems like half of what I learned this past year have come from the comments section after each of these essays – and when I say half, I mean, the good half.

One of the things that makes the current political debate so rancorous is that we do a lot of talking past each other, because the old labels no longer seem to apply. As one of my readers brilliantly pointed out in my comments section, it's not like the vast sensible middle of the nation is divided into Red and Blue camps, Republicans vs. Democrats, Liberals vs. Conservatives, Left vs. Right.

Today's politics are more like a Rubik's cube, where someone you may stand shoulder-to-shoulder with on one subject, can become, with a simple twist of the issues, a bitter opponent in some other fight.

This is where *Whittle's Theory of Political Reduction* comes in handy. (If that's too wordy we can call it *Bill's Electric Razor.*)

I contend that there is a single litmus that does indeed separate the nation and the world into two opposing camps, and that when you examine where people will fall on the countless issues that affect our society, this alone is the indicator that will tell you how they will respond.

The indicator is **Responsibility.**

Political Correctness, Deconstructionism, Trans-National Progressivism, Liability mania, Crime and Punishment, Terrorism, Welfare, Gun Control, Media Bias, Affirmative Action, Abortion, Education Reform, Social Engineering – all of it – will divide people according to their idea of Responsibility.

I suspect that there are really only two schools of political thought, and these are based on competing theories of how the human creature is constructed.

Again, a caveat about the ever-changing quicksand about labels. But with that said, it appears that people we generally group as 'the left' are convinced that society is responsible for pretty much everything that happens in our lives, that group responsibility trumps individual responsibility because they see the forces of the group – culture, history, economic background – as overwhelming determinants to individual outcome.

Those on the other side see *individual* responsibility as the final arbiter of human behavior. The United States of America is, without question, the most individual-centric nation in the history of the world. We have enshrined in the structure of our culture impressive guarantees of individual freedoms, and because of that, we see an enormous spectrum of behaviors – some noble, others…shall we say, 'colorful,' and some completely vile and disgraceful – that are the natural outcome of allowing people a great deal of personal freedom. Such a society will produce a US Constitution, a Bill of Rights, a *Voyager* probe…and unlimited episodes of *COPS* and *The Jerry Springer Show.*

We all profess to be in favor of more freedom. Freedom is the Platinum Visa card. We all want one. *Responsibility is the credit rating.* Not so much enthusiasm for the kind of discipline needed to earn one of those.

I talk often about evidence, and the idea that we owe ourselves a worldview that conforms to the facts we see around us. And to be fair, we have to admit that there is some evidence that people who believe in group responsibility can point to.

B.F. Skinner is perhaps the most famous of the Behavioralists. He did brilliant and groundbreaking work showing how much of behavior is based on conditioning. These experiments were highly predictive – when applied to rats. Somewhat less so, although still very compelling, when applied to monkeys. Erich Fromm makes a convincing argument that much of human behavior is based on avoidance of responsibility in his classic *Escape from Freedom*.

But to understand whether or not these experiments – and this theory of humanity –accurately reflects how we are built, we have to get to one of the thorniest philosophical issues since the dawn of human history: namely, is there indeed such a thing as free will? Because if there is *not*, then we are in fact products of our environments, our cruel or loving parents, our materialistic, ruthless or nurturing state, our religion or lack of it, our economic status at birth, and all the rest. If there is no free will, then Ted Bundy and Timothy McVeigh and Osama Bin Laden and Saddam Hussein are just automatons responding to root causes in the environment, mere executors of a pervasive, systemic disease rather than the authors of private agendas and the owners of the consequences of their actions.

If, on the other hand, there is something about being human that transcends Skinner's box and his wire frame monkeys, if we do indeed, through the unique capacity of self-awareness, have the ability to see how actions we commit that harm others could be unpleasant because we can imagine them being done to *us*, then we indeed are ourselves responsible for our actions. If this is true, then in the moment of the act of murder, or rape, or torture, we are presented with the most heartfelt pleas for mercy and hideous cries of agony, and nevertheless **make the decision** to continue our barbaric actions. If this is so then we, alone, bear the responsibility for what we have done, and while childhoods of horror may have steered us to that moment of decision, they do not absolve us from the consequences.

It has been our long, bloody and noble history to rise to this idea of individual responsibility; because if it is indeed correct, then it – **alone** – is the liberator of ourselves as a species. Individual responsibility frees us from our past, from the fate of our birth, from the millennia of class and caste and of failed ideas that have kept so many in bondage for so long. If we indeed do have the ability to control our own selves, then we can free our own minds from the river of history and experience.

Those on one side see individuals as rafts on that river of culture, swept along inexorably downstream, perhaps capable of a weak paddling, displacing our paths a few feet from side to side. I on the other hand, and others like me, see human potential as a powerboat, a nuclear-powered hydrofoil, one capable of cruising side to side at will, as easily able to race against the current as with it. I don't believe people are rafts adrift in the destiny of their culture. I think all people have propellers, whether they use them or not, and rudders too. And rather than commiserating with people about the rapids that they endure and the battering that is their lot in life, we should be teaching them how to start those engines, take the wheel of their own futures, and steer themselves *wherever they damn well please.*

This issue of free will has been debated since we've had language. It's not going to be resolved on these humble pages. So which view to adhere to: individual responsibility, or the predominance of culture? I say there are vast sets of evidence to prove that *both* are correct. So here's what I believe. I agree with the left on this: I do think we are indeed the products of the doctrines that have been fed us since birth. How else to explain the wild differences in human culture from a single species with no detectable biological propensities for intelligence, cunning, hard work or success? The fact that some cultures are free, fair, open, safe, creative and prosperous, while others are cruel, corrupt, repressive and poor – all while using the same raw human materials – means clearly culture plays a predominant role.

Which is why we must all *fight*, fight tooth and nail, fight to the death if need be, to defend this freakish idea that we are individuals responsible for our own actions. Because when we do, we have taught ourselves how to break those chains of history and birth, energized our own destiny, and inoculated ourselves culturally against the dictates of culture.

We are the first group of peasants to transcend the *idea* of peasantry. Here in America, we believe the words of the often-despicable Huey Long, *Every Man a King*. We are, as a direct consequence of this philosophy – the belief that the common man can be trusted to wield great responsibility – the most successful, creative, powerful, wealthy and free individuals who have ever lived. We are, indeed, in the words of a man who understood more about human freedom and its costs and responsibilities than any of us, *"the last, best hope of earth."*

Many years before his election as the nation's 16th President, this man, Abraham Lincoln, spoke at the Young Men's Lyceum of Springfield, Illinois on January 27, 1838. It is worth our time to whisper these words aloud, to ourselves, to be sure that we understand what he is saying across a gulf of a century and a half of differences in rhetoric and speech.

He said:

We, the American People... find ourselves in the peaceful possession, of the fairest portion of the earth, as regards extent of territory, fertility of soil, and salubrity of climate. We find ourselves under the government of a system of political institutions, conducing more essentially to the ends of civil and religious liberty, than any of which the history of former times tells us...We toiled not in the acquirement or establishment of them – they are a legacy bequeathed us, by a once hardy, brave, and patriotic, but now lamented and departed race of ancestors. Theirs was the task (and nobly they performed it) to possess themselves, and through themselves, us, of this goodly land; and to uprear upon its hills and its valleys, a political edifice of liberty and equal rights; 'tis ours only, to transmit these, the former, unprofaned by the foot of an invader...to the latest generation that fate shall permit the world to know. This gratitude to our fathers, justice to ourselves, duty to posterity, and love for our species in general, all imperatively require us faithfully to perform.

*How then shall we perform it? – At what point shall we expect the approach of danger? By what means shall we fortify against it? – Shall we expect some trans-atlantic military giant, to step the Ocean, and crush us at a blow? Never! All the armies of Europe, Asia and Africa combined, with all the treasure of the earth (our own excepted) in their military chest; with a Bonaparte for a commander, could not by force, take a drink from the Ohio, or make a track on the Blue Ridge, in a trial of a thousand years. At what point then is the approach of danger to be expected? I an-swer, if it ever reach us, it must spring up amongst us. It cannot come from abroad. If destruction be our lot, we must ourselves be its author and finisher. **As a nation of freemen, we must live through all time, or die by suicide.***

The idea of individualism, of personal responsibility, is the centerpiece, the gran-ite foundation, of the very *idea* of a free people. For that reason, it is under direct attack on many fronts from people, who, through motives well-intentioned or ill, find such an idea intolerable because a nation of individuals is immune to repression, coercion, social engineering and control by the elite. The threat, as Lincoln so eloquently foresaw, comes from within and it is here, now, well-estab-lished and growing.

We have to fight back. We have to fight back *hard*.

We have to fight back **now**.

How much damage has been done, so far? Consider this passage from *Prairie Justice*, by Will Bittle:

The American West: 1884

From afar, the only sign of the small homestead was a thin line of smoke from rising from the chimney in the small, wooden-frame house. A dusty porch overlooking a small corral, where horses were bred and raised. Out back, a small garden grew just enough vegetables for this small frontier family: a father, worn and weather-beaten, looking far older than his thirty-six years of rising before the sun. His wife, in the kitchen, baking a fresh pie for the two of her four children that survived to the age of four – but she too was bleached, severe, her hands those of a grandmother from years of lye soap and scrub brushes. A shot rang out from the woods beyond, and moments later, a boy of thirteen emerged, holding a dead rabbit by the ears, while a girl of six hauled bales of hay larger than she was from the barn to the small corral.

A small group of men rode up from over the nearby hills. The father made a move for his rifle, but squinting hard – his vision has been failing for years – he saw at the head of the party the local sheriff and deputy, along with five other riders, one of which appeared to be handcuffed, his head hanging in shame.

The wife stepped out off the porch, wiping her hands on her apron, and her husband took an unconscious step to place himself between her and the men that had ridden to the small homestead.

"Sheriff… deputy," said the homesteader, nodding. He was a man of few words.

"Howdy Luke," replied the big man with the badge, his stern face tightening into what was almost a smile. "That a huckleberry pie I smell, Sarah?"

"It is," she replied. "We got just enough for you and your men."

"Well that's right kind a ya, Sarah, but we're here on business." The sheriff turned to the handcuffed man in the middle of the posse. "Luke, you recognize this feller?" The Deputy knocked the prisoners dusty hat off and raised his chin. He was grizzled and mean, and his pale blue eyes made contact only for a second.

"Son of a bitch--!" Luke took the hunting rifle from his young son, cracked the breech to see if he had re-loaded – he had – and snapped it shut, leveling it at the man on horseback.

"That there's the son of a bitch that tried stealing my horses two nights ago! I missed him in the dark; I ain't about to miss him now! Move outta the way fellers!"

"See what I tole ya?" said the prisoner.

The sheriff frowned, shook his head, and looked down at the ground. He nodded at the deputy. "Show him the leg, Bob."

"Yessir"

Bob pulled up the prisoner's torn trousers to reveal a nasty red gash.

"Luke," said the Sheriff, looking down out of embarrassment, "I'm afraid I'm gonna hafta take you in."

"What the hell are you talking about, Pete?!"

The Sheriff sat straight in the saddle. His job was not a pleasant or an easy one.

"This here feller injured himself on your property, Luke—climin' over yer barb wire fence. He done got hisself a lawyer from Harvard university and I need ta take you in to get you deposed and such-like."

"It's all infected, too," mumbled the prisoner, sullenly.

"I cain't believe what ah'm hearin' here!" Luke shouted.

"Luke, his leg's all infected-like." The Sheriff surveyed the corral with a cool professional eye. "I notice that none a yer barb-wire there got any ah them OSHA-mandated cork tips on 'em. That's why this feller here got that nasty scratch on his leg."

"If'n he didn't want a leg-scratch or a hole in his head, he shouldn't a been in my corral a- tryin' ta steal my god-damn horses in tha middle a tha' night!" shouted Luke.

"Whoa, now, Luke! This here feller's had a rough time," said the Deputy, getting a little too worked up for his own good. "He was sittin' there at the Starbucks cross from the Dry Goods store ---"

"Naw, that Sturbucks ain't worth a tub a' spit!," said the prisoner. "Them fellers always put way too much sugar in their Grande Frappuchinos. Was the one below the whorehouse, right next ta tha saloon."

"Anyway," continued the Sheriff, "his pants got all tore up, and some t' other fellers started laughin' at him."

"Done lowered mah self-esteem," said the prisoner, more confident now. "Ya couldn't understand it – it's a horse-thief thang."

"You just can't go roun' lowerin' a man's self-esteem like that Luke. You oughts to know that," said the Deputy.

"You shut the hell up, Bob!" thundered Luke. He turned to the Sheriff. "Pete, that son of a bitch tried ta steal all my god-damned horses! That's all I got! We should be hanging that low-life horse thief! How the hell am I supposed to feed my family with all them horses gone?! We oughts ta shoot that thievin' sack a s--!"

"--That there's hate speech!!" said Deputy Bob, pulling out a notebook. "I'm writin' Luke's name down!"

The Sheriff's eyes narrowed to slits. "Now Luke, you listen to me now, and you listen good. As long as I'm Sheriff 'a this here county, we are gonna maintain a commitment to a diversity of ownership viewpoints. Do I make mahself clear?"

"So that's it," said Luke, eyeing the rest of the posse. Their hands rested nervously on the court-ordered injunctions and restraining orders they had strapped to their waists and legs. "You gonna hang me now, is that it?"

"Oh hell no, Luke! We're aimin' to break tha cycle ah violence! I rounded up the therapy posse so we could have ourselves a little man-to-man sensitivity trainin' seminar, maybe a little group drummin' and some visualizations, tell you and yer kids and the misses about some ah the root causes concerning horse-thievery and the like. Then we'll hafta safety-cork that barb-wire, get it up ta code. And I reckon yer gonna need to give this feller four, maybe five horses to make up fer the humiliation and sufferin' he's had to endure…"

"And throw in that huckaberry pie, too!" barked the prisoner. "I cain't even look at a horse no more without getting all nervous and twitchy-like!"

"That seems reasonable enough to me," said the Sheriff.

"Right! That's it!" Luke turned to his wife, disgusted.

The Sheriff looked down, shook his head. He dismounted in a fluid motion, spitting a bullet of chewing tobacco into the dust. He advanced on Luke with arms outstretched. "Well, now, I reckon it looks like someone here could use a hug," he said, his voice rattling like a sidewinder.

Luke turned his back on him. "Sarah, you pack up everthang we can fit. Jake," he said, turning to his son, "fetch Rachel and get the cover on tha' wagon. We're packin' up an' goin' where men are men and a man's word is his bond!!"

"Where we going, daddy?" asked the young man.

*"We are movin' ta **France**, God-damnit!" said Luke.*

Times have changed. There were some major problems with Frontier Justice: it was brutal, it was often error prone, and once made those errors could not be corrected by cutting down the offender, apologizing, and sending him on his way.

But Frontier Justice did have one immeasurably attractive virtue. It understood, in a way we are rapidly forgetting, the *difference between perpetrator and victim*. It realized that the former started into motion a chain of events, and that all of the consequences could therefore be laid at the feet of the individual person committing the crime. It recognized that as a creature with free will, a man at some point had to make a decision to do wrong, and that free-will decision to do good or evil was the centerpiece of their view, and mine, that we should treat people like adults and allow them as much freedom as possible, secure in the understanding that if they abused such freedoms, they would *pay the consequences*.

And even more importantly, Frontier Justice did not punish the victim. It was crystal clear and steely-eyed in this one essential element, the only one that really matters: it understood *who was responsible*.

A society, like any other complex mechanism, will seek, and eventually find, equilibrium. If you create a society with unparalleled human freedoms, you must build into it a corresponding counterweight, and that counterweight is the idea of individual responsibility for your actions. That's why you can do no better, as a blueprint for a happy society, than the folksy sentence, *Your freedom to swing your arm ends at my nose.*

Now if Freedom is the credit card, and Responsibility is the monthly payment, it should not come as a surprise to us to realize that human nature says we want the spending spree, but not put in the overtime to pay for it. And if this were just happening on a one-on-one basis, there would not be too much to worry about.

The problem is, there are many groups who have taken it upon themselves to preach the elimination of personal responsibility, and they are having a deeply corrosive effect on this experiment in self-determination. Some of these forces do it for money – personal injury attorneys come to mind – and others have darker and more obscure motives.

And so we have group identity advocates. Because if you can convince someone that they are not responsible for their failures and shortcomings, and that *someone else* is – not a hard sell if you think about it – then they will be willing to subsume their responsibility into that of the group, and with their responsibility goes their political power. Then all the responsibility of the group – and all their **power** – is concentrated in the hands of the very few who have led them to this position.

People like Jesse Jackson. Or Pat Robertson. Take your pick.

Who controls a nation of free individuals? **No one.** That is deeply unsettling to people who crave political control the way a heroin addict needs his fix. What would Bill Clinton have been without politics?

A wildly successful, Little Rock car dealer – that's what I think. And his wife? What of her? Who would have heard of this obscure partner in some backwater law firm? What power and prestige and ability to tell others what to do would she have wielded? And it's not just Democrats – Nixon was cut from this cloth. Truman – a Democrat – clearly was not.

What do you think drives such people? *Power.* **Control.**

How do you convince free people to surrender their power? Well, one way is to go in and take it by gunpoint. Sadly for them, Lincoln's – and our, *hardy, brave, and patriotic, but now lamented and departed race of ancestors,* foresaw this probability and put the gunpoint in the hands of the people. They assumed that if our system was worth having, if their theory of people was correct, then they could be trusted with such absolute power because they were willing to accept responsibility for it – as by and large, we have been.

So, taking our power was out of the question. Our power, and its concomitant responsibility, had been granted to us by the Founders. They'd have to talk us out of it. They'd have to **con** us out of it.

No one wants to give up power. But lots of folks cheerfully want to abandon responsibility. The two are flips sides of the same coin. Get people to abandon responsibility, and their power and freedom goes with it. *That's the way in.*

Lincoln was speaking of something overwhelming our innate power, the insurmountable power of free people. He saw, correctly, that such a thing could never happen. We would have to give it up, willingly.

As a nation of freemen, we must live through all time, or die by suicide.

Keep this in mind, my friends: when someone tells you *It Takes a Village*, remember that the corollary to that philosophy is *It Also Takes A Village* **Leader.**

Take a guess who that might be.

Give your responsibility to the group, and you give your freedom to the group. Freedom without responsibility becomes – very rapidly – a farce. When laws become farcical, the result is anarchy. Anarchy is unacceptable – so measures are taken to reduce freedom and increase controls on the population.

That is precisely what is happening at full gallop. Lets take a look at some case by case examples. When we are finished, you'll see who's responsible for this cancer, and even better, you'll learn who can stop it.

Before we go looking for trouble, we have to delve a little deeper into another thorny philosophical thicket.

How much freedom can we allow people?

The answer seems to be, *as much as they are willing to accept responsibility for.* But a deeper and more interesting question is this: if freedom is power, then how *much power are we willing to place in the hands of single individuals?*

To find that answer, we have to again try to connect with another rapidly-disappearing trait, one tied directly and causally to the idea of responsibility.

That second essential trait is **common sense.**

If we had read the above-mentioned *Prairie Justice* to actual inhabitants of the American Frontier, they would not have found it comical or ironic – they simply would be unable to follow it. It would, quite simply, read as Greek to them. The idea of punishing the property owner while rewarding the thief would so violate their common sense, their keenly developed sense of responsibility, that they simply could not believe what they were hearing, and that is because for those people, cold, hard reality stalked them right outside their front door, and moronic inversions of cause and effect would quite simply get you killed. That's why it was called *common* sense…it was the Minimum Daily Requirement of intelligence and logic that one needed to survive on a daily basis. Those who didn't have it were too stupid to live, and had been eaten by wolves or prairie dogs, depending on just how stupid they were.

Reality has receded far from the front porch in modern America, and in those isolated towers of law offices, bureaucracies and faculty lounges, all manners of thought inversions can grow and prosper. I recently heard of a woman who sued a car dealership. It seems her son had stolen a car from said dealership, gone on a joy ride – drunk, of course – and gotten himself killed. The woman claimed that if the dealership had maintained adequate security, her son would not have been able to steal the car and he'd be alive today.

This is madness.

Responsibility. Freedom. Common sense. Let's take a few snapshots of society today and see how these three essential elements come to bear.

And watch carefully, because if we apply *Bill's Electric Razor,* we will see that every one of the nasty modern monsters we are about to poke with a stick have only one thing in common, and that is this: *They all try to convince people to surrender their individual responsibility, and place that responsibility, and that power, in the hands of a governing elite.*

To be **Politically Correct** these days, you must accept the collectivist belief that words are like weapons, endowed with their own internal, innate power, and this power, like that of a chambered bullet, cannot be trusted to be used responsibly and so must be outlawed and banished from the community.

PC advocates have strict rules for what they call Hate Speech, and using such speech essentially makes you a criminal.

So much for the First Amendment. But the Bill of Rights never meant much to these people; indeed, they see it as an impediment to human progress.

Implicit in this belief is that I have the power to harm you by my use of language. Notice that all the responsibility falls on the speaker; the listener, the subject, is completely powerless, and has achieved the highest status with the group: victim. Note also that this worshipping of the victim, is in essence, the elevation of the most powerless and the least responsible to divine status. It is a very basic sleight of hand, that allows the controlling elites to maintain that they are only trying to help the poor and downtrodden, when in reality their actions are clearly nothing more than a naked grab for power that would shame the most ruthless corporate CEO.

Who decides what is hate speech? The group decides. If one person in the group seriously finds something offensive, then that term or phrase or entire concept is added to the list or proscribed terms, and this is how we get to office memo's being critical of the term "brainstorming" as being offensive to epileptic co-workers.

If we buy into this idea of Political Correctness, we do several things, all ruinous: we give other people the power to demean us, we remove any chance at reasoned debate on any issue, and most importantly, in a group of hundreds millions of professionally offended people, we come to a vocabulary of perhaps twenty or thirty words that have been so bleached of potential offensiveness and meaning that language itself becomes worthless.

If you have not read *1984* by George Orwell, you have deprived yourself of an entire education right there. There lies the eternal dictatorship, the ultimate all-pervasive Superstate. And how did such a monstrosity come into being? *By controlling language.* Not only controlling what could be said, but by so simplifying and infantilizing language that entire concepts become literally unthinkable because there were no words for them. Here we sit talking about Freedom, Liberty, Responsibility and all the rest. What if the act of speaking one's mind was described only as *"ungood."* What if the only adjectives applied to a life of subjection and servility were *"double plus good,"* the very words *subjection, slavery, servility,* and *submission* banished generations ago?

You look out into the street and see someone tearing down a poster of Big Brother; the offender is hauled away, never to be seen again. How do you describe such an action without *courage, audacity, rebellion, resistance* and *freedom?* You can't. You can't describe them to others, and you can't think about them yourself. *Ungood behavior.* You're a prisoner of your limited, puerile language, and that is precisely where the Politically Correct movement wants to take us, to a world where language and thought is rigidly controlled – by them.

How much better, how much stronger and healthier are we, when we dare anyone to use whatever terms they chose, and rather than sitting as powerless victims, rise in angry and righteous indignation to fight the human filth that use words like *nigger, spick, gook, mick, kike, dago,* and all the rest? How much more secure, how much more *inoculated,* are we when we can hear these words knowing that those who use them are discredited and terrified infants so out of ideas and argument that they must resort to such childish tactics to reassure themselves?

What words can hurt us when we refuse to be hurt by words? What simple and powerful wisdom is bound up in *Sticks and stones may break my bones, but names can never hurt me?*

I have been called a few choice names in the course of these writings, and I have quickly learned that I do not want to be admired and respected by totalitarians, willfully uneducated idiots, smug and jaded suburban revolutionaries, and apologists for dictators. If people like that agreed with me I would be ashamed of myself. I'm proud to anger those people, and whatever names they choose to call me I consider a badge of pride, considering their source. We can indeed judge ourselves by the loathsomeness of our enemies.

The defense against this kind of free – and repugnant – speech is not to put our hands over our ears, our eyes, and someone else's mouth. The way to fight this human virus is to do what we have been doing: hold those who use such language up to ridicule and scorn, to use our own words as a people blessed with freedom of speech, and to let such archaic and diseased notions and epithets die a quick death in the marketplace of better ideas.

It is a far more dignified, self-respecting and adult way to deal with life's travails than crying and stamping your feet when someone calls you a bad name. Name callers will always exist, even within the competing factions of a PC universe. If we have free will, we can control our own hearts. And if we let mere words hurt us, we have abdicated this responsibility, and given it to someone else.

It's like surrendering an impregnable fortress without a shot being fired.

And how does responsibility weigh on the issue of **Media Bias?**

Way back in ancient times -- before, say, 1974 -- the goal of a reporter was not to single-handedly bring down the government and become an international celebrity, but rather to report the facts as fairly and evenly as possible and provide the essential information that we use to direct ourselves as a republic. They had enough respect for the intelligence and decency of the American Public to allow them to make their own decisions.

They also knew that in times of war some things would have to go unreported for a while, so that the country and the free press could survive to read about it later.

But now most of the press – long a somewhat rumpled and disheveled but nevertheless elitist group – does not seem to be too happy with the decisions being made by the body politic, and have decided that the populace cannot be trusted with this responsibility. And so they color the news, not by out and out lying – although there is more and more of that, symptomatic of deeper rot – but by editorializing, by selective interviewing, by counting the hits but ignoring the misses.

They do not think we can be trusted to do the right thing. They, like most elitists, do not think the average American is up to the responsibility.

As a single example, CNN purposely withheld a number of Saddam's examples of bestial behavior, torture and repression, ostensibly to maintain "access." In fact, the elite determining what passes for news at CNN was opposed to the war, and decided *on their own* and *without disclosing this monumental decision* to present the war in the worst possible light. But if the price of "access" is the rote delivery of policy statements dictated by a mass-murderer – as claimed by a few CNN reporters struggling to hold on to some shreds of integrity – then what point is there to such "access" if all they do is mouth the party line of a dictatorship at odds with a nation of millions of free people? We expect that from puppets like Comical Ali – from an American news source, it is a disgraceful and shocking indictment of how elitist, arrogant and egomaniacal the news media has largely become. It is the willful destruction of the main pillar that supports our Republic. Such an act is a basic violation of a sacred trust, and I think such willing distortion ought to be legally actionable, tantamount nearly to treason or sedition.

It is profoundly, poisonously anti-democratic.

The press holds in their hand enormous responsibility; they bear on their shoulders the immense burden of trust that we have placed upon them. We have trusted that they will do their job of providing the people of this democratic republic the unvarnished information we need to make responsible decisions.

What we decidedly do *not* need is some arrogant man or woman deciding, consciously or unconsciously, that they will present information in such a way as to influence people according to their own inner ideologies. Sorry, but this is not acceptable. Their personal opinions entitle them to one vote, not forty million.

We ask them to report the truth. Their response, increasingly, is *you can't handle the truth!*

Who the hell are they to decide something of that magnitude? *Who do these people think they are?*

When you hear the Evening News report some new terrorist warning, and a slow-motion flag banner across the bottom proclaims *Americans living in fear*, who do you think is afraid: you, or some New York news editor? All of this verbiage about Americans living in fear, anxiety, gloom, terror? *They're* the ones living that way. We're getting up and going to work every day. Stop telling us how afraid we need to be, you pathetic terrorist-enabling weenies! We can handle the truth just fine; it's *you* we're worried about.

The Press has the responsibility *to report facts.* We have the responsibility to inform ourselves enough to make reasoned political decisions. How we make those decisions is none of their business. *Give us the information and then get the hell out of the way.*

Note to Dan, Peter, Tom, Wolff and Aaron: *trust us. We can handle it.*

That's not a plea, by the way. That is a threat.

Trust us, or we will find someone who will.

Deconstructionism. If ever there was an intellectual movement specifically tailored for a certain type of mental illness, this must surely be it.

Deconstructionists believe in collective responsibility and the dominance of culture over individuality to such a degree that they maintain that one of the most striking examples of free will – the ability to write down what one thinks about something – is so colored by culture that the *author himself* has no real idea what he is saying.

Who, then, can truly know what Lincoln, or Shakespeare, or Hemingway was trying to say? Well, you can't simply read what they say and take it at face value. Any common idiot can do that, apparently. What the hell fun is it being better than everyone else if everyone else can get the same information that you can?

No, to understand the true meaning, you have to take several college courses where some obscure and petty failed writer – a man with a bust of Salieri on his mantelpiece – will deconstruct the cultural and environmental factors and tell you what a real author was *actually* saying.

This level of arrogance is beyond my ability to parody, frankly.

Again, very popular with the professionally outraged crowd, because it allows them to overcome one of their most glaring deficiencies, namely, the lack of any facts or respected opinions to support their lunatic theories. So if they can, by fiat, announce that what Adam Smith *really* meant in *The Wealth of Nations* was simply that – once you strip away the white, male, European, patriarchal and materialistic / hateful culture that he swam in, was that we should all share and reduce greenhouse gases and most especially give money to the demonstrators, *for they are as the salt of the earth.*

This is not coercion of responsibility; this is highway robbery. The idea that a band of nitwits with too much free time on their angry and sweaty little hands, can sit in a small sub-basement classroom at Mediocrity U. and tell **Shakespeare** *what he was really trying to say* is simply the most vile and reprehensible hijacking of responsibility and authority it has ever been my unpleasant experience to see.

That is why, when I deconstruct Deconstructionism, all I see is a group of pathetic, talent-free, self-hating fourth-raters secretly sending out a message for someone with some common sense to ride into town and hang them all.

It is my firm belief that in any decent society, in any civilization worth living in, the healthy and the fit have a moral obligation to render assistance to those in need. None of the people I consider friends and ideological companions cares to live in a country where children are starving on the streets. And we don't, despite what the *BBC* or *Pravda* or *The New York Times* would have you believe. Actually, that comparison was unfair to *Pravda*.

Welfare, as envisioned, was designed to provide assistance to people who through economic downturns or other swings of fate, were *momentarily* unable to care for themselves and their families. This is a noble idea, and one of many prerequisites for a decent and honorable society.

Furthermore, we must accept the fact that through disabilities of birth, or injury, or chronic illness, many people will be unable to make their own way in this world.

And of those unfortunate people, there will be a significant number who lack the family and personal support networks available to others, and who will need to depend on public assistance *for the rest of their lives.* These, too, are deserving of our help, and it seems to me that a decent society has a moral obligation to provide care and comfort for those with such afflictions. A nation as successful and prosperous as we are can not only afford to assist these people; a people as decent and generous as Americans will *insist* upon it.

That was the plan.

The problems is, as I mentioned before, that we no longer have a safety net; we have created a safety *hammock*, where an entire subculture of millions of otherwise capable people have come to rely on public handouts for their livelihoods, with no intention whatsoever of assuming responsibility for their own lives.

I can truthfully state that I do not know the numbers, or proportions, of people on welfare who have no business being there, but they certainly appear to be significant.

If we are to speak frankly and intelligently about this issue, we must recognize that there are two sides of this coin of responsibility. The first is the obligation society has to the poor, outlined above.

What is not discussed is the reciprocal responsibility; *namely: what obligation does the poor have to society?*

I think there's a simple answer for that, much simpler than most people realize. I think that if we have a moral obligation to help those in need, then those in need have a moral obligation to recover and stand on their own feet *as quickly as possible.*

Let's take a relative compassion test, shall we? Who is more compassionate: those that want to limit the helping hand in order to allow someone to get back on their feet, gain an education, recover their self-esteem, manifest their self-worth, and lift themselves from the crippling depths of poverty, or someone who wants to hand them an endless supply of meager checks, just enough to destroy their self-respect, hobble their motivation, and sentence them, and their children, and their grandchildren, and *their* children, to squalid and wasted lives?

I oppose the creation and maintenance of a class of people perpetually on the dole because we simply can not afford it. And I'm not talking financially – we have the money to do that until the end of time. We cannot afford the *human cost*. We cannot afford to squander entire generations of Einsteins and Sagans and Mozarts and DaVincis by condemning them to a life that consists solely of pushing a lever and getting a food pellet.

We need all the help we can get in this struggle toward a more perfect Union. Training people how to remain passive, dependent and miserable is not noble, it is not just, and it is least of all compassionate.

But being the person who brings those benefits home from Washington does, I have noticed, put a fair amount of power, prestige and money in the hands of those elites that call themselves "Champions of the Poor."

If *I* were elected Champion of the Poor, my first goal would be the elimination of my job in as short a time as possible – by teaching people how to care for themselves, how to succeed and thrive and prosper – in other words, how to be poor no longer. Not by their own bootstraps – I'm not that naïve. But we, together, should be able to provide the assistance to get this much-needed human potential out of the stagnant swamp that forty years of public assistance has put them in.

We have thrown a lot of money at this problem, for nearly half a century now, with no noticeable improvement. Maybe the answer is not to throw just money, but to throw *attitudes*. It seems worth a try. I don't see how we could do much worse.

We could be here all day doing this, but we won't. Just a few more quick observations, then it's back to the cave until next we see the Bat Signal on a cloudy and threatening night.

I got started thinking about responsibility over the huffing and puffing done by the Perpetually Outraged regarding the death of Uday and Qusay Hussein. We were told they had been "assassinated," that the US had "murdered Saddam's children." We, of course, were the ones to blame. *We* were the criminals. We were **responsible.**

There is so much revealed in such an attitude that a rational, responsible mind recoils as if having picked up a white-hot iron bar.

First of all, a brief review of the facts will show that an offer was made for them to surrender – multiple times. I do not recall Lee Harvey Oswald shouting down to the Kennedy motorcade advising the President to get out of the limousine before someone got hurt, nor does history record anything of John Wilkes Booth slipping a note to Lincoln warning him that if he came back for the second act then grave consequences would result.

Those were assassinations. This was a raid to apprehend or kill two of the most despicable mass murderers in human history. The offer to apprehend being repeatedly made, and responded to with gunfire, pretty much rules out assassination to anyone but disgusting and reprehensible opportunists who will forgo the deaths of 300,000 – three filled Superbowls of innocent families -- in order to see their own man or woman win the next election.

Then the critics harp on the use of *overwhelming force.* 200 plus soldiers, Humvees, helicopters… and yet, who would be shrieking the loudest if fifteen or twenty or a hundred US servicemen had been killed in this operation? The *audacity* of such a claim boggles the mind, given its proponents endless quest for second-guessing military failures.

Who really believes that these two murdering bastards would put their hands up and march out to face the populace that they had tortured, murdered and raped for so many years? Who believes Hitler would have walked out of his bunker, hands in the air, and surrendered to Soviet authorities for a trial? What astonishing lack of comprehension does such a position reveal? What more evidence does one need to realize how deeply, fatally isolated these people are from the world they claim to criticize?

But here is the final outrage, one that makes all the others Sunday-school peccadilloes.

How dare these people, *how dare they*, absolve these two mass murders from **the responsibility** of the deaths of so many tens of thousands of men, women and children, simply because they cannot get over their loathing of the President of the United States? These people have the nerve, the unmitigated gall, to claim the moral high ground? What depths will such people not wallow in?

Imagine that you are a seventeen-year-old girl tied with electrical cords in a basement in Baghdad. It's Monday evening. Uday Hussein, a young psychopath given godlike power over life and death since birth, was driving his pimpmobile on Friday afternoon, and saw you walking home from your university classes. He ordered you into the car, took you to one of his compounds, and raped you for three days, sharing you with all of his sycophants. Then, when your family had the temerity to question what might have happened to you, they were brought to this basement. You were raped repeatedly in front of your father and mother, your younger sister, too – just so she could see what was in store for her. Your 7 year old brother then had his brains blown all over a wall in front of the entire family. Then your parents were killed, or you were killed, or your sister – the order doesn't matter, since none of you are getting out of this room. Inhuman wails of agony, pleas for mercy, begging, promising, mothers offering to be raped in place of their daughters, fathers begging to be killed if only they will release his family – all of this. Perhaps you'll be raped to death, or beaten to death; perhaps electrocuted with a wire brush plugged into a wall as salt water is thrown onto your lacerated body.

Maybe father will be placed into one of the industrial shredders – head first, if you can imagine such a thing…that would mean Uday is feeling merciful. Feet first will take a few moments longer. No, looks like it's feet first for him today.

And you? What is your last thought, a pretty seventeen year old girl majoring in Chemical Engineering, say? What is the last thing that crosses your mind before the lights go out on you, your future, and the future of all the children you will never have?

We know, from the pathetic, forever-scarred and infinitesimal minority that escapes such living hell, that the one thing they call for in their last plea to a God that did not save them, is for justice.

Justice.

That those who did these evil things, that laughed while lives were destroyed by their own hand, face the **responsibility** for their actions. Not to live life comfortably after the massacre of hundreds of thousands, like that cannibal monstrosity Idi Amin, who lived like a sultan for thirty years after his abominations, courtesy of our good friends the Saudis.

Justice for these animals – And Qusay, though less flamboyant, was by all accounts more prolific in this hellish competition – justice for that girl and her family and the hundreds of thousands of other *real people* who died appalling deaths in darkened dungeons – Justice for them came when these miserable bastards faced the fact that they were trapped, cornered, and going to die. There was going to be no last minute rescue for them, just as there was none for those untold Iraqi families that pampered western idiots dismiss with a wave of their rhetorical and oh-so-compassionate hands.

No, they were trapped, and they were not getting out of that place alive. I hope they were terrified. I hope they shivered and cried in fear. I hope they had, in those four hours, a *glimmer*, a faint, animalistic, dim recognition that this is how it must have felt for those objects they tortured and destroyed in their palaces of mayhem and grief. Uday and Qusay got a lot less than they deserved, but they did not get away. They did not escape justice. They did not escape responsibility. And they did not escape the United States of America, last best hope of this earth for all her manifest flaws and failures.

Who *did* escape responsibility? Those who called this an assassination. Those who turned a blind eye to children's graves and acid baths and rallied to the defense of these murdering bastards. They go about their lives today, looking for new apologies for Saddam and Osama and Fidel and Stalin. They walk our streets today, safe and secure, protected – rightly – from retaliation for their moral bankruptcy by the society they despise.

———————————

If we accept responsibility for our own actions, we are indeed worthy of our freedom.

This idea of individual responsibility is a new one. It works. It needs to be defended. If only a small portion of the mass of humanity can see clearly that this is the key to escape the bondage of history, class, race, sex and economic status, then that is simply a message we need to preach to anyone who will listen. Many will not hear it. Perhaps most will not.

As for me, I don't give a flying damn about being in the side with the most adherents. I want to be on the side that is *correct*. Remember, there was a time when three or four people on the entire planet believed that the earth was round, and the *entire rest of the species* said they were demonstrably wrong, insane, and should be burned at the stake.

Finally, I promised I would tell you who is responsible for the mess we find ourselves in.

Proceed into your bathroom and take a long, hard look in the mirror.

I also promised to tell you who can get us out of this fix. Well, **keep looking.** While you're looking, *make a decision.*

When we surrender our responsibility, when we say we are not capable of facing the consequences of being allowed to smoke, or own a handgun, or ride a motorcycle without a helmet, or drink hot coffee, then we have gained nothing and given away all. There are people who will gladly assume our responsibility in order to have our freedom and our political power. It's a buyers market.

As a nation of freemen, we must live through all time, or die by suicide.

We've been warned.

STRENGTH

May 22, 2004

First of all, let's start this little journey by mentioning **The Gloom.** *Fallujah. Abu Ghraib.* Bodies hanging on bridges. Prisoners standing on boxes.

Listen troops, let's get this straight right off the bat: it's only a catastrophe. It's nothing more than a major disaster. I'm not being cynical, or arch, or "ironic." I am deadly serious.

We have seen two months of what looks like non-stop catastrophe, and we will see more, and maybe worse, before we are through. Here is my well-reasoned, historically researched, deeply nuanced opinion: *Buck up.* This war will be over when we say it is over, and not a second before.

When Santa Ana's men ran up the red flag and his band played the *Deguello* -- "The Throat Cutting" -- it must have made the men and women in the Alamo sick and weak in the knees. But it did not have the demoralizing effect that the Mexican dictator intended. Rather, it hardened the defenders. They did not run, and we are not going to run either, and Dan Rather and Ted Koppel and the rest can play all the goddam dirges they want to.

The Alamo itself was a military disaster, a catastrophe. And when Sam Houston retreated from and kept evading Santa Ana's army, he was called a coward and a traitor – afraid to fight, not tough enough to do what was necessary. Sam Houston was a deeply flawed man, but he had thick skin and that in itself goes a long way when you are planning deep. Sam Houston didn't give a tinker's damn about Glory or Honor. Sam Houston wanted *Texas*. Like the equally wily and patient George Washington before him, Sam Houston wanted to *win*. And they did win. And that is why there will be no major metropolitan area named *Kerry*.

We ran from Fallujah, we hear; *those murdering bastards are laughing at us. We're not tough enough to win.* Uh, not quite. Hundreds of those murdering bastards are dead. They are not laughing at anything.

The Fallujah bridge pissed off a lot of Americans. It really made us see red. Would we be disgusted enough to walk away, or furious enough to go in and indiscriminately slaughter thousands? The architects of that atrocity must have thought they nailed that perfect tic-tac-toe move: we go one way, they win on the other. Quoth Den Beste: *the object of Terrorism is to provoke an overwhelming response.* And the response to that response is the political and strategic goal of the terrorist.

Al Sadr, you less than magnificent bastard! *We read your book!*

Blah, blah...war is lost...blah blah blah... disaster, wreck and ruin... Only it turns out that the United States military may have produced a few life-long professionals who actually hold victory more precious than crowing loud. Many of us value reason over emotion, and reality over wishful thinking. Well, we did not level Fallujah, and we did not do it because those bodies on that bridge were *bait*, pure and simple. We didn't take the bait.

Or, I should say, our military didn't take the bait; *I* took it, hook line and sinker. I wanted to level the goddam city and then walk away and let them kill each other.

Now, as Al Sadr's support evaporates; as his militia thugs are being hunted and killed by shadowy Iraqi ghost armies and extremely corporeal Marines; as his fellow Mullahs condemn him; as Iraqi demonstrations against him and all that poison and ruin he represents continue to rise; as his headquarters are destroyed, his most vicious 'soldiers' killed in their own backyards, playing defense in an urban environment by Marines whose skill and tactics stagger credulity for their expertise and success – now, we must ask ourselves: did you want to feel good or did you want to *win?*

I want to win. I was an idiot for taking that bait. And I thank God daily that America makes better, smarter people than me.

The average Iraqi knows full well we can bomb and pummel the hell out of anything we want. But this was different. This took patience, and a willingness to get inside the enemy strategy. This took commitment, and persistence. It was *cunning.* These people know how strong our military might is; no need to re-teach that lesson. But strong and *cunning?* Strong and cunning and *patient?* That puts the Arab imagination into overdrive.

The threat of the vast Shiite uprising that loomed in early April has largely evaporated. Things are still very tense. They may again get worse; they may become horrible. But we will win this because we are not going home until we do. This is slowly beginning to dawn on some of the hardest heads in Iraq. When Iraqi leaders start saying things like *we'd better help the Americans stabilize the country, because they will not go away until we do* – well, that is precisely, exactly the kind of victory we need. We need that *attitude.* There is a shred of can-do self-reliance in those words. Al-Sadr will either end up like Uday and Qusay or Saddam. Those are his remaining choices.

Fallujah still stings proud people like me. I want them to admit the obvious: that we kicked their ass and can do so again at the drop of a hat. But confidence, the confidence borne of real strength, tells me I might perhaps be wrong. Victory may be more important than my personal pride; indeed more important than the pride of the US Marine Corps. The Marines are all about pride, but their mission is Victory, and nothing gets between a Marine and Victory.

So the next time you hear this *Graveyard of Americans* bull, do what I do: close your eyes, picture Colonel Klink, and remember that *no one has ever escaped from Stalag 13.*

Because we did not take the bait, because we so clearly were not the staggering, drunken, imbecile Giant we are accused of being by our European betters, we denied the Syrians and the Iranians the general, nation-wide uprising they so dearly wanted. Idiots. We vote in *November.* They played their hand *now.* Kerry and Bush are in a dead heat after eight weeks of unrelenting **catastrophe** for Bush. And there is such a thing as catastrophe fatigue.

On May 7th, 1864, the Army of the Potomac had once again been thrashed at the hands of Robert E. Lee. Their newest commander, US Grant, had been beaten, and beaten badly, in his first contest with the legendary Southerner. Beaten worse than "Fighting Joe" Hooker had been on the same ground at Chancellorsville.

Beaten as badly as Burnside, and Pope, and McClellan had been beaten before the endless retreats, the shame, and the false hope of a never-ending parade of new commanders. They were a beaten Army. And as they marched out of the Wilderness to camp back in Washington, they had nothing to look forward to but new commanders, new catastrophes, new humiliations, and new defeats.

But when they came to the familiar crossroads, a buzz ran down the line. Some solders described it as a wave of emotion – disbelief, mostly – others, as static electricity. It was a murmur, then a shout, and then a cheer. They were not turning North. They were turning South, trying to steal a March on Bobby Lee! They had been beaten and bloodied as badly as any time in their seemingly endless string of utter defeats. But now they were marching South, to try again.

The simplest farm boy in that line that night knew, with certainty, that they could suffer as many catastrophes and disasters as fate could throw at them, for while they might be defeated again and again, they only had to succeed once.

So remember this; tattoo this in backward letters on your forehead so you can read it when you brush your teeth each morning: The most deadly, most awful and destructive war in our history was won not by a series of tactical and strategic masterstrokes, but rather by an endless, relentless series of monumental, hair-rending, soul-destroying blunders, missteps and debacles…that **never stopped** until they had won total, complete, utter, victory.

When Lee announced the surrender of the Army of Northern Virginia at Appomattox, many of his soldiers wept. As it began to dawn on them, and they started along the winding dirt roads that led to home, they would say things to each other like *One Johnny Reb was worth ten Yankees on the battlefield* and *Give us time to get a crop in and we'll go back and lick 'em again.* They were proud and tough people trying to retain their pride in the face of the worst defeat ever suf fered by Americans. We didn't club these people to death to show them they were wrong. We left them what was left of their pride; we'd need those people to be good citizens again someday. Victory is enough.

That takes strength.

Catastrophes are only catastrophes; disasters are only disasters: they are not the end unless we decide they are. And so, let us, right here and now, decide that they are not the end. Because this is something we need to understand, something we need to feel deep in our bones: We are so strong, as a nation, that nothing can stop us when we set our minds to something. Nothing. We can only stop ourselves. All the players know this to be true. Al Sadr knows it. France and Germany know it. The Jihadis know it. The UN knows it. You and I know it.

Because we, the American people, are the only ones who can decide whether or not to give up in failure and defeat or carry on to the victory of a free and stable Iraq, we find we *ourselves* – the common, average American – are to be the battleground. We are the soldiers. We are the weapons. We are the targets of the enemy strategy.

Our hearts, our spirit – that is the front line. All the players know this, too. This is our war, more than it is the Marines' or Al Quaeda's.

Our war. **Ours.**

So we need to find the strength to fight this war. And this search will not be a quick or easy one, for our strength lies both obvious and on the surface in some places, and in other places, very, *very* deep.

This is a critical, essential search, for the manifest strengths and beauty of our Western Society have been under such sustained attack, for so long, that we are beginning to believe this parade of lies launched against us. We have to stop it. We have to fight it. And we have to beat it. On this everything else depends.

This will be a long and circuitous journey. I'm sorry; I wish it were not so. But we must, we **must** find the strength we need to sustain our spirits against an onrush of negativity, pessimism, defeatism and despair that is so deadly precisely because it is so antithetical to the natural character of the American people.

Morale, my friends. Morale. Humor and confidence are our best friends now. And so, as we begin our journey through Mordor toward the heart of Mt Doom, this mission to defeat this pernicious attack on our strength, remember this:

Americans eat disasters and crap hand grenades. And I got your quagmire right here.

It seems fairly incredible to me that I have to spend some time on whether or not Radical Islam – which we will, for the sake of the discussion, call Islamist – is really a threat to the West in general and the United States in particular.

But the fact remains that those determined to weaken our will are methodically trying to undermine every aspect of what we Westerners refer to as "reality." So, like a giant and unusually serious game of Whack-A-Mole, we have to spend time going around clubbing arguments that should be blatantly obvious.

Remember, links in a chain of argument. Grab the hammer and tongs, and let's get to work:

To those who claim that Islamist terrorists do not pose a direct, immediate and potent threat to the United States, I would like to condense the next four thousand words of this argument thusly:

One of the most vilified people on the internet right now is Charles Johnson at **Little Green Footballs** *(http://littlegreenfootballs.com/weblog/)*. It is the only website that I will check at least twice a day. Charles has been called a racist, a bigot, and much worse. He is personally threatened daily. Charles is attacked personally, and with a viciousness rare even among the most vicious out there, because there really is no other defense against the arguments that LGF makes, many times a day, than to attack the man.

But Charles Johnson is not the issue. I could counter with the fact that I have met him several times; he is, like Steven Den Beste, an extraordinarily gracious, soft-spoken and gentle man. None of this matters.

What does matter is what Little Green Footballs does on a daily basis. Charles Johnson does not sit down and write five essays a day on why he thinks Radical Islam is a deranged and poisonous and growing Death Cult. Charles simply links to newspaper articles, usually from Arab and Islamist sources like Arab News and Reuters, that show without question that Radical Islam is calling, daily and nightly, for the destruction of the West, the murder, enslavement or conversion of its citizens, and the establishment of a world-wide Caliphate where *Shariah* – Islamic Law – is the only law.

This is not his opinion. This is not the opinion of Western editorial writers. This is a filter (and of course it's a filter – that's why it is useful) that looks at Islamist thinking and behavior daily and shows what Islamists are saying and doing *in their own words*.

I and many others view *Little Green Footballs* as the equivalent of the Cold War's D.E.W. Line – the Distant Early Warning radar system that searched the Polar skies, looking for incoming threats. This is why Charles is attacked personally. He is attacked *personally* in an attempt to discredit him and his website because the fact remains that almost everything he links to are articles *by Islamists*, about Radical Islam – and what they say in their own words is so totally compelling, damning, and down-right blood-curdling that anyone not seeing the danger brewing does not deserve to be part of this argument.

Now, the source of this hatred towards the West is the source of endless books and analysis and articles and thesis papers. To this interminable Gordian Knot of causes and effects and counter-causes and grievances, I can only add this:

I don't care.

If someone is coming toward me in an alley, knife drawn, I do not give a damn why their socio-economic status may have had an influence in coloring their worldview regarding income redistribution. To take such a position rather than preparing to defend yourself is **suicide**, and we will come back to this later because it is a key to understanding what is going on out there.

Radical Islam is a religious cult based on constant, never-ending warfare. I personally am aware of no other religious tracts that are as filled with page after page of conquest, strategy and military jargon. Islam rose to prominence under the sword, and the Prophet was, above all else, a military commander determined to spread his faith by conquest and enslavement. Islam has rules for when prisoners should be released, ransomed, sold into slavery or have their throats cut. As a matter of fact, Islam has rules for *everything*. What to eat, how to wash, where and when and in which direction to pray. Islam has rules for the treatment of animals and the treatment of women. There is no part of daily life that is not specifically addressed, sanctioned or outlawed by Islam.

And contrary to post 9/11 spin, the most accurate translation of Islam is not *"peace."* Prior to 9/11, the nearly universally accepted translation of the concept of Islam was *"submission."*

Of course, submission sounds a little more prickly to American ears. Matter of fact, it's hard to imagine a word that would so enrage the American psyche than the concept of submission. "Tyranny," perhaps, but tyranny is only what we are expected to submit to. Americans have fought against submission and Tyranny since there have been Americans. That's what we *do*. That is who we *are*. And ever since the Revolution against submitting to the tyranny of King George, American revulsion with the entire idea of submission has been watered each generation by fresh waves of immigrants who have fled here *escaping submission*.

And here are two final thoughts on this issue:

First, Islam philosophically divides the world into two camps – this is *Islam's* definitions, not mine – *Dar al-Islam* and *Dar al-Harb*. Dar al-Islam is the *House of Submission*. Dar Al-Harb is not the *House of Infidels*. It is the **House of War.**

I, and others who see a terrible threat in the growth of Radical Islam, did not invent this term. It is considerably older than my humble self; besides, I do not speak Arabic. It is *their* term. And unlike people determined to hide until this problem goes away, I am determined to take Islam at its word.

Second, consider this: Muslims are angrily at war with Buddhists in East Asia. Muslims are at enraged with Animists in Africa. Of course, none of this approaches the sheer hatred that Muslims bear towards Hindus in the South Asia peninsula. And this foaming hatred blanches compared to the white-hot fury Muslims feel to the Christian American Crusaders. And this fury is but a candle to the incandescent, boiling, supernova of murder they feel toward the Jews.

Does anyone beside me detect a pattern here? You know, my Dad told me once, *"Bill, if more than three people in your life are utter, total, complete, miserable bastards then maybe it's you."*

I am not a religious person. I do not have a horse in this race. But everywhere I turn in the world today, I see Radical Islam – and not the United States – at war with *everybody*. And I have no choice but to conclude that this is not a blip or a hiccup. It is a growing threat. And it needs to be met head-on. Right now.

Have I slandered 1.5 billion people? I don't know. Have I? I speak of Radical Islam. I speak of people determined to kill and terrorize to impose their religion on the rest of the world. If you are a Muslim who is against these practices, you have my respect and admiration. And, as with all other religions in the United States, I will as passionately defend your right to practice your faith in harmony and goodwill as I attack those who may carry the Crescent far, far away from your peaceful and devout beliefs. But I will not pretend I do not see and hear what I see and hear every single day, just because you may not like to hear it. That is not something I or millions of my countrymen will submit to. Accept, or at the very least, *understand* that right now. I say this for both our sakes. More on this later.

The philosophy of Radical Islam is at war, not only with America and the West, but with everything that is not Radical Islam. So, do they hate us? Yes they do. Judging from their street demonstrations, and the rhetoric issuing from their madrassas, does anyone seriously doubt that if millions were given a button that would wipe us from the face of the earth, they would push it?

I don't see how any rational person could deny this is so.

They are working on that button, by the way.

WHACK! On to the next mole.

Those who would have you doubt America and the West want you to believe that there are many legitimate grievances that Islamists have against us. They argue that they are only acting against American and Western aggression, colonization and arrogance. So it's all our fault and if we'd just come home and mind our own business everything would be dandy.

Unfortunately, when you actually listen to the Islamists talk about their "griev-ances" (hey, Reuters? These "quotes" really do perform as advertised!), they will start at the Crusades and work their way forward, in no particular order. Sadly for those who want you to believe they hate us for what we do rather than who we are, Uncle Sam was not at that fight – a fact that might be apparent had their historical knowledge predated 1968. Americans were not only quite spectacularly underrepresented at the Crusades...we in fact do not make much of a dent on the Islamist bloody roll-call until the middle 1970's. Before then it was the Franks and the Spanish and the English and just about everyone else.

Why are these people still seething about things that happened a thousand years ago?

Well, because it's been that long since Islam was a dominant force in the world. It's like watching a Red Sox fan pining for the days of the Babe and the lost glory of that 1918 season.

The truly remarkable, astonishing and galling issue here is that while the multi-culturalists are the ones shrieking the loudest about understanding different people and different values, they are the ones absolutely least willing to take themselves at their own words and so they consistently apply western thought models to people who think **nothing** like we do.

We are a co-operative society. Compromise, agreements and webs of trust run through our culture in mind-blowing levels of complexity. The most virulent Islamist Arabs, on the other hand, live by completely different rules and values, and time and again we who should know better by now refuse to try to see things through Arab eyes because the view is frankly so jaundiced and horrible we really can't believe what we are seeing.

Honor and shame trump everything in that world. A pithy sentence, eh? So instead, think about what it would take for you to kill your own daughter with a knife, or with your bare hands, because she was seen in the company of a man not her husband or a relative? Think about that. Think long and hard. What kind of hatred and shame could drive a human being to do such a thing? What kind of pressures does that society bring to bear on an individual to make him capable of *that*? How different is their view of women, of family, of honor and shame? What would it take for you to murder your daughter with a knife, or a knotted cord – with your own two hands and against her pleading, her protestations, and her begging for her life? If your response wasn't *"there is nothing that could make me do that,"* then stop reading right here and get the hell off my property.

Multi-culturalists will respond that Honor Killings are not the norm and not representative of Islam and life under *Shariah*. We can debate the exact numbers of these horrors for days, but the fact remains that no matter how many individual cases there are, there is de facto legal protection for committing these crimes. When Islamic schoolgirls attempting to escape a burning building with their faces uncovered were sent back inside to die *by the religious police* rather than dishonor Islam …well, that is a brush that will carry a lot of tar.

There is a simple enough reason why these Islamists so hate and despise the West, and America especially. It has little to do with our foreign policy. We have taken the side of oppressed Muslims in Kosovo, Chechnya, Kuwait and many other places. We spend billions of dollars a year in aid to Egypt. We're still waiting for the love to pour in.

No, this is not about reason, as we understand the term. This is about shame, it is about denial, and it is about transcendent revenge. Shouts of *Allahu Akbar!* were not overdubbed by western propaganda agencies as they sawed through Nick Berg's throat and twisted off his head. Those are authentic.

As they got down to their filthy work they were screaming, over and over in a fit of religious ecstasy: *God is Great!* Nick Berg was nothing more than an animal sacrifice to them. *That* is Radical Islam.

The only thing that will appease them is your blood. All of it. Remember that.

They are the willing architects of their own brutal oppression. They are dirt poor – not because of what was done to or stolen from them, but because of what they have done to themselves. This harsh, vicious, bitter patriarchy of control and domination has systematically and methodically wrung out of life the smallest joy or happiness. The Ayatollah Khomeini, the Santa Claus for your eternity in hell, famously remarked that:

"Allah did not create man so that he could have fun. The aim of creation was for mankind to be put to the test through hardship and prayer. An Islamic regime must be serious in every field. There are no jokes in Islam. There is no humor in Islam. There is no fun in Islam. There can be no fun and joy in whatever is serious."

And yet, in a very different desert on the far side of the world, sits... *Vegas.*

There was no issuance of demands prior to 9/11. 9/11 was not a response to acts taken by the United States government. 9/11 was never about what we have done. 9/11 was an attack on **Who. We. Are.**

In the world today there exists a 21st Century society with unimagined freedoms, opportunities and protections for the individual. Opposing it is a 12th Century religious cult bound in concepts of tribalism, shame, revenge and envy.

The presence of Las Vegas makes a mockery of these people's lives. They have been taught that they are God's own chosen people – but they are *humans*, as human as we are. And so, shackled to an ideology determined to wring every precious drop of enjoyment out of life, they look across the world to see a group of people enthusiastically breaking every commandment they were ever given, and not only do these heathens succeed and prosper beyond the wildest tales from the Arabian Nights, but they are enjoying themselves beyond any measure as they do so.

These tortured souls can vaguely guess, lying in bed late at night, that even the lowest and most common working man or woman in America can, once a year, travel to Las Vegas and live a few days in luxury unknown to the grandest Caliph in the very flower of their history.

You've got to admit, if that were you – that would *suck.*

The success, the strength – indeed, the very presence of the United States tells them that their religion has been lying to them. They, who follow every stricture, who submit to every admonition, who put away every single shred of enjoyment have been told they are the chosen people of God, and that the World shall become their domain and its citizens their slaves and concubines.

Not happening.

This fact is not lost on them. They are told it is because they are not devout enough. They are pointed toward 19 Warriors of the Faith, pure in heart, and what they can accomplish against the Great Satan. What other explanation can they accept? That their entire religion, their entire culture, their entire history of failure, torture, hardship and ruin is their *own* fault? That it will not, it **cannot** change, and must be discarded? That there is nothing for them but more of the same endless misery, while everyone else in the world grows richer, freer, and happier?

No. That is not going to happen. We are their test. God has promised them the world, and, if you will forgive the trendy internet reference: **all our base are belong to them.**

To them, we and our pursuit of happiness are intolerable. More intolerable is the incredible appeal our culture has for people – especially young people – all around the world.

Our 21st Century society can easily survive the cultural appeals of their 12th century one. The reverse is certainly not true. Radical Islam, without Jihad, without the promise of elevation and achievement through death, cannot survive in the world we have created.

One way or another, it is going to be Them or Us. Everybody knows this, and no one will say it.

Because this conflict is about who we are, rather than what we do, defeat for us means not stepping back from places where others claim we have no business, but rather the destruction of this society, and the values upon which it is based.

And so the attacks on our foundations continue, a concerted and coordinated effort to define our history and our culture as being unworthy of defense and antithetical to humanity's greater good.

Having spent untold hours hovering in the electronic cafes, meeting halls and sewers that link us in this world wide web, I see a disgust for and frankly a complete disbelief in the amount of patriotism displayed by the average American.

I have also seen ugly, mindless displays of American pride and arrogance. In some of this, I think, I see the hurt and disbelief, and the growing sense of betrayal and shock at the abandonment and slander coming at us from those formerly thought friends whom we have helped often and dearly in the past when *their* existence was threatened and their own buildings lay in smoke and ruin.

Those friends that have remained are especially dear to us now. I suspect we will not forget either camp for a very long time indeed.

There was a time when most every nationality expressed a burning pride in who and what they were and had become. I have always understood and admired this essential pride in one's self and their extended national family.

Many in Europe, especially, have renounced such feelings of nationalism. Nationalism has not played out all too happily in Europe, and so we, who have had nothing but success in this regard, are expected to toe the line and voluntarily scrap our shiny new automobile because the neighbors went and ran theirs over a cliff.

What is not apparent from history is the simple fact that being an American is a choice. It is a choice we have all made to be here, or to come here, either ourselves, or our parents, or their parents. It is a choice new millions make annually. And any of us can leave, at any time. No one not a part of this experiment, no one who does not hold the truths we live by to be self-evident, can have a glimmer, a nanosecond *flash* of how deeply and brightly that pride burns inside so many of us.

This is a strength – I believe the *only* strength, when all is said and done – that has the power to stand up to these forces of darkness gathering once again in the margins of the world. It is another reason why those who would strangle liberty, individuality and joy hate and fear us so greatly.

And so the attack on our self-image is essential to weakening our fundamental strength. And it has been accelerating where we are the most vulnerable, in our schools and universities, launched by the most self-obsessed, pampered generation in our history: mine.

Do you disagree?

Well, let's start by looking at how we view ourselves now, in our antiseptic, safe and bland reality, against how we viewed ourselves in the crucible of our existence when our personal lives and the life of our Republic hung in the balance.

On one hand, we're lucky. We've got a history that is so packed with heroism and courage and strength that the hard part is figuring out which example to start with. It could be much worse, *n'est pas?*

History is woven from a collection of snapshots, flashbulbs in a dark room revealing instants frozen in time and memory. Behind the boilerplate of historians are moments so fragile and ephemeral we can catch and preserve but the thinnest fraction of them. After the Civil War, many millions of delicate glass negatives were used as panes in greenhouses all across a nation determined to forget the horror and sorrow and move on with life once more. How many proud or grim expressions have simply faded slowly away in the sunlight of the succeeding years, ghosts lining the walls and ceilings of hothouses in Maine and Alabama, growing dimmer, and fainter…and…*gone.*

On the eve of that nightmare, that horror that so many had seen coming for so long, history and chance have snatched one of those snapshots back from eternity. Study it. Take your time. Soak it up. Even better, whisper it aloud, if you dare – these words need human breath again. It is a dried and brittle flower, pressed into the book of our collective memory; a snapshot of American thought from 143 years ago…

Shortly before the first great battle of the Civil War, a Major of the 2nd Rhode Island Volunteers wrote to his wife in Smithfield.

July the 14th, 1861
Washington D.C.

My very dear Sarah:

The indications are very strong that we shall move in a few days – perhaps tomorrow. Lest I should not be able to write you again, I feel impelled to write lines that may fall under your eye when I shall be no more.

If it is necessary that I should fall on the battlefield for my country, I am ready. I have no misgivings about, or lack of confidence in, the cause in which I am engaged, and my courage does not halt or falter. I know how strongly American Civilization now leans upon the triumph of the Government, and how great a debt we owe to those who went before us through the blood and suffering of the Revolution. And I am willing – perfectly willing – to lay down all my joys in this life, to help maintain this Government, and to pay that debt.

But, my dear wife, when I know that with my own joys I lay down nearly all of yours, and replace them in this life with cares and sorrows – when, after having eaten for long years the bitter fruit of orphanage myself, I must offer it as their only sustenance to my dear little children – is it weak or dishonorable, while the banner of my purpose floats calmly and proudly in the breeze, that my unbounded love for you, my darling wife and children, should struggle in fierce, though useless, contest with my love of country?

Sarah, my love for you is deathless, it seems to bind me to you with mighty cables that nothing but Omnipotence could break; and yet my love of Country comes over me like a strong wind and bears me irresistibly on with all these chains to the battlefield.

The memories of the blissful moments I have spent with you come creeping over me, and I feel most gratified to God and to you that I have enjoyed them so long. And hard it is for me to give them up and burn to ashes the hopes of future years, when God willing, we might still have lived and loved together and seen our sons grow up to honorable manhood around us.

My dear Sarah, never forget how much I love you, and when my last breath escapes me on the battlefield, it will whisper your name.

Forgive my many faults, and the many pains I have caused you. How thoughtless and foolish I have oftentimes been! How gladly would I wash out with my tears every little spot upon your happiness, and struggle with all the misfortune of this world, to shield you and my children from harm.

But I cannot. I must watch you from the spirit land and hover near you, while you buffet the storms with your precious little freight, and wait with sad patience till we meet to part no more.

But, O Sarah! If the dead can come back to this earth and flit unseen around those they loved, I shall always be near you; in the garish day and in the darkest night – amidst your happiest scenes and gloomiest hours – always, always; and if there be a soft breeze upon your cheek, it shall be my breath; or the cool air fans your throbbing temple, it shall be my spirit passing by.

Sarah, do not mourn me dead; think I am gone and wait for thee, for we shall meet again.

Major Sullivan Ballou was killed one week later at the first battle of Bull Run.

The most remarkable thing about this letter is simply how ordinary such thoughts were in that day. Many, of course, have heard of this letter thanks to Ken Burns and his amazing documentary, *The Civil War.* Many have said it might be the greatest love letter ever written. And I would agree, but look deeper…

Major Ballou is, in effect, writing this letter as an *apology.* It is an apology to his wife and sons that his love for his country has called him away, to leave that which he loves so dearly alone and undefended in a world very much harder than our own. Until I read the unedited letter I myself never suspected that Maj. Ballou was an orphan; how bitter it must have been for him to willingly condemn his own two children to a fatherless existence in the days before life insurance and Social Security.

Look at how this man views his country. Here he stands, a beacon of love and sacrifice against the gloom of historical anonymity; a man ready to sacrifice his overwhelming love for his wife, his children and his life for a cause which he believes supercedes them all. More than anything, this letter speaks of a selflessness and gratitude that surpasses modern understanding. There is not a shred of victimhood, not a whiff of regret or bitterness from start to finish.

There are people who will read this letter and cry. I am one of those people. To me, the sentiments expressed with such casual eloquence are the absolute pinnacle of what the endless human struggle entails: *Courage. Honor. Duty.*

And yet, and yet…for all those hard virtues, how much love is in this letter? How much joy? How much beauty? How much pride and dignity? How much confidence? How much compassion? How much sacrifice?

How much **strength** is in that letter?

There are people who will read this letter and call men like Sullivan Ballou idiots and fools. They will mock those values and say they wasted their lives, and abandoned their children, to die horrible deaths at the hands of their brothers for no reason other than foolish jingoism and false glory. Such people will say that he was a mere cog in the interests of rich and powerful men struggling only to grow their own wallets.

But Sullivan Ballou is above their derision and deconstruction. He had a level of courage and moral clarity so far beyond these critics that it goes through them, invisible and undetected, like an X-ray.

Those people will never know what he knew, and what some of us struggle to retain today. It is beyond them, as far beyond them as Shakespeare is to a slug or a sponge. I pity these gutless, heartless, soulless, guilt-ridden, self-obsessed, self-hating people. But every generation, it seems, we glorify the self ever further, place *personality* further above *character*, and steadily create from the security and prosperity provided by better men and women a wave of smug, unprincipled, ungrateful Narcissicists who can see nothing beyond the nearest mirror and hold nothing sacred but themselves. *Nothing* is worth dying for to such people, because to them, the end of *them* means the end of *everything*. I once heard such a tower of self-obsession, Dr. Helen Caldicott, admit exactly such a thing on Public Radio. One of the reasons she fights so hard against nuclear war, she said, was because she can't shake the idea that if she were to die that would be the end of…well, the entire Universe.

I wasn't shocked that she said it. I was only shocked that she *admitted* it.

And you mark these words: in another 143 years, people like you and me will still be reading this letter and weeping at its selfless, immortal beauty, while people like Ted Rall will be as anonymous and forgotten as some crude pornographic cartoon carved in an outhouse wall in 1861.

In 1861, this love for and obligation to the ideals of America was common. The selflessness, the recognition of things greater than one's self – earthbound, temporal realities like the ability to say what one wants, go where one wants, to live a life free from the dictates of the powerful, and the freedom to defend one's self and family from the depredations of the cruel and the ruthless – these qualities were common, if not ubiquitous, of the America of 143 years ago.

Let's look at another snapshot, shall we? Here's one that's a little more recent – October 2nd, 2001. Here is a song from the point of view of someone free and powerful, admired and loved; a person possessing the most fabulous gifts imaginable, a voice that has known no hardship, no fear, no illness and no enemies capable of even giving challenge, let alone loss and defeat:

SUPERMAN
By Five for Fighting

I can't stand to fly
I'm not that naive
I'm just out to find
The better part of me
I'm more than a bird...I'm more than a plane
More than some pretty face beside a train
It's not easy to be me
Wish that I could cry
Fall upon my knees
Find a way to lie
About a home I'll never see
It may sound absurd...but don't be naive
Even heroes have the right to bleed
I may be disturbed...but won't you concede
Even heroes have the right to dream
It's not easy to be me
Up, up and away...away from me
It's all right...you can all sleep sound tonight
I'm not crazy...or anything...
I can't stand to fly
I'm not that naive
Men weren't meant to ride
With clouds between their knees
I'm only a man in a silly red sheet
Digging for kryptonite on this one way street
Only a man in a funny red sheet
Looking for special things inside of me
Inside of me
Inside me
Yeah, inside me
Inside of me
I'm only a man
In a funny red sheet
I'm only a man
Looking for a dream
I'm only a man
In a funny red sheet
And it's not easy, hmmm, hmmm, hmmm...
Its not easy to be me.

It's not easy to be me. Dear God, no – the horror of it all. Immortal, impervious…faster than a speeding bullet, more powerful than a locomotive, able to leap tall buildings in a single bound. *How gauche. How tacky. How totally uncool.*

This modern Superman – this symbol, this *America* – hates who he is and what he has become: imprisoned in his ridiculous red and blue sheet, desperate to go up, up and away, as far away from himself as possible. There he stands, in a filthy city doorway: stooped, cynical, a broken man, digging for Kryptonite – digging for *death* -- on this one-way street – to Hell. **Suicide.** Ah, there you go. He'll be dead and then we'll all be sorry.

So this is Superman for the new millennium: a charcoal-gray, lower-case 's' on a black T-shirt, curled on a filthy mattress in the basement, hands pressed to his ears to tune out the screams for help from Lois Lane whose ankles he can see as she is murdered up in the alley. **Superman:** cowering, whimpering, the ultimate victim, who dies from stomach cancer at age 24 from endlessly using his X-ray vision to stare at his own navel.

Gone is the icon of great strength in the service of great good. Gone too is a Superman raised by a simple, honest man and woman on a farm in Kansas, who taught him that there is a difference between good and evil, right and wrong, and how to recognize it, and what to do about it. In his place sits a brooding, whining victim, an emotionally abandoned child raised by a Belgian nanny in a mansion in Bel Aire, hating his father for not producing his student-film screenplay. If our original Superman had nightmares, they were no doubt about the times he had *failed* to act, *failed* to save, *failed* to rescue. This Superman fears nothing more than being caught doing a good deed – *like there's any difference between "good" and "evil." They're just words, cultural relics from a bloody past leading us ever deeper into the darkness of a pointless and meaningless future. It doesn't matter anyway. Nothing matters. Not even me.* Especially *me.*

The Superman – the America – that most of us love and admire is lovable and admirable because they both personify the ideal of **strength against evil** -- and not just brute force, physical strength, but something far more rare and precious: the ability to tell right from wrong, and the courage to do something about it.

Somewhere along the way some people have let their compassion for the weak and the victimized in society trump everything else – everything. A growing number of people no longer wish to protect the weak and defend the victim – they wish to *become* them. As champions of the victimized, it stands to reason that the more victims, the more important the champion. And so the cult of the Victim continues to grow. And since it takes strength to oppress the weak and the defenseless, but strength and *courage* to oppose it, those without courage have made strength the enemy instead of oppression.

Of course, for a class of people that fetishizes weakness and idolizes victimhood, the entire archetype of a Superman simply has to go. Good and unimaginably strong? Please! After all, how will the Big Brains in the teacher's lounge be able to control such a boy? Idea! Perhaps we should drill into this Kent kid the notion that if we can't all fly faster than a speeding bullet, then no one should. It's not fair to all the other kids at Smallville High. Yes, that might work: he's a sucker for wanting to play fair and do the right thing. After all, better we should all drown when the dam breaks than lower anyone's self esteem.

No, this fellow's *got to go.*

Of course, you can't just walk up and kill Superman. No. Too strong for that, the bastard. We'll have to talk him into committing suicide.

And that is exactly what some people have been trying to do for no less than the 66 years Superman has been with us.

Tracking down and cornering the cause of this unending, mindless attack on one's own society – this urge to suicide, this mindless assault on the very idea of strength, this **death wish** – leads us down many winding and serpentine paths. I for one do not believe in conspiracies. So what could possibly explain why so many people feel the need to attack the most free and expressive society in the world and glorify the most awful and odious?
One analogy continues to fascinate me:

We know that allergies result when the defense mechanisms of the body's immune system mistakenly attacks healthy cells, falsely recognizing them as foreign and dangerous. The body's defenses essentially go to war against the body itself.

Here's what intrigues me: new research seems to indicate that the cleaner and more sanitary the environment we live in becomes, the more likely we are to develop allergies. Allergies appear in much, much lower numbers among farm kids, who are exposed to all manner of infectious elements – not to mention the cuts and scrapes and so on caused by actual, physical work. And as we become more and more obsessed with 'disinfecting' everything in sight, allergies skyrocket.

What seems to be happening is this: the more we are exposed to real infection, the easier it is for the immune system to identify foreign cells from host cells, since there are dangerous foreign cells in abundance. These infectious agents constantly demand new antibody production, and the line between "host" and "other" is clearly and continuously redefined. In excessively antiseptic environments, that level of discrimination appears to break down due to lack of use, and the body's immune system turns on itself.

These allergy attacks range from the mildly annoying to the almost instantaneously fatal.

And a serious and potentially fatal allergy attack is precisely what I believe is happening to Western Civilization today.

Consider this:

If you genuinely, honestly believe you can compare George Bush to Adolph Hitler, it is only because you are so removed from exposure to the genuine horrors of the Nazi regime – routine street beatings, confiscation and destruction of businesses, homes and property, then deportation and extermination of millions of your own countrymen – that you are functionally incapable of the most basic and fundamental level of discrimination. If you can compare Abu Ghraib to a Nazi death camp with a straight face then you have never been to Abu Ghraib, or a Nazi death camp, or *either* – that is patently obvious, and it would be comically so if the stakes were not so monumentally high. Having never been exposed to genuine evil, you have literally no conception **whatsoever** of what it looks and smells and tastes like.

(Immigrant Americans from Poland or Russia or Cuba, or Iraq, for that manner, exhibit virtually none of this madness. They know what a real secret police presence feels like.)

Let me clarify this if I may. Senator Kennedy claims Abu Ghraib is simply Saddam Hussein's torture chambers "under new management – U.S. management." Taking him at his word – a somewhat iffy proposition right out of the gate – he apparently cannot see the difference between the humiliation and bullying of enemy combatants, which is shameful, disgusting and reprehensible, and the gleeful, mocking murder, torture and gang rape of over 300,000 innocent men, women and children -- which is something worse.

So Senator, here is a helpful analogy which you may find useful: The difference is about the same as pulling over and leaving a young female secretary on the curb in the rain, which is shameful, disgusting and reprehensible, vs. leaving her trapped in the car at the bottom of a river while you look at the bubbles and ponder the political repercussions.

Which is something worse, Senator.

Americans living today have never known torture or oppression or state-sponsored murder, and so it becomes nothing more than a rhetorical concept for most of us. People who defend Saddam and Kim and Castro have no idea at all about what that life entails. None. And so, in their safe and antiseptic little worlds of coffee shops and chat rooms, it all reduces to rhetoric. And since, in the end, it's nothing but words anyway, they feel they can win an argument because their rhetoric goes up to eleven.

Bushitler.

In extreme cases – sadly rising in frequency -- these people not only hate America. They hate everything. They see nothing in American history beyond slavery and the Indian Wars. They often claim to live, or would prefer to live, in more refined, decent and civilized nations, like Canada and Britain and New

Zealand: as if white, English-speaking Canadians grew out of the ground like corn on an empty, Indian- and Eskimo-free horizon, or the thousand years of English conquest over India, China, Africa, Ireland, Scotland and Wales was in a parallel universe, or that the warlike Maoris invaded and took over the North and South Islands from the peaceful, indigenous white settlers. As if France were not the most blood-soaked patch of land on the surface of the earth, as if Russia's leaders never so much raised a hand against its own suffering people, as if Scandinavia was not the epicenter of centuries of rape, pillage, murder and misery, as if the Aztecs said *gracias* in Castilian Spanish as they cut the living hearts out of their prisoners. As if the Spanish themselves had never known the Inquisition, Italy no Papal Wars or Duces or Ethiopias, as if Belgium had no Leopold and Leopold no Congo, as if Germany…well.

As if African slaves were only held by whites and Christians, as if Japan has practiced nothing but calligraphy and origami for a millennia, as if South America was a spotless white linen of freedom of expression and individual rights, as if China was a champion of democracy and the common man, as if Indians never spat on anyone, as if, as if…as if the entire bloody history of conquest and war and displacement were the unique domain of America alone, or, equally absurd, that we deserve to die for not being born perfect and without sin – as they, in their own self-obsessed, one-person Universes expect everyone else to be.

And so they trot out every single example of human atrocity as if they were Atticus Finch sweating under the heat in that courtroom in their mind; these snipers and critics and 'activists' who have no plans of their own, no solutions, no answers to these dirty and difficult and eternal issues, and so sit in the warm cocoon of perfection afforded the man who attempts **nothing**. And while better men and women – better men and women *by every measure* – struggle and fight and bleed to make the world a better and safer place, they grow more and more disconnected from the essential ugliness and brutality that is half – and only half – of this flawed and broken and hopeful and noble human existence.

And because we are all born with this legion of devils inside every heart, more than anything else in the world they hate themselves. Carrying all the guilt of the world on their stooped and broken spirits, their eyes cast so far down that they can see nothing of nobility or progress or redemption of any kind, these people are *broken*. They are miserable, bitter, cynical husks. And we all know what misery craves.

See them for what they are: nothing more than the Comic Book Guy on the Simpsons: *Worst. Country.* ***Ever.***

They are useless people. They have heeded the last and final boarding call and pushed back from the gate of reality. They have left the building.

Don't argue with them, don't engage them. They want to make this about rhetoric and sophistry, which they fetishize, and not about the simple difference between right and wrong, which is a world where they cast no reflection.

So is this nation, this culture, worth fighting for? Are our lives even worth defending?

Let me offer two answers; one hard-headed, pointy and practical; the other warm and fuzzy and easy to cuddle up to.

Okay, left brain: this is for you.

Hardly a person reading this has not sat, probably many times, on board a commercial jetliner, munching a terrible sandwich while watching television on a little screen at seven miles above the earth moving faster than the musket ball that ended the life of Sullivan Ballou.

The sheer mundane frequency of this miracle should be enough on it's own, but I ask you to look much deeper.

Think, for a moment, about the endlessly intricate, stunning web of trust, cooperation and genius required to make this happen. Drop the obvious elements like the pilots and the air-traffic controllers. Forget the armies of people who set their alarms every day to go and build, fly and maintain these wonders.

What about the chemist who determined the correct mixture to get that reprehensible purple dye just right for the fabric on the seat back covers? Who engraved DIANE's name tag? How many hundreds of men cut how many grooves in how many trees to make the rubber that seals the handles on the restroom faucets? What were the names of the aerodynamicists who designed the wing section *before* the one actually finalized in the design of the airplane? Who made the air traffic controller's coffee? What were the first words spoken between the parents of the person who cleaned and vacuumed your seat?

What were the names of the guys that laid the cement for the VOR station you're navigating by, back in the 60's? Who churned the butter in that little plastic container? Somebody forged the bolts that hold down that seat seven rows up? Who? Who delicately put into place that little paper diaphragm in the microphone the flight attendant is boring you with? The person who dry-cleaned the co-pilots uniform – nice guy? Creep? Who pumped the gas into the little tug that pushed the plane back at the gate? Come to think of it, this crappy TV show you're watching? Who edits this garbage? What do we know about *that* guy?

You don't see any of this, of course. You think nothing of it. But there it is. And this molecular structure does not run as deep anywhere else in the world. You're it. You in 37B.

Now ask yourself if those five hooded murderers, those 19 hijackers, and those endless seas of raving, chanting, flag-burning lunatics could, together, manufacture one #2 pencil. You know, a perfect, yellow, three-cent pencil – including the dyes for the enamel paint, the glues and presses for the wood, the mined copper alloy for the band, the chemists to make the graphite and then there is the eraser – and no one knows what *that* is made of.

This web that keeps us alive and safe and free needs many things to thrive. Trust. Communication. Mutual respect. Genius. Hard work. And mostly passion.

Fear will kill it all. It will fall apart and unravel into smoke.

All the virtues of science, all the genius of seven thousand years is refined and built into the structure of this Western Society. If we lose this now, humanity will not see it return. To paraphrase Jimmy Doolittle, a great pilot and greater patriot, *"we could never be this lucky again."*

And finally, for you soft-hearted, touchy-feely right brain types: a small quiz. Don't worry: no grades, no trick questions, and no time limit.

If you are a Feminist: Do you think that women should be treated with respect and equality in all matters, and allowed to reach their fullest potential as individuals by making their own decisions? Or do you think that they should be kept locked in the back room, that they should suffer beating or death for being seen in the company of a man not her husband or relative, that she should never be allowed to study or drive a car, and that she must remained covered head to foot when outdoors?

I'm for the former. Which are you for?

If you are a homosexual: Do you believe that sexual orientation is a private matter between consenting adults, that all people deserve the same measure of dignity and respect, and that you should be allowed to live your life and love the person you choose without intimidation and fear? Or do you believe that homosexuals are an abomination in the eyes of a vengeful God and should therefore be executed?

I'm going with "A" on this one, too. What do you think?

If you are an artist, a writer or a singer: Do you feel that free expression is the soul of the artistic impulse, that artists have the right to explore whatever depths of emotion or feeling that their muse may drive them to, and that the free expression of the artistic impulse should never be inhibited no matter how offensive others may find your personal journey? Or do you believe that society should place strict limits on what is permissible expression artistically, and that some entire studies – music, for example – should be removed from society to prevent moral decay and people straying from the Word of God?

I'm taking the first one again.

So my real question is, if you agree that the former choices are better than the latter, why do so many of you take the side of murdering theocrats like the Taliban, or state-sponsored terror regimes like Saddam's when they are in opposition to a culture that provides legal and cultural protections and freedoms unparalleled in human history?

I'd really like an answer, if you can spare the time. And so would a lot of folks.

Now while we're changing the sets and costumes for the final act, how about a brief intermission? Let's take a hypothetical, shall we? Something we've all seen on the old idiot box?

Breaking News!

Police are at the scene of an urban standoff. Here are the details as they come in:

We can see right away that this is not a good neighborhood. Crime is rampant, and, as in most crime-ridden communities, a lot of nasty stuff goes on every day.

Now it seems that one lunatic – your standard heavily-armed psychopathic loner – last week had gone next door and shot the hell out of the neighbors. Of course, those neighbors were not exactly the Cunninghams or the Waltons, so there was no 911 call…but *still*.

Anyway, it's a few days later and it looks like he's done it again: now he claims he owns the entire back yard of the people out back. SkyCam 6 is running aerial footage of him kicking down the fence, going into the neighbor's house and shots being fired. The camera work on the ground is shaky as the crews duck for cover, but you can hear the screams from inside. Lots of covered bodies seen coming out and being placed in ambulances.

The police arrive, and now he starts shooting at them; just goddam *unloading* on them. They shoot back, forcing him back into his house; he is severely wounded. They tell him to disarm and come out with his hands up. He shoots out the windows and keeps taking potshots at the police.

A tense standoff occurs. 13 hours go by, during which time, the neighborhood Roach Coach arrives on the scene. The police allow the man inside to buy food as a gesture of goodwill. The guy in the roach coach sells him a turkey sandwich for $150 and a can of Coke for $75.

As the standoff continues, we can hear him shooting his family inside. The screams are muffled; sounds like he's got them down in the basement. A few of them manage to make it out the side and back doors; one or two escape. Most are shot in the back. And as the hours grind on, the shots, and the screams, continue. So do the potshots at the police cordon outside.

Finally, the police realize that cannot afford to wait any longer. The negotiations have accomplished nothing except to give the lunatic more time to shoot more of his own family members and presumably reload. The only one arguing to continue negotiations is the guy running the Roach Coach: he's made more money selling $80 hot dogs and $200 ice cream sandwiches for 13 hours than he has in his entire career. The police make a final offer: *come out with your hands up!* The response is yet more potshots. The SWAT team gets into position.

They storm the house! Gunfire! Screaming!

The Crazed Loner runs out the front door, lowers his assault rifle at the police, and is cut down in a hail of bullets.

A liberal arrives on the scene, now that the danger has passed and the area is secured. He walks over to the dead lunatic, removes the gun from his hand, pulls back the bolt on the lever…***empty!*** He removes the magazine. Empty too!

"This man could not have hurt anyone," he shrieks! *"The gun wasn't loaded! He was murdered in cold blood!"*

He turns to the TV audience, grabbing the microphone from the reporter…no, wait. Looking closely, I now see that the reporter has gestured wildly for him to step into frame and he is handing him the microphone, smiling, and making 'go on' gestures.

"Did he come into the police chief's home and try to kill him? He did not!!

The liberal is really getting religion now. He visibly shakes; his eyes bulge and his forehead goes white with rage! *"The man who ordered this assault,"* he screams, spittle flying in righteous indignation, *"knew all along that this gun was empty!!"*

*"He lied!! **He lied and people died!!"***

There was a time when a person making a statement as ridiculous as that would be tarred, feathered and ridden out of town on a rail. It would have been good for a laugh for all concerned. In fact, if the social consciences of today had one particle of the wit and genius that Mark Twain had, they might have said, as he did: *"if it weren't for the honor and glory of the thing, I'd just as soon walk."*

Sadly, these are different times. Why, just one of them unshaved, baseball-cap wearin' fellers I seen on TV would take the feathers from 150 geese and four miles of highway asphalt to cover adequately!

No, today such mock-serious people drive to work in new Hondas with GREENPEACE stickers on the bumper; they get 35 mpg to your SUV's 17 mpg, so they are **Saving the Planet** while you are trading **Blood for Oil**. See how easy it is?

Remember all the outrage there was from these people about a *pre-emptive* war? Remember how President Bush was vilified on the left for floating *the very idea* that in a world of hidden weapons and shadowy, deniable delivery systems that we might have to attack an enemy before he has the capacity to cause us incalculable harm? Remember all the flak he caught for that?

The Cambridge dictionary defines **Pre-emptive** as *something that is done before other people can act, especially to prevent them from doing something else.*

So I'd like to know how it is a *lie* that we didn't find something we told everyone in advance we were determined to stop *pre-emptively.* One – *one* -- of the reasons for going to Iraq was to prevent Saddam from acquiring and using Weapons of Mass Destruction, weapons that no one denies he once had, he once used, and continuously tried to obtain again. No serious person can deny this.

We *have* prevented Saddam, and Iraq, from acquiring and using Weapons of Mass Destruction. The only other way to prevent him from doing so would have been to continue the sanctions, and the torture, and the mass murder – indefinitely. That's fine, as far as some people are concerned. So long as they don't have to watch GWB on TV anymore.

It is true that Saddam had managed to convince the President, and the Congress, that he was further along with these programs than he actually was. In fact, it appears that many in his own regime had lied to him regarding this progress, and these lies and communications were intercepted, analyzed, compared to his known previous efforts, and presented to the President *and the Congress.* Those politicians now howling that President Bush lied to them were accessing the same information he had. The record of them condemning Saddam's WMD programs has filled volumes. Presumably, even a Congressman is capable of weighing evidence and making his own decision. Page after page after page shows they reached the same decision, based on the same evidence, that the President, the former President, the British Prime Minister, The Secretaries of State and Defense, and countless other bright people from all across the political spectrum had done.

Does anybody actually think that the President would make such a case, knowing full well that no WMD's existed? Do you honestly think he planned this action based on a lie, and therefore pinned his entire political career and the Nation's credibility on the hope that everyone in the world would *forget* if none showed up?

The WMD intelligence was clearly at fault regarding Saddam's progress toward WMD's. This does not affect by one particle the fact that Saddam had repeatedly used chemical weapons, had at one time a universally acknowledged nuclear weapons program, and had enormous amounts of biological weapons material the destruction of which he could not provide documentation for. These are undeniable facts.

And if you are one of the people howling with outrage over the fact that significant WMD's were not discovered, perhaps in the future we can count on your support the next time some genius wants to gut and field dress the entire military intelligence establishment.

Saddam's progress was irrelevant to the motivation. The man had used them before, and if he obtained them, would use them, or threaten to use them as he has done time and again. He was pre-emptively – don't forget the outrage! – stopped in these designs, and so the risk of an Iraqi nuclear or germ or gas attack on the US or his neighbors has dropped to zero. Maybe the threat was overrated, based on his previous predilections. But that threat is zero now. I spell that M-I-S-S-I-O-N A-C-C-O-M-P-L-I-S-H-E-D.

We've become hated overseas for this pre-emptive action, and it often seems to me that this alone is why so many Americans have opposed it; not because it was necessarily the right or wrong thing to do in and of itself, but because it makes us *unpopular*. This is our vital weakness, this desire to be loved by the rest of the world. How many currently opposed to the War in Iraq would change their minds had it been cheered and applauded by the French and the Germans?

But what difference would that have made to the rightness or wrongness of the action?

Consider this: we know, for a fact, from records and interviews with top German OKW (Army High Command -- *Oberkommando der Wehrmacht*) commanders, that large segments of the Nazi army command structure were violently opposed to Adolph Hitler's decision to violate the Treaty of Versailles by placing a small contingent of troops in the demilitarized Rhineland. These Generals, in interviews after the war, had agreed that if the French had placed so much as a *platoon* in their way and contested this violation, Hitler would have been immediately overthrown in a military coup. These officers were astonished that the French made no such response. Hitler knew his enemy far better than they did.

A platoon. 30 or 40 soldiers, applied to simply *stand in the way,* would have seen Hitler overthrown. So think about this...

What if President Franklin Roosevelt, seeing this failure to enforce Versailles – which, like UN 1441 et al., was an international agreement designed to contain a militant and dangerous nation – decided to unilaterally place a regiment or two in the Rhineland and force the Germans to comply with the agreement they had signed?

What would have happened is this:

The widespread and extremely vocal pacifist establishment would have decried it as an unwarranted act of aggression against a far weaker foe who was, after all, only moving within the bounds of their own country. We would have been accused of beating up on a poor, battered and defeated nation whose leader had done nothing but build roads and schools and hospitals, all because our President feared the international competition or still harbored a sick desire for revenge against a weak and essentially harmless member of the family of nations.

Americans, rather than being loved as the good-natured liberators of 1944 and '45, would be hated as swaggering militant aggressors wherever they went. And what would we have to show for it?

Nothing but the prevention of 50-odd million deaths and the destruction of a continent.

I swear to God, you just can't please some people.

The United States and her many allies went to war in Iraq for many reasons besides preventing Iraq from developing Weapons of Mass Destruction; not the least of which was to give the United Nations a chance to show itself for what many wanted to believe it really was: a champion of world security, willing to enforce its resolutions to preserve peace and stability...rather than a morally, intellectually and financially corrupt debating society with no goal other than tony Uptown addresses for cousins of tin-pot dictators and a chance to bash the West from the pulpit in its very heart.

Two more bear mentioning. I believe that one of the unstated reasons for this war was to return the oil wealth of Iraq to the Iraqi people, to rebuild their infrastructure and fund the restoration of the fabric of their society. To those who claim we launched this war to steal their oil I refer you to your local gas pump.

Oil is an essential resource for modern society. To those on the far left, all I can say is that without oil there would be no trucks to deliver the entitlement checks. The United States remains dependent on foreign oil – both less so and more so than other industrialized nations. Those of you howling about the improprieties of this as an ethical basis for war had best be reading these words in book form by candlelight. Anyone using electricity to do so while they whine about ethics are hypocrites who as usual want to have things both ways in order to preserve that essential fix of moral superiority that seems to be the only thing to make life worth living for the Bitching Classes.

Liberating Iraq from the depredations of a madman accomplishes many political goals: first, it means we can remove the troops from the Sacred Sands of Saud. They were there, at the Kingdom's reluctant request, to make sure that Saddam didn't go postal again and pull a Kuwait to the southwest this time, instead of the southeast. Presumably, this will make the nasty stain on the cave wall at Tora Bora rather pleased. It was the only coherent political demand Osama bin Laden ever made in his life.

More importantly, I believe it is part of the Administration's daring, farsighted and unspoken vision to establish a replacement supply for Saudi Arabian oil. Once that economic pistol is removed from our heads we will be in a better position to deal with the very heart and source of all this unpleasantness. We *pay for* the oil and gasoline we use. Being able to send that money via the gas pump to an Iraqi school or hospital, while at the same time putting us gradually into a position where we can ask some pointed questions of our Saudi buddies without fear of economic meltdown … well, that's just a twofer.

Finally, there is the moral argument. Not just the liberation of Iraq from three decades of fear and torture that reached down to every single person in that poor, battered and abused land. We who have never lived in fear might have expected more from the Iraqis during this past year, but we do not know what three decades of terror will do to a people, and we are having this discussion today because many among us are determined that we shall never know.

When the brave and the bold lie in shallow graves next to their wives and husbands and children, where does that leave Iraq in its search for a Washington or Jefferson, or a Lincoln, or a Roosevelt, a Truman or a Reagan? We who will stand up and fight for freedom do so because it is what our fathers and their fathers have done, and as Lincoln so hauntingly described, the Mystic Cords of Memory do indeed stretch back from every battlefield and patriot's grave to touch the hearts of we who are alive today. How deep would our courage lie had they been taken out in the night among screams and squealing tires, never to return?

There are many who are claiming that the moral argument came only after the WMD's turned up missing. Re-reading my own thoughts on this matter, I found them co-existent and roughly equal. Having attacked one side of the rationale for faulty intelligence, they now attempt to discredit the other half for the mortal crime of having not given it top billing.

Again, to the crossroads of our being: the North launched the Civil War to restore the Union. Many in the North opposed abolition at the outset. But the war changed them. And on that night those soldiers turned south toward eventual victory, it was the Battle Hymn of the Republic they were singing.

As he died to make men holy
Let us die to make men free

The war, and its awful arithmetic, had elevated them and Lincoln too. The Better Angels of our Nature had touched us, once again.

The primary reason for us to be in Iraq is not to liberate her people so that they can be free. It is, quite bluntly, to liberate her people so that **we** can be free.

Freedom, prosperity and progress are antithetical to the Death Cult rising in that region and spreading its hatred and violence throughout the world. Iraq presents an opportunity, a chance, for a different way.

A free and stable and prospering Iraq demonstrates to everyone on this Earth that Arab society can be free of both secular and theological totalitarianism alike. A functioning, modern Iraq, where people can live their lives free of fear and oppression, where they can worship as they themselves see fit without imposing their beliefs on a neighbor or having them imposed on oneself, where they can perform the simple miracles of going to work each day, earning a living and coming home to a night of television with the family without knowing terror every second of every day: *that* is what will set them free.

Syria, Iran, Al Qaeda and all the rest fear this very greatly. If we succeed in Iraq – we and the Iraqis, together – they know that their own downtrodden and oppressed people will start asking pointed questions about their own corrupt and joyless societies. And when it is possible to be a Muslim, and have a sense of quiet pride that does not come from death and revenge but from hard work and a safe and prospering family…well, I believe – we, many of us believe – that they will follow Frankie's advice.

They will Choose Life.

They are human, like we are. They will choose life over death. I believe this with all my heart.

My friends and my countrymen, this is one of those rare things worth fighting for. It is worth dying for. It is even worth killing for.

Take the number of people Saddam has murdered in unmarked graves – at least 300, 000 and rising, and add to that the number of his own conscripts he has killed in wars against Iran and the various coalition forces deployed against him.

No less than **a million Iraquis** have died at his hands. No less than that, surely. In the twenty-five years or so that he had absolute power, that averages to 40,000 men, women and children a year – no less.

This past year, despite the number of casualties we inflicted, there were perhaps thirty thousand Iraqis who were *not* killed because we invaded that country. Next year there will be forty thousand more – **forty thousand** who will survive, and have children, and grandchildren, because we did what we did in 2003. And the year after that, another forty thousand will live. Ten years from now, which in the world of our critics might have been year three of Uday or Qusay's reign, there will be **five hundred thousand people alive** – because of us. Because of what we did. Because of what we are fighting and dying to do today.

Don't abandon those people. Do not make meaningless the deaths of our own sons and daughters – and, for that matter, their sons and daughters. We can end this thing for the nearly unbearable, awful, horrific cost of around a thousand American lives – and not a bill far, far worse, which will come due to us if we fail now.

We – humanity – can prevail. We must not lose hope. We must not abandon our ideals. Disgrace and dishonor such as Abu Ghraib we can learn from, and correct, and redeem. Do not abandon this fight now.

Not while we are winning. Not while success in within our reach but not yet within our grasp. Not this time.

This is the right thing to do. And we must continue to do it. We must.

Find the strength. We have it in abundance. Find it. Hold on to it. In our hearts – as in the hearts of that very different and yet identical people we have bound ourselves to in this endeavor – victory and salvation lie. Together, we together – we are the weapons, we are the targets, and we are the battlefield.

———————————

Throughout this collection I have done my best to try and show how deeply my life has been affected by the miracle that is this country and the family that is her people.

We have been doing a lot of arguing lately, this family. Many things have been said in anger. Well, these are critical, dangerous times…we can all agree on that much, at least.

But we are a family, whether we like each other or not. We are in this together. I would never urge any free man or woman to take sides contrary to their principles, and our principles vary as widely as our places of origins, our accents and our skin colors – no two exactly the same.

I am asking you now, as one voice among millions – nothing more – not to cease criticizing the government, the President, or our actions in Iraq. Without the crucible of heated debate among passionate believers we *will* lose our way.

All I ask is this:

Do not destroy this house. Do not destroy this house to make a point. It is a magnificent house, a grand and sturdy home to us all. Do not let the stains upon her floor cause you to set her aflame. We have fought amongst ourselves for as long as we have been a people; that will never change, and in its own unpleasant, annoying and wonderful way, it *should* never change.

But for our sake and for those across the oceans: argue about the paint. Argue about the sleeping arrangements. Argue about how best to wash those stains where they appear.

But for the sake of all who have gone before us here, and all who will come after: help me defend this house.

DETERRENCE
October 06, 2004

Watching the Presidential debates of September 30th, and the subsequent reactions to them, has left me once again with the sad realization that there are many millions of people who prefer a man who says the wrong things well over one who says the right things badly – and in the case of the first debates we are talking about saying very, very stupid things well and intelligent things very, very badly.

Now I don't mean stupid in a *bad* way. I fully credit John Kerry with the intelligence needed to analyze, dissect, and evaluate a position and without mechanical aid quickly and accurately use advanced trigonomic functions to determine the most popular position on a wide range of complex issues – a feat that requires a very quick mind indeed.

So it's not *dumb* stupid, those statements he made in the first debate. It's more of an entirely understandable, eminently defensible, very common *fossilized* kind of stupid that we saw from the Senator. It was the stupid of a man claiming to have new ideas and new plans based on shared assumptions and models that no longer apply to reality.

President Bush seemed stupid in comparison because he seems to only know three things in all the world – and it is our great good fortune that he is right about all three.

In a moment, we'll look at what both men said, and through a very specific filter: not their Aggregate Presidentiality, or their respective Molar Charm Ratio. We're going to look at what both men believe in respect to **deterrence**: whether their positions increase or decrease the likelihood of further attacks on the US.

That's it. That's all. That's the sum total of this election for me. We've survived boobs and crooks and idiots and charlatans of all stripes and colors, struggled through booms and recessions, surpluses and deficits, and wars on poverty and drugs and crime and General Public Lasciviousness and come through just fine, and we will again.

But the nuclear destruction of the heart of Manhattan, or Long Beach Harbor, or the Capital mall – these things are serious business and as Sam Johnson once said, the prospect of being hanged in the morning tends to focus the mind.

As I have been willing to accept that George W. Bush is no longer a hard-drinking frat boy but rather a sober and responsible adult, then so too am I willing to allow that John Kerry has matured since his secret meetings with enemy leaders during a time of war. I myself cast my first presidential vote for Walter Mondale.

There is no decent excuse for any of these behaviors; and I only wish that my own lapses of judgment had been less embarrassing and more explainable… *cannibalism*, say, or something of that nature.

So I am willing to put the Moonbat and Wingnut nonsense aside for the moment, and grant that both men – and their supporters – have in mind the same objective when they talk about national security.

We both look at this:

And we both want to make sure that it – or worse – does not happen again.

We don't want it to happen again.

We want to **deter** it from happening again.

And all of this rage and fury and spitting and tearing up of signs, all of these insults and spinmeisters and forgeries and all the rest, seem to come down to the fact that about half the country thinks you deter this sort of thing by being *nice*, while the other half thinks you deter this by being *mean*.

It's really just that simple.

Now if sociology were a real science, we could set up experiments. We could, in fact, do what just about every one of us – Liberal or Conservative – has, in our heart of hearts, secretly wanted to do: send that 50% of idiots on the other side packing – I mean, really packing, as in, *out of the country*, for good – and let history show we were right after all.

We imagine an America made up exclusively of tough-minded Conservatives would be a far better, a safer and stronger place, than an America composed of nothing but compassion-filled Liberals.

They, of course, think precisely the opposite. And I have, over the past two years, determined that internet comment threads do not hold the answer to this predicament.

Theirs, and ours, are usually just cheerleading sessions, full of sound and fury and signifying nothing but a soothing reduction in blood pressure brought about by the narcotic high of being agreed with.

We can't, alas, deport all the left wingers and they cannot, damn it, silence all the right wingers. We are stuck with each other. Each sees the press as biased toward the other, and each gapes in awe and amazement that the other side could possibly feel the same way.

And although we cannot run an experiment to look into the alternate futures to glean the best result, to determine the relative benefits of being *nice* or being *mean* – for those,

ultimately, are the choices, believe it or not – we can at least look back to see which seems to have produced the best results in the laboratory of history.

It all comes down to carrots (liberals) or sticks (conservatives). By the way: if you're in a rush and need to run, here's the spoiler: You can offer a carrot. Not everybody likes carrots. Some people may hate your carrot. Your carrot may offend people who worship the rutabaga. But no one likes being poked in the eye with a stick. That's universal.

I'm a stick man. I wish it were different. But part of growing up – in fact, the essential part of growing up – is realizing that *wishing does not make it so.*

Folks, it's time to reach down deep and get in touch with our inner adult.

I used to be a carrot man. Like most larval liberals, I grew up in a life that would be unrecognizable to all but the thinnest sliver of humans that ever lived on this great rock in space – that thin, thin sliver being everyone and everything you and I know and take for granted.

Reality – meaning the wolves – have never been so far from the door as they are today. So believing in the power of goodwill and friendship, of handshakes and agreement and compromise, of trusting to the good and noble in mankind was easy for me, for the consequences of being wrong in that belief cost me nothing at all. I'd never been robbed, raped, beaten or victimized in any way. That belief in goodwill, compromise, concession and trust grew as a result of being surrounded by decent people in a well-ordered, lawful society, with a long history of compromise and cooperation.

I can remember saying, in college, that if someone broke into my house and stole my television, well that was fundamentally just, because after all, I was white, male, educated and could make enough money to afford an endless line of televisions.

This view of the world was tempered somewhat, when, a few months later, I awoke to the sound of my window being opened and the sight of the upper torso of a man climbing in over the sill. By the way, it was only much later that I realized that it wasn't *my* TV he was there to steal. He was there to steal *my dad's* TV – he paid for it, not me. Once I had to go to work and earn money to pay for things my mood changed somewhat. I put in forty hours of misery, boredom and early mornings for that TV, and some *yayhoo* just walks right in and takes it? Screw that! You want a TV? The McDonald's on 13th and University is hiring.

Folks, some people who steal and rob are not fundamentally bad people. Some of them are desperate, some of them are stupid, and some of them are just plain lazy. Some of them, though, are psychopaths who'd kill you for a nickel and think nothing more about it – they'd trade your life, and the life of your spouse and children, for two hours of getting high and it would not bother them **in the least.**

Nations are governed by people. People are noble and base, honest and corrupt, brutal and gentle and all the adjectives in between. Yes, even Americans!

The success of democracy, it seems to me, is that there is always a counterweight to the most mendacious and the most harebrained of human activities. It's harder to fool all the people all the time.

Dictatorships, on the other hand – well, you're down to the limits of one man's sanity, ego, vanity and judgment. And when you consider the kind of person it takes to rule absolutely and totally the lives of millions of others – many of them more intelligent, educated and capable – then what you are left with is a giant, enormous, destructive Iron Giant – a state – with a tiny, desperate, paranoid, perpetually fearful psychopath pulling the levers. Dictatorships put the power of millions, the muscle and capability of entire nations, behind the guy with the gun in that dark alley.

It is a prospect to make sane people shake with fear. Surely we can agree on this much. Surely we can agree, no matter our political persuasion, that there are mean, bad, violent people who care nothing for inflicting violence on the inno-cent in order to get what they want. And since those people exist, we should also be able to agree that such people can – even in the heart of people as civilized as the Germans – ride to power and employ that hatred and reckless disregard for human happiness multiplied by a hundred million.

That's reality. It's undeniable. I wish it were not true… but wishing does not make it so. Paging the Inner Adult… white courtesy telephone, please.

It would be nice to live in a world full of liberals. I say that as a staunch conserva-tive. It would be nice to live in a world that behaved like a Hollywood party or a university campus, filled with kind, educated people with lots to lose, who cher-ish art and culture and are incapable of brutal, violent acts. If all the world were filled with decent, compassionate, rational people, life would be a bouquet.

But it's not. There are bad people who do bad things, and there are bad countries run by bad people who do bad things who eat the kind and gentle people for breakfast. There is no denying this. Therefore, liberals are insane. I speak from experience here.

It's a damn shame, it really is.

———————————

Reasonable people can take the most cursory look into the world – the Western world, anyway – and see successes everywhere, but perfection nowhere to be found at any price.

Because I try to be a reasonable person, I don't fault the government for not preventing 9/11 only because ultimately the government is made up of ordinary people, and ordinary people, like me, could not fully imagine or grasp what we were seeing that day *even while we were seeing it.*

I tuned in when the first tower had just gone down. The first images I saw that morning were of one tower and a cloud of smoke. *Funny*, I remember thinking, *I thought there were **two** World Trade Center towers.* I was sure I had remembered wrong. I didn't see the first tower go down. Skyscrapers don't just *disappear.*

Vapor lock.

When I saw the replay of the first plane hit, the first words I said that weren't mumbled, awestruck and unpublishable were simply these: *There's no way airline pilots did that. Those were not our pilots.*

That was the only coherent thought I had for six hours.

We like to say that the world changed that day. What a ridiculous, self-centered thought. The world didn't change. Our *illusions* about the world changed. The scales had (mostly) fallen from my eyes in the years leading up to that morning. My travels (and travails) through the Dark Realm called "Reality" had almost completed my conversion. But many, many conservatives were born precisely at 9:17 am EDT, when United 175 flew past the burning North Tower – an accident? – and exploded through the second, on the morning of September the 11th, 2001.

And everything we thought we knew about deterrence changed at 9:17 too – although I am sorry to say it hasn't fully sunk in on certain people.

Nineteen people – some barely literate – killed almost three thousand of the most highly skilled and productive citizens on the planet. I told my Dad that morning I just saw our Pearl Harbor. He immediately replied, "No you didn't. After Pearl Harbor we knew who to attack."

He was right. That's the point of terrorism, of course. *Deniability.* 9/11 was an attack on the US by Islamicist fanatics, orchestrated by Egyptian strategists, staffed with Jihadists recruited from around the Arab world, and paid for largely by Saudi religious zealots. So why not launch the attack with elements of the Egyptian and Saudi air forces? Because within six hours there would have been no more Egyptian and Saudi air forces, and within six weeks, no Egyptian and Saudi governments, either. Our deterrence against conventional attack, or even nuclear attack from a nation-state, is so credible and muscular that such a thing has become literally unthinkable.

But how do we deter people who *want* to die? How do we deter people who need only the skill and the means to push a button on a briefcase, or open a box cutter and be prepared to do bloody work with it? How do we deter the assassin lost in the crowd at the Super Bowl? How do we deter enemies who are so dispersed, so ethereal and fragmentary, that hostile governments can arm and shelter them knowing full well that we will not retaliate with a nuclear attack against millions of genuine innocents in Cairo, or Tehran, or Riyadh?

If a suitcase nuke detonates in Times Square, or Long Beach harbor, or outside the Capitol building, what do we do? Nuke Mecca? Incinerate Damascus? Because – so help me God, I tremble to say it – that is exactly the response our enemies would hope for. They care not a whit about their own people because they have no allegiance to anyone but themselves and their vision of a vengeful and bloodthirsty *Allah.* A million, *ten million* innocents under American mushroom clouds are just that many more martyrs gone to paradise. It is they, not we, who dream of a clash of civilizations, with its promised sweeping away of the decadent and godless by the blood and faith of the Believer.

We might yet be able to stop this on the cheap. If we do not, I fear the day will come when 3000 civilians and 1000 American soldiers will look like a very, very small bill to pay.

What we learned on 9/11 is that there are people out there who are not deterrable. Given the chance – given the weapons – these people will strike without any regard to consequences. The ultimate horror of a world enveloped in nuclear fire is just peachy keen with them if it will bring about the New Caliphate. *We love death the way you Americans love life,* they say. They are not kidding. They are serious. You can pretend otherwise, but that will not make it change. There are people who are determined to kill us for who we are and what we believe. They can not be deterred.

But they can be **defeated.** And the people they depend on for survival *can* be deterred.

I initially had many doubts about George W. Bush. Actually, that's not quite fair. The truth is, I despised the man. But then something happened.

I was walking across the studio lot to my car on the night of September 20th, 2001. I ignored the NOT A WALKWAY! signs in the grip and lighting department: cutting through the building saved me having to go around three giant sound stages to get to my car. Barricades had been put up on the back gate, and security guards were checking our trunks for explosives and running a mirror under every vehicle that drove onto the lot. And you couldn't hear a jet fly over without wondering... what *if?* What *now?*

You may remember those days. I do.

It was getting dark as I walked down that narrow corridor, flanked by enormous movie lights and innumerable c-stands. And there, at the desk, was a group of six or seven grips watching a small color television in perfect silence: an ancient TV, the greens and oranges radioactive and bleeding – the Acid Channel.

I watched George W. Bush give the best speech I have ever heard: better, by far, than FDR's Pearl Harbor address. Better, even, than the tinny, lilting, lisping sound of Churchill's immortal call to fight them on the beaches.

As I watched that speech unwind, I knew, instantly and unequivocally, that this President understood what we were up against, the moment he said:

We are not deceived by their pretenses to piety. We have seen their kind before. They are the heirs of all the murderous ideologies of the 20th century. By sacrificing human life to serve their radical visions – by abandoning every value except the will to power – they follow in the path of fascism, and Nazism, and totalitarianism. And they will follow that path all the way, to where it ends: in history's unmarked grave of discarded lies.

Yes, precisely: not desperately aggrieved parties, not freedom fighters, not anything more than thugs and murderers who want to impose their way of life on the world. Fascists. Ruthless, fanatical bastards sworn to our destruction.

Then, three paragraphs later, this:

Every nation, in every region, now has a decision to make. Either you are with us, or you are with the terrorists. From this day forward, any nation that continues to harbor or support terrorism will be regarded by the United States as a hostile regime.

This line, this doctrine – *either you're with us or the terrorists* – has drawn derision and scorn from the nuanced sophisticates from around the world. What they refuse to see is that in one brilliant stroke it cuts the camouflage away from terror, and in effect neutralizes the very lever that makes International Terror so effective a tool: *deniability*. More on this in a moment.

I sat amazed at the confidence and the vision President Bush outlined in that speech. I remember saying out loud, to no one in particular, "*I was wrong about this man.*" A few of the grips nodded in silence. None of us took our eyes off the TV screen.

It is my hope that in the months and years ahead, life will return almost to normal. We'll go back to our lives and routines, and that is good. Even grief recedes with time and grace. But our resolve must not pass. Each of us will remember what happened that day, and to whom it happened. We'll remember the moment the news came – where we were and what we were doing. Some will remember an image of a fire, or a story of rescue. Some will carry memories of a face and a voice gone forever.

And I will carry this: It is the police shield of a man named George Howard, who died at the World Trade Center trying to save others. It was given to me by his mom, Arlene, as a proud memorial to her son. This is my reminder of lives that ended, and a task that does not end.

I will not forget this wound to our country or those who inflicted it. I will not yield; I will not rest; I will not relent in waging this struggle for freedom and security for the American people.

And there stood a man I had not seen before – and sadly, have not seen often since – holding the shield of a dead hero in his hand, promising not to tire, or falter, or fail, until this vague and mysterious war was won. And I swore to myself, right then and there, that I would support this President, come what may. And in the intervening years, as the criticisms and hysteria rose in pitch to the point where only dogs can hear, I have stood by him and his policies, and I do so proudly, to this day.

But time and again I have wished and hoped to hear that music again, that calm, unruffled, determined voice. By now so many small people have carried so many lies so far – *BushHitler! Halliburton! Yellowcake! No Blood for Oil! AWOL!* – that we awake as the Sorcerer's Apprentice to find the broom shards have filled the cellars with an ocean of poison to debunk and to drain.

During the past two years I have been angry with the President; angry that common amateurs writing online in their pajamas (I favor a smoking jacket, fez and calabash pipe when I dash off these little gems) have to rise and defend the policies that we wholeheartedly agree with but which have been appallingly poorly defined and defended by the White House.

And then I had a bit of a revelation. Like Col. Kurtz, I felt I had been shot through the forehead with a diamond bullet. This happened last night.

I tried to enlist on September 12th, 2001. I knew a little about airplanes; maybe the Air Force would trust me to wash them or something so as to free up useful people. They asked how old I was, thanked me, and told me they'd give me a call if they needed me.

So here I am: feeling useless. But President Bush warned that this was going to be a different war – something unlike anything we had ever seen. The front line, at this critical time, is in the hearts and minds of our own people. That's where the real battle is now. That is our weakest point, our breach, our point of failure. We have not made the case to enough people and time is running out.

So maybe now, at this absurd point in this new kind of war, *we're* the crack troops, we old and useless pajama patriots reduced to printing up pamphlets to sell war bonds to the weary, to make the case for holding on to an unglamorous, uninspiring, relentless grind because that – not Normandy and Midway – is the face of war in this gilded age of luxury and safety and plenty.

Maybe that's our job. Maybe we can help cover some small gap in the lines.

We'll see. But for now, I will take up the sword of the *pajamahadeen*, and rise up: just another citizen-wordsmith, trying to put words and ideas where they are needed: into the stumbling gaps, exasperated expressions and defensiveness of a brave and exhausted man under a lot of pressure.

John Kerry has spoken now in front of the nation. We have, at last, a position that can be analyzed. I could use excerpts from their first debate to show that he is better spoken, or nicer, or taller than President Bush. I care about none of that. I am interested in one thing only from these two men: who will best deter the enemy? Who will best be able to stop a thousand 9/11's in a millisecond of religious ecstasy? That's all I care about.

We'll review the debate in the order in which it occurred.

Let's roll.

SENATOR KERRY: I can make American safer than President Bush has made us.

And I believe President Bush and I both love our country equally. But we just have a different set of convictions about how you make America safe. I believe America is safest and strongest when we are leading the world and we are leading strong alliances.

I'll never give a veto to any country over our security. But I also know how to lead those alliances.

This president has left them in shatters across the globe, and we're now 90 percent of the casualties in Iraq and 90 percent of the costs. I think that's wrong, and I think we can do better.

Four years ago, I would have voted for this policy in a heartbeat. This is what I mean by *not stupid in a dumb way.* But it is stupid in an *ignorant* way.

It's stupid because it is a precise example of how to fight the last war. We are in a World War right now. It is being fought all across the globe and the consequences of winning or losing this war will effect every person on the planet. It is World War IV. If you can't see that then you are either not paying attention, or are mollified by our spectacular successes over the past three years.

I credit John Kerry with the genuine desire to protect this nation, because the alternative to believing that is the back alley short-cut to insanity. He has, in mind, precisely the correct formula used to protect the ideals of Liberal Democracy and ensure its victory in WWI, WWII and the long, twilight, Cold War fight of WWIII.

Allies and alliances defined the First War. After four years of mind-shattering horror, the European powers had fought themselves to utter stalemate – and those trenches might yet today mark the borders between Germany, Belgium and France were it not for the arrivals of the American allies. Don't misunderstand me – we did not win that war on the battlefield. That credit goes to the British and the French. But the endless supply of American troops disembarking, full of confidence and optimism and raw heroism, convinced Hindenberg and Ludendorf to desperately roll the dice on the spring 1918 offensives before they faced a million fresh American troops, full of fight. But defense was king in that war, and the Ludendorf Offensives failed. The counterattacks succeeded. The *alliance* won that war.

The *alliance* won World War II – that is beyond dispute. Without Britain hanging on during the lonely and dark opening years, where would the Western invasion have come from? Soviet Russia defeated almost 70% of the strength of Nazi Germany, and the United States defeated Japan single-handedly at sea, and with a great deal of help from the British and Australians and New Zealanders in brutal island jungles. An *Alliance* won that war – not us. Not us alone.

For almost fifty years, the most successful *alliance* in history had the guts and the commitment to put American cities on the line in order to prevent Soviet tanks from crashing through the Fulda gap. American, and to a deteriorating degree, European taxpayers built and maintained the armed forces needed to keep half of Europe free while the other half slowly rotted under the weight of an ideology so corrupt that it can now only thrive in the hothouse environment of the western coffee shop or faculty lounge. That, too, was an *alliance* victory.

If John Kerry were running for president in 1916, or 1940, or even 1976, he would have my enthusiastic vote, for the alliance of the US and the European powers is what saved Europe and the world not once, or twice, but three times in a single lifespan. One might expect some gratitude and respect for this, but as I say, the scales fell from my eyes some time ago.

But this is not 1916, or 1940, or 1976. Europe, ruler of the world in the first war, had become a military freeloader by the end of the third. Europe was not able to muster the military muscle or political will to extinguish a genocide **within**

Europe – and things have gotten worse since then. The French nuclear carrier, the *Charles de Gaulle*, returned from her sea trials with a reactor room flooded with five times the allowable level of radiation and with one of her propellers at the bottom of the Atlantic. She borrowed a screw from her predecessor, the *Foch* – which was faster – and now sits in port making impressive appearances during national holidays and furthermore showing that if God exists he has both a sense of justice and a sense of humor.

The Germans cannot deploy an effective force beyond her own borders. The Russians – the mighty Russians – could not call up so much as one decent ten-man special ops squad when she and her children needed them the most. Japan has constitutional restraints – drafted in American English – preventing her from deploying her defense forces overseas: a fact that has given me many nights peaceful sleep. And as for China… even if she decided, out of the kindness of her heart, to commit her forces to help her arch-rival…who do you think, Senator, would benefit the most from us sharing our weapons, tactics, logistics and intelligence with *China?*

An alliance would be nice – if the allies could shoulder some of the burden. But the sad, inconvenient, disappointing fact is that there is only one army on the face of the earth that can fight on the same battlefield with the United States; whose forces, technology and training rival ours in quality if not in scale, and whose trust has been forged by three world wars when we have stood alone, together. That country is Great Britain, one of the members of what Senator Kerry called the *"trumped-up, so-called coalition of the bribed, the coerced, the bought and the extorted."*

The sad fact, the unpleasant reality of 2004 is that there is only one nation in the world that is of any strategic value on the battlefield, and that ally is with us as she has always been, a staunch friend through many dark nights who deserves something better, I perceive, than slander from a man proclaiming himself the greatest diplomat since... well, since *himself.* I will say this for John Kerry: he is a man unrivaled in his own esteem.

An alliance of European powers is a chimera that no longer holds any significant value. That is a critical point. It is an essential point of delusion embedded in Senator Kerry's world view. He waits for rescue from a knight long dead and moldering, sitting beneath a withered oak tree in rusted armor.

That's point one.

Second, you cannot even throw the cloak of wishful thinking over Senator Kerry's strategic nakedness, because as those of us in pajamas are well aware, the governments of the Grand Rescue Alliance – that is, Germany and France – have both announced publicly and in the most clear language available that *regardless of who wins the election in November,* **they are not coming to Iraq.**

That is not my opinion, that is not a product of the Republican Smear Machine…**that is an official statement from the governments of the nations in question, stating unequivocally that they are not going to be a part of a coalition that is against their interests even if it is lead by an American who went to Swiss schools and speaks fluent French.**

Is it possible to put this any more plainly? They do not have any meaningful capability, and they are publicly pledging that their lack of meaningful capability **is…not…coming.**

As a final thought on this essential issue, consider this, from your own personal experience: I have found that the only thing worse than doing a hard, dirty, thankless job by yourself is depending on help from someone who will not be there when you need them. We have a few good friends in this fight: Britain – the Aussies, God bless them – the Poles and the Italians and a few others: 4am friends who will drive 300 miles in a snowstorm to help us when we are broken down on the side of the road. Those are friends. Those are the people we need in a tough and dirty fight. Those people deserve gratitude and honor, not scorn and mockery.

Senator Kerry, your powerful allies don't exist, and even if they did, they have plainly told you they are not coming. Welcome to 2004, John. It sucks, I know. That's just what we're dealt.

SENATOR KERRY: I have a better plan for homeland security. I have a better plan to be able to fight the war on terror by strengthening our military, strengthening our intelligence, by going after the financing more authoritatively, by doing what we need to do to rebuild the alliances, by reaching out to the Muslim world, which the president has almost not done, and beginning to isolate the radical Islamic Muslims, not have them isolate the United States of America.

I'd consider voting for this policy. But John Kerry has a 20 year record of having voted against every significant weapons system the US has deployed during his term in office. This is an assertion on the Senator's part; words from a man who has been steadfast, constant and consistent in his ability to say what he thinks his audience wants to hear. His voting record – the *put your money where your mouth is record* – is the polar opposite of this assertion. I'm taking the walk over the talk on this one.

Now, assume for a moment, that you are one of the Islamicist enemies of this nation. President Kerry has outlined a plan to reach out to the Muslim world and isolate you. President Bush, on the other hand, predicates his reelection on the premise that he will

…pursue(d) al Qaeda wherever al Qaeda tries to hide. Seventy-five percent of known al Qaeda leaders have been brought to justice. The rest of them know we're after them.

By the way, for about seventy of that seventy-five percent, you can go ahead and substitute the word "killed" in place of the more delicate "brought to justice."

As a deterrent, I honestly and regretfully don't think our terrorist enemies are much deterred by the thought of dying. I think they are fully ready to die. People who are fully ready to die in order to kill you and your family, who are undeterred by death, are likely not to be terribly concerned by the thought of being *isolated* in a more **sensitive** approach to John Kerry's sworn mission to hunt down, and isolate, chastise and severely reprimand terrorists.

Terrorists don't seem to be too afraid of stern language. But I do notice, that while the fear of death does not seem to deter these people, the fact of **being dead** does significantly decrease their operational effectiveness. That's a casual observation on my part – no real Harvard study to back it up. More of a hunch, really.

75% of known pre-9/11 al Qaeda killed in three years. Where's my calculator...? 75% divided by three equals uh…25% a year. *Well I'll be a blue-blooded socialite!* Why, at the rate of 25% a year, I calculate that ol' Dubya will have bagged the whole lot of em in …*one more year!*

I say let's give him the chance.

Quagmire! *Quagmire!*

No, not this season's fashionable entry: I was referring to last seasons' quagmire, Afghanistan.

*PRESIDENT BUSH: Ten million citizens have registered to vote. It's a phenomenal statistic. They're given a chance to be free, and they will show up at the polls. **Forty-one percent of those 10 million are women.***

The fact is that liberal feminists, when all is said and done, would rather have a man who can turn a witty phrase over a nice Cabernet Sauvignon than one who liberates a nation of women, and gives them the vote, to boot. What refined morality they possess.

You know what our enemies really fear? *Women.* Women scare the hell out of them.

Hey, there's no shame in that: women scare the hell out of me, too, only I don't shoot them in the head in their burkas in front of a cheering crowd in a soccer stadium. And in that regard, I find I am exactly like the Taliban…*because they're not doing it either.* They are dead or in caves. Has this president deterred atrocities coming our way from Afghanistan, home of the International Jihad 2001 Road Tour? You're damn right he has. I have a word for how that makes me feel.

It's an archaic, old English word, no longer in common usage. It's pronounced, "GRAT-eh-tood"

You liberate the women of the world and Islamic Terror evaporates. They fear this the way we fear interruption of our Cable TV service. It is the death knell for their tradition of dominance and brutality, and it is not just the sight, but the very *idea*, of liberated, independent and unafraid women that causes them such hatred and revulsion when they look to the West.

Ladies, President Bush has freed the women of Afghanistan, and shut down the state-run rape and torture of women in Iraq. And for every one of those women who was raped and tortured to death, remember that half the entire country lived in daily fear of being spotted by some Ba'athist pig with too much time on his hands as he hid behind the tinted windows of his limousine, cruising the streets of Baghdad or Mosul or Basrah looking for a little fun.

Senator Kerry, on the other hand, has not only said, he has *promised* that he will do no such thing.

———————————

SENATOR KERRY: But we also have to be smart, Jim. And smart means not divert-ing your attention from the real war on terror in Afghanistan against Osama bin Laden and taking if off to Iraq where the 9/11 Commission confirms there was no connection to 9/11 itself and Saddam Hussein, and where the reason for going to war was weapons of mass destruction, not the removal of Saddam Hussein.

Somewhere, in an infinity of alternate universes, there must be a place where at this very moment, Ben Stein is wandering the wasteland of Tora Bora with clip-board in hand, stumbling over the rocks, never looking up, and saying, *"Osama..? Osama..? Osama..?"*

God, the restraint that the President must have when that murdering bastard's name is mentioned in derision as a sign of Bush's incompetence. It's practically superhuman.

First of all, you may recall that three years ago, the President – correctly, in my estimation – pointed out that this was not a criminal manhunt for Public Enemy Number One, but rather:

Americans should not expect one battle, but a lengthy campaign, unlike any other we have ever seen. It may include dramatic strikes, visible on TV, and covert opera-tions, secret even in success. We will starve terrorists of funding, turn them one against another, drive them from place to place, until there is no refuge or no rest. And we will pursue nations that provide aid or safe haven to terrorism.

"Secret even in success..." An interesting phrase, that. What does that mean?

Osama bin Laden has not been seen since the battle of Tora Bora in December of 2001. Remember now, this is not someone like Abu Nidal, a genuine terror mastermind described by the US State Department as *having carried out terrorist attacks in 20 countries, killing or injuring almost 900 persons. Targets include the United States, the United Kingdom, France, Israel, moderate Palestinians, the PLO, and various Arab countries. Major attacks included the Rome and Vienna airports in December 1985, the Neve Shalom synagogue in Istanbul and the Pan Am Flight 73 hijacking in Karachi in September 1986, and the City of Poros day-excursion ship attack in Greece in July 1988*

Abu Nidal was rightfully phobic about being photographed. Anonymity was camouflage to him: incredibly tight operational security, even plastic surgery. The man wanted to remain unseen. In fact he did remain unseen, retiring in his golden years to a nice apartment in Baghdad until he was assassinated by Saddam just before the war to maintain the well-established fact that Saddam had no ties to terrorism.

 No *living* ties to terrorism. Well, to *that* terrorist. It's all very nuanced and sophisticated.

Contrast this behavior to that of Osama bin Laden, who did not operationally plan the 9/11 attacks (see dead underlings, above) but was rather the figurehead for an international organization of many thousands of fanatics, their numbers much thinned now.

Osama made endless videotapes. Lecturing, preaching, instructing, firing an AK-47: all the things that make young jihadis feel funny in the pants. After 9/11, he wowed 'em in several tapes gloating and laughing over the attack and its aftermath. He was reliably heard on the radio during the final phase of Tora Bora, then…nothing.

Maybe he escaped. It's possible.

Then came the videotape condemning the Israeli incursion into Ramallah and Jenin…only it didn't. The US corporate scandals? Silence. Anniversary of Holy Tuesday? Cue the tumbleweeds.

The freaking invasion of a Muslim country by the Great Satan, and this new Caliph, the Leader of the Oppressed, cannot bring himself to shoot a crummy VHS in front of a white wall condemning this outrage? This glory-seeking egomaniac, the New Saladin riding the White Horse across the desert, who practically put out a 10 DVD commemorative set every time the US so much as hiccupped, is now suddenly silent, and has been for three years?

You may call that a Terror Mastermind. I call it a greasy wet spot on the wall of a cave in Afghanistan.

The man is **dead.** Dead, or just possibly captured. The likelihood of him having been killed at Tora Bora by US "outsourcing" was rising with his deafening silence concerning each American counterstroke and became 100% when nothing was heard from the late Osama after the US invasion of Iraq.

Does President Bush know what became of him? I would say, very likely. We know what did not become of him: he didn't become a Martyr. He did not become the symbol of Glorious Death resisting the Great Satan. He did not become a Symbol or a Cause or an Example to Them All.

He became, if you will pardon the expression, AWOL. Bugged out. Handed in his walking papers. Fizzle…poof. *Gone.*

Brilliant.

Unfortunately, I do not have fake (but accurate!) documents to back this claim up. I just have common sense, a psychological history, and the ability to see Naked Emperors. The man is dead – just possibly captured; he has been for years.

Now, do I fault President Bush for not announcing this? I do not. For the President to not disclose something so beneficial to himself, politically, must mean that there is a reason of great magnitude behind the official silence. Are we, the American People, entitled to know what this secret is?

We are not.

We are not for the same reason we were not entitled to know that allied cryptographers won WWII by breaking the Japanese and German codes and having the good sense to shut up about it. But don't dare breathe such sentiments to the current editors of The New York Times. Had those people been running the paper in 1943, tomorrows headline would have read:

AMERICAN AND BRITISH CRYPTOGRAPHERS BREAK JAP AND NAZI WAR CODES – ALL FUTURE ENEMY MOVEMENTS NOW KNOWN WITH CERTAINTY BY ALLIED HIGH COMMAND.

I suspect that if I live another ten years, I'll be sitting watching the History Channel some night in my pajamas and all will be revealed to me. Until then, I'm happy not to know. I know some people have a hard time with that. Go to hell. This is serious business. Not everything is about you.

Has President Bush deterred bin Laden from repeating his attack on the US? I don't honestly see what Osama can do these days, what with him being in several thousand crispy pieces and all.

One nice thing about those hyperbaric bombs, developed by that Vietnamese immigrant who fled to the US after certain people's ideological heroes overran her country and likely killed most of her extended family: they make a small boom, release some nastiness, and then make a much louder boom. I hope that son of a bitch knew what the sound of that first little boom meant.

And now, finally, the *piece de resistance*, the Main Event. Iraq.

SENATOR KERRY: Well, where do you want me to begin?

First of all, he made the misjudgment of saying to America that he was going to build a true alliance, that he would exhaust the remedies of the United Nations and go through the inspections…

…And we pushed our allies aside.

Yes, after only thirteen brief years of Iraq's causus belli of repeatedly and energetically violating every clause of the cease-fire agreement that stayed the US hand in 1991 when he was down, out and routed, and after only fourteen barely-have-time-to-pee months of non-stop, back-to-back UN sessions, resolutions, meetings, condemnations, threats, blocked inspections, harsh language, sanctions, embargoes and Saddam's willful disregard of international protest, the Smirking Chimp ordered the raring-to-go German, French, Russian, Chinese, Japanese and Belgian armored divisions out of theater so that he could have his unilateral war.

Thanks for clarifying that opaque moment in history, Senator.

And so, today, we are 90 percent of the casualties and 90 percent of the cost: $200 billion – $200 billion that could have been used for health care, for schools, for construction, for prescription drugs for seniors, and it's in Iraq.

The inference being, I suppose, that a more sophisticated foreign policy and lack of Texas accent could have persuaded France, Germany, Russia, indeed, the entire UN – all with their hands deep in the oily pockets of Saddam – to put their billions back on the table and step up like good fellows to trade their cash for some decent-sized share of the casualties…three or four hundred killed, perhaps, something in that ballpark. Yes, exactly: the Kerry team, using the same impeccable diplomatic finesse they displayed in calling the desperately courageous leader of Iraq a "puppet" and our true, abiding friends a rabble of bribed, coerced, bought and extorted lapdogs, will convince the most selfish, perfidious and unreliable "ally" in human history to step up and do the right thing because *he* is asking them?

And *Bush* is arrogant?

But wait! There's more!

John Kerry, in his bones, cannot envision winning a tough fight. He supported the effort in Iraq when we had a three-week victory, just as the anti-war activist and enemy collaborator is now John Rambo gunning down commies in a hail of bullets. But now that things are just a dirty, nasty, slugfest – a war that is nothing more or less, in fact, than French premier Clemenceau's description of *a series of catastrophes that results in victory* – as it has in Afghanistan, and Germany, and Japan, and the Confederacy and as it most pointedly did **not** in Vietnam, he says he alone can save us from *the wrong war at the wrong time in the wrong place?*

US marines are killing Ba'athist remnants and Syrian and Iranian mercenaries at an incredible ratio, which, I might point out, is a damn sight better than the 150 to one against us that those 19 hijackers pulled off on 9/11. The insurgency in Iraq is burning casualties at an absolutely insane and unsustainable – indeed, *ruinous* pace. Why?

Well, they have been paying close attention to Senator Kerry and his history, and saw how unsustainable, devastating, insurmountable NVA and VC losses during the Tet offensive bought victory because we decided we had had enough. Because we were told we were nothing more than a modern day horde of Genghis Khan and the people whose freedom we were fighting for did not have the guts or the spine to stand up for their own defense.

Today, that nation – Vietnam – remains a basket case while the rest of Asia rocketed out of the stone age.

That is the model Senator Kerry has for Iraq. I'm not claiming he's malicious. Not at all. I genuinely don't think he gives much thought to Iraqis or Vietnamese at all.

I do know what he does give a lot of thought to, and that is the melodious sound of the phrase, *President Kerry.*

PRESIDENT BUSH: I don't see how you can lead this country to succeed in Iraq if you say wrong war, wrong time, wrong place. What message does that send our troops? What message does that send to our allies? What message does that send the Iraqis?

Yes, almost got it, Mr. President. But what the hell does this policy say to **our enemies?** Does this deter attacks on our troops? Or does it say, in the clearest and most unmistakable terms, that as long as you blow up our men and women, President Kerry will begin plans to pull them out as soon as the hand comes down on Inauguration Day?

Does it not ultimately say that this "mistake" was another War Crime? That it was an unjustified and unwarranted attack on an innocent and harmless nation? Does this not make any future preemptive action on the part of President Kerry for all intents and purposes impossible to achieve? Does this "Global Test" non sense mean every single nation in the world must approve of our pre-emptive actions, including the one we mean to invade to defend our people? No? How many then? 90% of the globe must agree? Fifty percent? France? *Who?*

But of course, there's a four point plan at www.JohnKerry.com that will "change the dynamic on the ground." Yes, this plan on a website will stop Improvised Explosive Devices from detonating. This plan will bring the sworn enemies of this nation into a series of binding arbitrations that will convince them this is all one jolly misunderstanding. This plan – *unlike any military plan in human history* – will survive contact with the enemy, and his intentions, his will and his capabilities will melt away like the morning dew because Senator John Kerry has a four-point plan at www.JohnKerry.com.

Finally, and most tellingly, Senator Kerry says that Iraq is *"a long, long way from the fight on terror."*

Senator, you might choose to read some history: it might broaden your perspective. The last time this country was attacked, it was by the Imperial Japanese Army and Navy, whose capitol city was Tokyo.

The first land battle the US Army fought was at Kasserine Pass. Kasserine Pass, Senator, is in Tunisia. Tunisia is in Africa. Africa is a long, long way from Japan.

Tunisia did not attack the United States, Senator Kerry. Tunisia, in fact, was a far, far more innocent battlefield than Iraq, which had spent the preceding decade, and then some, committing overt acts of war against British and American aircraft flying missions to enforce UN mandates.

US troops fought in Tunisia – and they fought badly; infinitely worse than they do in Iraq – because people of vision and courage and great intelligence perceived that this was the first, best front against an enemy that straddled the entire globe.

We did not begin our war by launching an armada of landing craft filled with Marines on a suicide mission from Hawaii to Tokyo. We did not send fleets of transports to get shot down over Berlin carrying fifty divisions of paratroopers.

We attacked in Tunisia because it was the soft underbelly of a powerful enemy. There is a word for this type of action, Senator Kerry, and that word is "foothold." It is a place where the enemy is weak. It is a place we can capture, fortify, defend and launch further attacks from. As Tunisia, so Africa. As Africa, so Italy. As Italy, so Germany.

We were not attacked by the natives of the Marianas, or the Solomans, or the Marshall islands, and yet these innocent people died along with our troops. It was part of a *strategy for victory,* Senator. I know you understand the term 'strategy.' It's the other term that seems to me to stick in your craw as I examine your entire career.

Here's something you might want to read up on aboard the campaign jet: bright people have done studies on what the operational limits of a terror cell are. It's actually kind of... biological. See, as a terror cell grows in members, it gains not only mutually-reinforcing enthusiasm, but capability. However, the bigger the cell, the less secure it becomes.

Zarqawi's cells having been fighting us from the day Saddam's statue fell. So I ask you, Senator: if there were no terrorists in Iraq, where did these organized units come from? Did they parachute in? Saddam's Fedayeen are not and did not behave as a defeated military unit, but as an organized, cell-based structure. Where did they come from? And poor, unlamented Abu Nidal? And how many others?

When operating outside of rogue nations, law-enforcement pressure limits the cell to about 80 members, and the operational center is much smaller. Any larger and the cell fragments into smaller, more secure, but less capable splinter cells.

However, when protected by a nation-state, such as Syria or Iran – Iraq and Afghanistan having been wiped off the blackboard in this regard in a puff of chalk dust, and Libya having suddenly found religion – there is effectively *no limit* to how large and capable a terror organization can become, since there are no law-enforcement pressures limiting its growth.

Putting a democracy – even a very bad democracy – in the heart of the Middle East is a dagger at our enemy's heart. It is as if Canada were overrun to the degree that Afghanistan once was: intolerable. It draws all the enemy's resources. It provides a mortal example that people of Arab lands can live in freedom, and eventually, prosperity. A free Iraq is a fatal, deadly poison to the Ideology of Death that threatens this nation and the world.

The essence of deterrence, Senator, is to cause uncertainty in the mind of your opponent. The missile defense system, which you oppose, does precisely this. It doesn't matter if it has a 3 out of 5 success rate. Fifty such anti-missile installations enormously, in fact *fatally* complicates an enemy's ability to plan a first strike or, far more likely, to issue nuclear blackmail.

You have made it clear that you would cancel the bunker-busting bombs that cause uncertainty – **deterrence,** Senator – in the minds of unstable lunatics like Kim Jung Il and the Iranian Thugocracy.

They do not have to guess what you will do, Senator: you have already given that away, in the same way you gave away the atrocity fictions the Vietnamese Communists were torturing your "Band of Brothers" to obtain, without success.

President Bush believes that a free and democratic state provides a shockingly clear example that there is another way for Arab peoples to live. He believes, as I do, that all people want to live free and determine the course of their own lives. You claim that this is a mistake. You seem to be determined to fulfill that prophesy.

You lack the vision, Senator, to see this as a many-front war. You lack the insight to see how the sight of Saddam crawling from a hole inspired an identical self-possessed lunatic to give up Libya's nuclear weapons program. Iraq **deterred** Libya, you eternal defeatist. And all of the rest of the former free-range dictators now hang on the results of this election to see whether they will get a man who has capitulation in his very marrow, or one who has weathered unbelievable pressure, slurs and insults, and very likely thrown away his second term, to face reality and *do something*. Something unpopular. Something that he knew would make his poll numbers go *down*.

I know. I know, John. Inconceivable.

Senator Kerry, I do not desire to be President of the United States. I will settle for being the head coach of the Florida Gators. I have a four-point plan on how to win against the Tennessee Volunteers. My plan is foolproof, and it will change the dynamic on the field. I place little weight on the fact that the game I have in mind was played several weeks ago: that is why my four-point plan is so perfect! I have analyzed all of the Florida errors, and they will not be repeated when I replay that game in my head.

And I might add I have won every Monday morning game I have ever quarter-backed.

Vote for me.

POWER
October 01, 2003

Lately I've been reminded constantly of a remark that James Lileks made to me in an e-mail regarding the Writing of Essays and Other Deep Thoughts. He's a perfectly ripe mango of annoyance, that fellow; if the man weren't so funny and spot-on I'd like and despise him far less. But no – my admiration for him continues to grow and soon murder will be the only way for me to adequately express it.

We were talking about this process in an e-mail exchange, and he said that when we chase the rabbit down the hole we never know where it's going to come out again. That's it exactly.

I've been chasing a particular rabbit for months now; had it cornered in the back of a cave. I'd gotten out the knife and was prepared to make short work of it, when suddenly the little bastard launched itself fifty feet through the air, landed on my neck and started tearing at my jugular. I've been fighting with it since.

I've been thinking about **Power**. Thinking about what real power entails, and more importantly, wondering if there is a way to defeat that ancient and highly reliable adage and perhaps find a way for a nation – mine – to wield power, enormous power, without being corrupted – enormously.

The use of power is straightforward, and throughout history we see salvation or ruin as a direct result of the application of power. But the *moral* use of power: *that* is a Jackalope; it's a Snark – easy to talk about, but damned hard to catch. But chase it we must, because the United States is a moral country, filled with decent and generous people, and we can see that the few times in our history when we did not fight a moral cause produced stains on our honor and history, and wrote a page or two identical to the volumes of horrors inflicted by nations and empires with no such moral inhibitions and restraint.

The United States is often referred to as a childish country, an adolescent nation, young and strong and stubborn, but unsophisticated and unseasoned. Up until a short while ago, there may have been some truth to this, for there is one adolescent quality that has long marked the American psyche when involved overseas, and that is the desire to be liked by everyone. As we mature as individuals (and this is not a universal phenomenon – yes, I'm talking to *you*, Sheryl Crow), we begin to realize that not only is it impossible to be liked by everyone… it is, in fact, repugnant. I do not want to be admired by murderers and rapists and liars and wife beaters. I want to be admired by good and decent, intelligent and just people, and in order to achieve this I need to do things that make me despised by their opposites.

As we began to fight back against the worldwide terror network, their corrupted ideology, and the states that harbor them, I and many of my fellow countrymen were shocked to discover all of the sympathy and affection generated by our status as victims suddenly evaporated the moment we decided to utilize our power to try to put an end to this threat. We were counseled by our moral superiors that terrorism was a fact of life in this new millennium – best just to ignore it as much as possible, and not make things worse by poking it with a stick. And as for all those new skyscrapers and super-jumbo airliners and all those other dreams... forget it. Too much of a target. Who would ever want to inhabit the building replacing the fallen towers? The terrorists will just blow it up again. Better to build a park or something less provocative.

How very...*French*.

Well, we chose a different path, and we have now two years of data to see the results of this experiment. And we also have to ask ourselves some tough questions regarding the use of power. Does fighting back reduce or enlarge the threat to our country? What are the diplomatic costs, and do they exceed the benefits gained from unilateral action? And because we are a moral nation, most importantly: how do we know when the application of our vast power is justified, not only for our own self interest, but also in the consequences to those on the receiving end of that power?

This subject is too important to screw up, frankly. We – 21st Century Americans – need to understand *power*. We need to understand the perils and traps that have throughout history ensnared nations and empires, and turned once noble ideas into bloody disasters.

It is a painful process. It means turning a cold, unwavering eye on some of our own worst excesses. It means rooting out and examining our own failures, disgraces and shortcomings, and pointing out, in broad daylight, the stains of dishonor on our beloved flag unflinchingly and unfailingly.

We need to do this. We need to do this *now*, all of us. Because we are at another of those fulcrum points in history – all of us, together – where the decisions we make will shape a century. We hang in a moment of space and time where one thing, and one thing only, will determine whether we will advance into a century of science, freedom, tolerance and marvels, or fall back into a dark age of tribalism and terror, of religious fundamentalism armed this time with the very weapons of God.

We look out at an uncertain and unformed future. And the one thing we can all agree on is that the single unique force shaping that world in the coming decades will be American Power. Upon how that power is used, or squandered, or perverted, hangs the future of humanity. How, in this coming age of shadows, do we find our way? How do we do what is right and honorable in a sea intentionally made grey by those who would quickly lose a stand-up fight of good versus evil, black vs. white?

How in fact do we fight and defeat the enemies of freedom, of invention and science, of tolerance and compromise, without, as James Lileks wrote, *"waking up to find we had become what we hated the most?"*

I thought this was going to be pretty straightforward. And then I ran into a voice that knocked the wind out of me.

I was offered a chance to spend four days in the stunning mountaintop home of the scientist-millionaire – and old friend – that I profiled in **TRINITY**. I took it. One look out the window and you could feel your mental horizon expanding. There, in a view extending for at least a hundred miles, one could see, on a clear day, perhaps four or five signs of human settlement – a few single houses. And these could be easily ignored. What lay around every switchback in the magnificent lower western corner of North Carolina was America in all her pristine glory – almost untouched, man's presence so light and scarce that it can be easily removed with a quick pass of the mental Photoshop.

Things were looking promising. Now all I had to do was sit down and write a few hundred thousand paragraphs on military power and the need to use it when the time arose.

Then the flash.

As I was minding my own business during the first few minutes in this magnificent house, this shrine and testament to the fruits of hard work, daring and ingenuity, I saw bookshelf upon bookshelf of interesting titles.

I walked straight toward the nearest, walked right up to it in fact – as close as I am to these very words. And there, right in the dead center of my field of vision:

Mark Twain on the Damned Human Race, a collection I had not even heard of.

Now it would help if I could explain the kind of effect Mark Twain has on the mind and soul of the American writer. There is no better way to pass a period of hard work than by dipping into small, bite-sized, individually wrapped pieces of Mark Twain. And I soon found out that this would indeed be a wonderful way to pass the hard and backbreaking work of sawing, hammering and hinge fitting that I was about to face when constructing a gallows to hang myself – for that is the reaction writers have when they read Mark Twain.

I crack open the book before I put my bags down. The very first line my eyes land on is this:

To my mind, Judas Iscariot was nothing but a low, mean, premature Congressman.

I'll just go home now.

Sorry, no escape. I'm hooked again, *doomed* again. I'll just unpack my bust of Salieri and place it up here on the monitor. He'll be a source of great comfort, no doubt, the next time I try to describe the smirk on Michael Moore's face, the look that Twain caught on a similar creature a century ago when he wrote that he had *"a smile all over his face and looks as radiantly happy as he will look some day when Satan gives him a Sunday vacation in the cold storage vault."*

I admire and respect much of the man that was Teddy Roosevelt, but in my opinion there is no doubt whatsoever that the fourth face on Mt. Rushmore should have been Mark Twain's. Washington, Jefferson, Lincoln --- and Twain: easily the four greatest Americans – to my mind, the four greatest *people* – that have ever lived.

But I very soon discovered that *On the Damned Human Race* is not *The Innocents Abroad*. It is an angry book, a ferocious indictment of humanity, and most especially America, the country that he skewered mercilessly with the sharpest wit ever granted a mortal person, and a country that through four decades of criticism and remorse never was anything other than the object of his deepest love. It is a glimpse into a world that is long gone, but one that is echoing through a century passed, for me, now. For Twain is writing about the Spanish-American War, and the Philippine rebellion: our one true effort to try our hand at actual imperialism. And what he has to say about Power is not refreshing.

*"True, we have crushed a deceived and confiding people; we have turned against the weak and the friendless who trusted us, we have stamped out a just and intelligent and well-ordered republic; we have stabbed an ally in the back and slapped the face of a guest; we have bought a shadow from an enemy that hadn't it to sell; we have robbed a trusting friend of his land and his liberty; we have invited our clean young men to shoulder a discredited musket and do bandits' work **under a flag which bandits have been accustomed to fear, not to follow;** we have debauched America's honor and blackened her face before the world…"*

(Emphasis mine – BW)

A galaxy of talent divides us, but I know I have at least one critical element in common with Mark Twain. We both love America. And people who deeply love America need to hear his words regarding the massacre of 600 Moro tribesman in a remote crater during the mop-up of the Philippine campaign, a century ago:

"We did not exterminate the Spaniards – far from it. In each engagement we left an average of 2 per cent of the enemy killed or crippled on the field.

Contrast these things with the great statistics which have arrived from that Moro crater! There, with six hundred engaged on each side, we lost fifteen men killed outright, and we had thirty-two wounded…

The enemy numbered six hundred – including women and children – and we abolished them utterly, leaving not even a baby alive to cry for its dead mother. **This is incomparably the greatest victory that was ever achieved by the Christian soldiers of the United States."**

(Emphasis Twain's)

Damning words. Fatal. Fatal words. And:

"The next headline blazes with American and Christian glory like to the sun in the zenith:

Death List Is Now 900.

I was never so enthusiastically proud of the flag until now!"

If you were looking for words to prevent the American colossus from stamping out a poor, weak, brown-skinned country – say Iraq – you could not do much better than to invoke Twain and his essay, *To the People Sitting in Darkness.*

You could bring down all of his thunder and wrath and compassion and unquestionable moral power and invoke him to bring American troops home, all across the globe.

You could do it. But you would be wrong.

Before the War in Iraq, before Afghanistan, before 9/11/01 as a matter of fact, I was surfing the web and came across a very interesting animation at the Lockheed website.

It was a demonstration of an entirely new kind of warfare. It was stunning.

The computer-graphics scene was a remote airbase in a distant valley in the dark of night. Two – *two!* – shadowy forms appear on the ridgeline, in ragged cloth Ghillie suits, and lie down to become just two more bushes on a moonless ridge several miles from the enemy base below.

High overhead, several alien, bat-like UCAVs – Unmanned Combat Air Vehicles – orbit the battlespace. Without a human crew, they can remain on station for days, replaced by others when they return to refuel.

It is like an attic full of bombs, hanging in the rafters, 24/7.

The two forward observers – Special Forces guys – are armed with a laser rangefinder. These two men now wield the firepower of a battalion.

Looking through the telescopic sights, they put the crosshairs on a bunker and pull the trigger. An invisible laser ranges the target to within an inch or two. Since GPS tells the rangefinder where it is, it calculates the angle and distance to the target and passes the coordinates of that bunker up to a military communications satellite. This then beams it down to the unseen, unheard UCAVs orbiting tens of thousands of feet above, which in turn enter the bunker's coordinates into a GPS-guided J-DAM smart bomb.

The men on the ridge continue to mark targets. A control tower. A transport airplane. A fuel depot. A hospital is spared. And so on.

And then, after receiving authorization, the UCAVs open their bomb bay doors, the J-DAMs fall through any weather, and those targets simply disappear. When a convoy of tanks and Armored Personnel Carriers tries to make a run for it, repeated updates of the target designator take them out, too.

Then the two men pack up and disembark, on foot, for several miles, where they will uncover a camouflaged ATV and exit the area for recovery by helicopter.

I described this animation to my friend Richard Riley, who works in aerospace. He described this type of warfare as having, in effect, *The God Button*. It is an apt description. We see something, point at it, and it goes away.

Various companies are now flight testing these very UCAV's. Deployed from an aircraft carrier, with a range of, say, 1000 nautical miles and carrying advanced optical, IR and radar sensors, these vehicles will be able to loiter unseen and unheard at 40,000 feet and target *individuals.*

I think the most remarkable weapon deployed during the Iraq war was the GPS-guided JDAM bomb that was modified to have it's warhead not enhanced, but removed and replaced with ordinary *cement.*

It did not get a lot of press coverage, this weapon. But think about this for a moment: 500 pounds of precision-guided cement falling from a height of 20,000 feet or more is a weapon that is designed to destroy a single room in an apartment building, or an individual car in a traffic jam -- without damaging anything around it.

I must say that for a racist, mass-murdering nation of Nazis bent on terrorizing poor brown people by blowing as many of them to bits as possible, this is rather an anemic effort. How many American and British lives were lost in Iraq due to our self-imposed reluctance to level, at the merest lift of a finger, the building of city block from which our troops were taking fire? How bitterly disappointed must be the barking moonbats of the lunatic left, that we who had the power to kill hundreds of thousands of civilians to limit our own losses saw fit to stay our own hand? Unilaterally, without prior UN approval. There was not a solitary Belgian in sight to instruct us in morality.

Remarkable.

But I digress...

The United States, today, has the capability to push The God Button and make targets disappear. We are fast developing battlefield lasers that can shoot down incoming *artillery shells*. Such a system can aim and correct a directed energy beam on a target instantaneously. No artillery barrage, no missile attack, and least of all, no incoming aircraft will be able to penetrate a fully functioning energy-weapon defense. We are testing such systems at this very moment.

Small wonder, then, the rest of the world is coming to realize that US power is not collapsing or slowing, but rather accelerating, and accelerating *rapidly* away from the rest of the planet. And so we should not be surprised to see so many efforts to constrain and derail that power.

So it is time for hard questions: how much power is enough? Who can wield such power without being corrupted? And if we voluntarily relinquish this power?

What then?

It never fails to impress me that we best gain insight on the most complex of issues not by boring in closer, but rather by stepping back – and the further back we step, often the clearer things become.

When all is said and done, discussions of power and morality seem to hinge around a single idea – or rather two conflicting ideas regarding the nature of power.

Those that would have us disarm, withdraw, apologize and retreat make the assumption that by removing American Power from the world, the planet will become a harmonious village of diversity and mutual respect. Remove American capitalism, and the world's people will trade solar cars for indigenous beads, our European moral betters will hand over their cash to the third world until all are perfectly equal, and everyone will live in a sustainable ecological paradise. Remove American cultural power and Britney will be replaced with Beethoven, and an exquisite and reasonably priced *Pate de Foi Gras Existentialist Meal* can be had at a corner drive in where the former McDonald's once stood.

This is utter nonsense. It has never been true for a single page of the history of the Damned Human Race. There has never – **never** – been a day in human history when some form of power has not flooded the world, or competed to do so; and those times when the power was most one-sided reveal themselves to be the times of greatest relative peace, stability, and advancement of that quaint notion known as *civilization*.

This is not merely a European construct. We see this iron rule in Inca and Aztec histories in South America, in Shaka's Zulu nation, in Chinese empires and Japanese Shogunates, Native American tribal relations, and wherever else we turn our eyes.

The idea that all would be well if only America would retreat from the world and stay at home is a pernicious and seductive one. It appeals not only to those that hunger after the freedom to do mischief in our absence as it does to our natural sense of isolationism.

It has been the mantra of communists, totalitarians and elitists of every vile stripe for well over a hundred years. It is utterly and completely wrong. Political power has never been removed from the world – it has only been replaced. And so our choice – *now pay attention you No Blood For Oil types* – is not between power and no power. It is a choice only of **what kind of power will fill that vacuum.** Chinese? Russian? European? We have seen all of these before. The horrors they have inflicted, with far less absolute power than the US wields, do not leave me pining for those alternatives. Someone is going to be the world power, or tear the world apart fighting for it. And no matter how hard we may wish it, the winner will not be a Blindfolded Jury of Archangels.

That is an unpleasant realization. It does not bestow glory on the human animal. Mark Twain:

"I am the only man living who understands human nature; God has put me in charge of this Branch Office; when I retire there will be no one to take my place. I shall keep doing my duty, for when I get over to the other side, I shall use my influence to have the human race drowned again, and this time drowned good, no omissions, no Ark."

We have some very hard decisions to make as a nation, and as a people – and we have to make them, *now.* There is no perfect power. There is only human power. History shows that the best we can hope for is that the most decent, least flawed power – the British, for example – will, despite their horrors and massacres, displace people who are far, far worse.

It's really that simple.

We have to face the fact that we are imperfect creatures; that as long as there remain brutal and savage dictatorships power is not something that can or *should* be put down or put away, because power dispersed among hundreds of millions of fundamentally decent people displaces and curtails the murders and genocides of those forces that would rush in to fill their place.

We must face the hard and bitter truth that good people can walk away from a fight, but when they do, bad people will have the field and we have seen the horrors they can inflict.

For there are indeed good people and bad people. We have been, on the whole, the best-behaved, most generous and benign power in the history of the world. But we have had our Ft. Pillows and our Wounded Knees, our Moro Craters and My Lais. We are not immune, no matter how deeply and fervently so many of us wish we were.

We are Twain's people: fallible, often greedy, prone to vanity and pride over our institutions and successes. We are all this and more. We have committed bloody acts and disgraced our flag and our honor, and written shameful pages in a history that cannot be erased.

Face it.

We *have* to. We have to do it, now, openly, honestly. We have to look our weakness and our sins full in the face, and accept them, and unlike past occupiers of this position, unlike, for example, the Japanese who still refuse to face their responsibilities in World War II, we must undergo – daily if necessary – the painful and humiliating airing of our worst excesses, and stare right in the face the reflection of our own flawed nature.

But unlike our hand-wringing, self-loathing, paralyzed elites, we must do this not to become immobilized with shame and doubt, but rather to have the confidence and moral clarity needed to be able to act when action is essential, to act when all others are paralyzed by the shame of unexamined atrocities, to act when *only* action can save this world from the relentless drag of human entropy that cannot abide creativity, freedom, tolerance and success.

Because now, at this moment, this fulcrum point in history, we need American power more desperately and urgently than at any time in memory. And we cannot allow the past errors of a fundamentally decent, generous and kind people to prevent us from acting at this critical moment where inaction and paralysis could doom the world.

There is loose in the world a cancer, a cult of death and destruction, a force that loves nothing but destruction and pain and revenge for slights real and imagined. We face people whose hatred and rage sends them into fits of ecstasy at the thought of their own children being blown to bloody shreds so long as they can kill as many innocents as possible. And the higher we build the more fervent and hardened their desire to bring us down.

It is a sickness, it is a disease – it is, in fact, the last animal howling of rage and impotence at a new idea of humanity that is, at a long, bloody and terrible price, fighting and winning a war against racism, sexism, religious extremism, tribalism, conformity and slavery.

It is a war for and against the liberal freedoms of the West, for and against the idea of self-determination, personal liberty and responsibility, human creativity, diversity, and freedom of expression.

It is a fight to the death for and against a culture that can build marvels like skyscrapers and airliners, acts of technological and creative daring, and fill them with individuals of every nation and religion and color united by their desire to work hard and get along with one another, people who have traded in machetes and blood feuds for letter openers and water-cooler gossip. We are fighting a nihilistic force, a force that creates nothing and would destroy this entire world for their place in the next if given the means, a force that hijacks – both literally and figuratively – these miracles of industry, creativity and compromise and brings them down in blood and fire and ruin.

It is a fight that we cannot avoid. Despite the bleats of terrified apologists and appeasers, this is not a fight against what we have done, but rather a war against who we are and what we believe and represent. That is why we must remind ourselves, *daily* remind ourselves, that all these miraculous things we take for granted are *not* the natural state of man, but new and terrifying ideas for millions of people shackled to the past, ideas that must be fought for and maintained by force if need be. Maintained by **power**, the vast power generated by freedom and creativity and cooperation.

And yet, we woke up on the first day after the world had changed, woke up to find the plainest evidence possible that we are at war with yet another enemy of civilization and progress, and what did we see?

We saw the rest of the Western world cowering in fear and self-hatred, awash in the disease of self-doubt and myopia that comes from decades of success and luxury – the same disease that brought Rome from the stability and growth of the Pax Romana to the decadent and self-loathing horrors of Caligula. We saw a few friends – pitifully few; *painfully* few – ready to stand and fight this disease, this death cult of Terror. And of the rest?

They have traded in their power, their means of self-defense, for 35 hour work weeks and months of paid vacations and pre-paid health care and covered it with a patina of moral superiority that masks a rotten and tottering foundation. They have become cultures unwilling to pay the price to defend themselves, cultures so pessimistic and cynical that they have – literally and without rhetorical flourish – lost the will to live to the degree that parents outnumber their children and birthrates plummet through replacement levels and into the basement of collapse and ruin.

And so who is willing, who indeed is even able to fight back in the defense of skyscrapers and bridges, of jetliners and miracle drugs? Who will stand and fight the forces that wish to tear down our cities, shroud our women, burn our science, execute critics, torture the different and destroy our new and alien ideas of personal freedom and responsibility, ideas that have lifted billions from the perpetual fear and horror that have been the lot of the Damned Human Race since man walked upright?

Who will fight for that? Who?

We will fight for it. *America.* Fallible, human, flawed America will fight. Australia – another tough and proud nation of free men and women will fight. Great Britain, that ancient champion of decency and fair play. Poland, who knows more about war and horror than perhaps any place on earth – she has shown she will fight. Israel. Israel who has borne this burden alone for decades...

Who else? Who else with high-rise offices and jetliners, computers and western freedoms, sits on the fence and flatters and bribes these forces that make no distinction among us, who see us as equally infidel – who else has bet their futures on diplomacy and compromise with an adversary that looks on compromise as weakness and diplomacy as nothing more than a means to get us to lower the drawbridge?

Up until very recently, Terror was growing because Terror worked. Now for the first time, Terror – Terror as a political tool – has been met with real *power*. Two governments have fallen, and contrary to the stated expectations of these savages, ours was not one of them. Terror, for the first time in modern memory, now has attached to it negative consequences. Consequences that have been severe. Severe, indeed – fatal in a great many cases. And all of a sudden, Terror does not look like such a great bargain after all.

There is a word for this phenomenon. That word is *deterrence.*

Prior to Iraq, prior indeed to Afghanistan, we were told by the natural cowards that get paid by the catastrophe that to fight back would unleash world-wide *Jihad*. Suicide bombers would be a weekly – daily – occurrence at malls and football games. These deep, deep thinkers assured us that if we so much lifted a finger in our defense our society would collapse in the flames of righteous retribution. We defied these defeatists and fought back anyway. As I have said many times, this was an *experiment*. The results are *data*.

Al-Qaeda, Hamas, Islamic Jihad, and all the others have the means to launch a wave of suicide bombings in the US. It is not that very difficult. They have not done so. Why? Because if current events are any guide, such an action would mean the immediate end of *Hamas* and the rest of their ilk. They are cold-blooded murderers, but they are not idiots. The cost of terror – in the US at least – is nowadays higher than the rewards.

History is crystal clear on one point, and that is that power – the exercise of raw military and political force – is the only effective cure for dictators and fascists, whatever flag they fly. It is not only morally justified to confront such evil; it is immoral not to do so.

But suppose we had listened to Noam Chomsky and Cynthia McKinney and Ramsey Clark and Ted Kennedy -- that bulwark of personal integrity? What of their promises that the vast Arab Street would arrive from the ocean like Godzilla and smash our cities – *Arrgh! **Arrrrgh!!*** – if we so much as used harsh language during Ramadan?

Who now doubts that an American retreat after 9/11 would have reinforced what these Terror masters had been led to believe – that we were a weak and decadent people unwilling to fight to defend ourselves? And if these deep-thinking prophets of disaster were so spectacularly wrong then, why should we listen to them now?

If an American withdrawal had succeeded 9/11, what new daily horrors would we be facing in a world where any lunatic teenager could strap on an explosive belt and dictate policy to the greatest power in the history of the world? And who seriously believes that more recruits have flocked to al-Qaeda now that Osama Bin Laden is pasted on the inside wall of a Tora Bora cave than would have joined if he had ridden a white horse into Kabul after blowing up the World Trade Center, and sent The Great Satan packing in humiliation and defeat from Saudi Arabia – as so many of our liberal elites demanded we do?

It hasn't happened that way. What changed that equation? *American power* did. And don't you forget it.

My friend Steve Stipp mentioned in passing a fascinating thought experiment. If you had to design some foreign power to dominate the planet, what would you want it to look like? If there is to be a hyperpower, how would you design one that was least likely to run haywire and plunge humanity into a new dark age?

Would you want its people to have untrammeled respect for authority, like Nazi Germany, with a lock-step willingness to follow its leaders blindly, or would you prefer that it had a deep and passionate anti-authoritarian bend, where the soul of the rebel and the outsider and the little guy fighting big powers was manifest in all of its art and music?

Would you want it to be racially homogenous, like Imperial Japan, advancing out into the mongrel world as the sons of heaven, or the most racially diverse blend of people ever to form a single nation?

Would you prefer that it be driven by a rigid and ironclad ideology, such as the Soviet Union, or rather a hodge-podge of wildly differing and competing ideals doing constant battle in the marketplace of ideas?

Would you want it to be a religious dictatorship with a state church, acting on what it perceived to be the revealed word of God, as is the case with Islamic fundamentalists, or a secular nation with strict and inviolate rules keeping religious fervor out of the decision-making process?
Should it be administered by a small group of hereditary elites, as with Imperial Great Britain, or rather have political power dispersed among its fractious citizenry?

And finally, should it be a product of a culture long isolated from the rest of the planet with a low tolerance of outside ideas and philosophy, such as China, or rather one composed of all the nations and histories the world has to offer?

I have my own opinion. Your mileage may vary.

———————————————

It is generally agreed that throughout human history, there have been three distinct, world-changing revolutions: Megatrends that encompass far more than individual national histories. These three revolutions have been the Agricultural Revolution, the Industrial Revolution, and the Information Age.

Through human history, exceptional military, cultural and political power has been applied to create empires. I have argued elsewhere that by no stretch of the imagination does the United States fit such a profile. We control no Parliaments, we exact no tributes, we provide no Governors and we levy no taxes. Indeed, in the nations where the United States has a significant military presence, that force is there to protect rather than suppress, and huge sums of money are paid into these countries, rather than extracted from them at gunpoint.

But consider this, when questioning US motivation and US power:

During the Agricultural Age, the reward for empire was **land**. Land, livestock, and the people to work it were the source of all wealth in the First Age, and Empires of the period were marked exclusively by their thirst for land, from the Babylonians, Egyptians, Aztecs, Romans – all the way on up to the British.

The second age, the Industrial Age, is much younger, perhaps three hundred years old. There was a century or so of overlap with its predecessor, but Industrial Age imperial ambitions were not about land – they were about **resources**: Iron, oil, rubber, cotton – the raw materials that kept the factories of the time running profitably. The Japanese attacks in the Pacific in the thirties, and German aggression eastward, were motivated by imperial desires for resources.

The United States was born an agricultural nation. Its childhood and adolescence spanned the Industrial revolution, and now it is the leader in the Information Age. And here we see something completely unique in human history, something very telling and important regarding America's attitude to power and conquest.

During the Agricultural Age, the United States was founded on the prime agricultural real estate on the planet. Therefore, we as a nation never felt any first-age pressures for empire (although it certainly did drive the desire to enlarge the homeland westward to the Pacific).

During the Industrial Revolution, America again had no need to conquer and steal resources. Our oil supplies were more than adequate for the time, and we had ample supplies of iron ore and other natural resources.

That may be nothing more than good luck, but again, the American mindset has always been that we have at home the best of everything. It is the antithesis of envying, plotting Imperial ambitions.

And now we find ourselves predominant in the world. True, we still require industrial resources, and some of these – chiefly oil – do come from overseas.

But we have always been a nation of businessmen, and placing morality completely aside for a moment, Yankee common sense tells us it's cheaper to buy this oil – at prices set by the sellers, not ourselves – than it is to fight for it.

Since so many of our critics refuse to countenance the idea that we have morals and restraint, take them out of the picture if you like. What resources do Americans need that we cannot simply buy? What motivation do we have for invasion and war? What temptation to power? Let us not forget that the NO BLOOD FOR OIL slogans first appeared in Gulf War I – well over a decade ago. What oil have we stolen at gunpoint since that signal victory? Where, in fact, is there any sign whatsoever of us using our overwhelming military strength to take *anything*?

And consider this for the future: we are now leading the world into an economy based on information. The fuel of this new age is **ideas**. And where do all the great ideas seem to be coming from? The most cursory glance at the world of invention, art, science and technology show that these come, to a really staggering degree, from the United States. That makes three world-spanning epochs, and during all three, the United States is the only great power in history that did not to need to go abroad to grow powerful and prosper. Those that fear American power in the future might stop to consider that if current trends continue, we will – again – have no need to go forth into the world, because what good ideas that do come from outside our borders – and they are legion – are cooked up by individuals who almost universally want to come to America because here we admire and respect innovation, here ingenuity is rewarded – in cash! – rather than strangled and buried under ever-thickening, Kudzu-like mats of bureaucracy.

It's like oil loading itself on tankers and making their way to Galveston, or entire counties of prime farmland cutting themselves into sod and stowing away in container ships, to be opened and unfurled in Long Beach harbor complete with sheep and shepherds.

I will grant that from abroad, the prospect of this much American Power is intimidating and worrisome. But how much of this angst, I wonder, has to do with the internal temptations they feel at the prospect of such power at their own command?

Twain again:

"There is only one expert who is qualified to examine the souls and the life of a people and make a valuable report – the native novelist. This expert is so rare that the most populous country can never have fifteen conspicuously and confessedly

competent ones in stock at any one time…The native expert's intentional observation of manners, speech, character and ways of life can have value, for the native knows what they mean without having to cipher out the meaning. But I should be astonished to see a foreigner get at the right meaning, catch the elusive shade of these subtle things. Even the native novelist becomes a foreigner, with a foreigner's limitations, when he steps from the State whose life is familiar to him into a State whose life he has not lived. "

I am not one of those rare experts. I am certainly not Mark Twain. But I do grasp what he is saying here, and it bears repeating: Those foreigners who see in American power imperial ambitions do not know the soul of this country.

They see mechanisms and potentials, they see through the eyes of their own histories and cultures.

I know Americans, because I am one. I keep my eyes open. I listen to people talk. And I have never – I can stand naked before Angels and say this with a straight face – I have never, *ever* heard a single American acquaintance of mine talk of empire, dream of conquest, or glory in the idea of invasion. And I hang out with the mean, nasty, bloodthirsty hawks! There are millions upon millions who were not willing to use force even when we are attacked. The idea of invasion and occupation of a brutal dictatorship like Iraq has caused their heads to explode, to the point where a walk down Sunset boulevard in LA sounds like a fire at the Jiffy Pop factory.

I have had innumerable discussions about threats, actions, responses, contingencies and capabilities, but I have never, not once in 44 years, met an American who advocated invasion and permanent conquest for national gain.

Never.

I suppose many overseas readers have a hard time believing that. I'll also bet real money that just about every American that reads this is nodding his or her head in agreement right now, because once it is pointed out it is a startling, almost unbelievable statement. And it is true.

This is not because Americans are saintly people without vice. On the contrary. We are a proud, aggressive, clever, often violent and ambitious people. We are, on paper anyway, exactly the kind of people the world should worry about.

And yet Imperial ambitions are unknown to us. Why?

Well, I have a guess. My guess is that when fate deals you four aces and a king, you don't need to kick over the table and draw a pistol, and you damn sure don't need to discard and draw again.

We Americans know what we have here. We *know*. Even the dimmest of us know in their bones, in their genes, how good we have life in the United States. Some of it was luck; most of it – the vast huge middle of it – was hard work by ambitious, energetic people who did whatever it took to get here. We don't want to go back out into the world – our families did everything they could to *get away from the world to come here*. We are happy here. We want to barbeque and watch football games. We most certainly do not want to be stomping around Ethiopia or New Guinea or Belgium – it's a step down for us, *capishe?* There's not an American alive that would trade the rest of the World for the southwestern corner of Indiana. It'd be like Hugh Grant out on a car date with Divine when he had Liz Hurley waiting at home.

Stupid.

There are practical restraints placed on US power. There are economic reasons why business is preferable to war. I suppose if things got ugly enough, the entire world could embargo the US commercially, and I cannot imagine a set of circumstances – short of our national survival – that could justify the level of US aggression to make *that* bargain worthwhile.

But ultimately, the best guarantor of American restraint is…American restraint. Power is not a nocturnal gift from the power fairy. We posses unparalleled levels of political, cultural and military power because we posses unparalleled opportunities for creativity and success. Indeed, with the most energetic and ambitious people of the world constantly flocking to America, one could correctly state that we are a *refinery* of success.

The things that make America hum: hard work, self-criticism, openness to new ideas, ethnic and national diversity, tolerance and respect, and distrust of authority are not just what makes us powerful. They make us *worthy* of being powerful. They are the checks and balances that provide so many viewpoints and histories that there is not a country on the face of the earth today that an American army could invade without some of its soldiers invading their ancestral homes. It has an enormously inhibitive effect.

The fundamental decency of the American Character reverberates throughout our history. Immediately after the French and Russian Revolutions, huge numbers of people on the losing side were murdered indiscriminately. In Paris, the gutters ran red with blood and the guillotine saw so much action it must have tottered on the verge of catching fire. And the revenge taken on the kulaks in Russia was horrible almost beyond imagining. During the American Revolution, on the other hand, the winners fought a terrible and bitter war, and the losers… went back to their homes.

During our own Civil War, with a quarter of the population in open, armed rebellion, the Union captured the entire political and military leadership of the Confederacy intact. One man – the superintendent of the appalling Andersonville prison camp – was hanged for his command's monstrously inhumane treatment, but that was not punishment for rebellion. The rest of them: Generals Lee, Johnston, Bragg and Beauregard, not to mention President Davis, Vice President Stephens, and all the others – were released unharmed. Stephens immediately ran for, and won, his old seat in Congress!

Show me anywhere else in all the pages of history such national decency, forgiveness, and generosity. You can't do it. It is, like so much of our history, unique.

This fundamental moral decency was evident all throughout the Iraqi war. Countless times, US (and British) troops were under direct attack, and did not return fire due to the presence of civilians, or even due to the fact that the attackers were firing from mosques and we did not wish to *offend*, let alone kill or injure, the people who we were mocked for trying to save from themselves. There was, and is, no better look at the vast American military juggernaut, than that image of a young American soldier atop a Humvee, in a still-unsecured village, giving hip-hop dance lessons to a group of obviously delighted Iraqi children. I'll never forget it as long as I live.

———————————————

Earlier, I said you could invoke Twain to oppose the war in Iraq, but you'd be wrong.

You'd be wrong because although Mark Twain hated war – hated war more than any author I have ever read – he hated injustice and hated murder more. Reading Twain's condemnations of our actions in the Philippines, you are struck immediately and often that Twain's scathing rebuke and criticism, unlike that of lesser minds like Chomsky's, and far, far lesser minds like Michael Moore and the rest of the Hollywood Herd, was born of a deep love of America and a sense of shame at seeing her dishonored. Twain's voice is not that of a man convinced that we are the source of all evil in the world, but rather one of a man who loved America, who knew she was better than her actions of the time, who still felt she was a good and great nation that should have known better.

Mark Twain's voice rings across the intervening decades, as does Lincoln's, and Jefferson's, and Washington's, and all the others. But if Lincoln is the voice of courage, Jefferson the voice of liberty and Washington that of sacrifice, then Mark Twain's is voice of **conscience**. It is our own voice. It is the sound of rage and protest when we have lost our way. It is the rapier that nicks and slashes at tyranny and brutality under any flag, including and especially our own. It is the voice of justice and compassion, and it holds us to a very high standard indeed.

I have no special claim to knowing what was in the man's heart. But I cannot imagine that had he seen the images of torture and rape and murder in that poor, desperate country of Iraq, had he heard the pleadings of families torn apart by that brutality, and had he seen the courage, decency, kindness and generosity of our troops on the ground, and the extraordinary efforts they went to in order to prevent innocent suffering, I do not see how he could have possibly opposed what we did there, and continue to do.

"It is a worthy thing to fight for one's freedom; it is another sight finer to fight for another man's" he wrote at the start of the Spanish-American War, when we fought to free Cuba and stated we had no ambitions other than freedom for her people. That we ended up *"playing the European game"* in the Philippines broke his heart, as it breaks mine, a century later. He would have us (as we did in the beginning in Cuba) *"playing the usual and regular American game, and it was winning, for there was no way to beat it. The master, contemplating Cuba, said: 'here is an oppressed and friendless little nation which is willing to fight to be free; we go partners, and put up the strength of seventy million sympathizers and the resources of the United States: play!' Nothing but Europe combined could call the hand, and Europe can not combine on anything."*

We played the European game in the Philippines and stole a bit of empire. But we didn't have the taste for it; more likely, didn't have the stomach to do what was needed to keep it. We fought side by side with the Filipinos during World War II, and spent blood and lives regaining those islands. Then, on the 4th of July, 1946, we did what we should have done four decades earlier. We handed them back their country, as we have handed back every country and territory we have ever conquered with our globe-spanning power, and done it willingly, not as a parting shot after rebellion and failure. We shall soon enough do it with Iraq, once it awakens from its thirty year nightmare and gets back on its feet. It too, like the Philippines, is a nation we broke a promise to, and also one that we owe its freedom and independence by way of atonement.

We played the European game in Vietnam, too; came to the aid of an ally that has come up short on many occasions of late. There is a story that Ho Chi Minh wrote Washington with a plea for aid; his country, he said, only wished for its freedom from a colonial occupying power. Surely America could find sympathy with such a cause after our own birth under similar circumstances?

Perhaps it was a ploy. I don't know enough about it to say. But, if true, what tragedy, what heartbreak, was made from that decision to play the European game? I strongly support the toughness and courage the present administration has shown in taking this fight to the enemy. I am deeply convinced it is not only in our own interest, but in the world's interest. I also understand and respect that people of honor and integrity will disagree.

But do not for an instant take my support to mean that I trust this or *any* administration to be given a free hand to act without criticism, intense scrutiny, and dissent. I do not trust that the President – any president – will always do the right and honorable thing. But I do trust, I deeply and sincerely trust, **the American people.** I read history. We've earned it.

The day may come – and I hope I never live to see it – when we may again lose our way. And then, the cause *against* war will be so solid and so strong that we will not need giant puppets and infantile slogans to try and make a case for peace. If that day comes, those filling the streets will not be aging hippies longing for their youth or furious socialists itching for revolution. On that day, the streets will be filled with middle America, **Silent America,** the great sensible, decent core and soul of the nation.

And I will be there, too.

I never ceased to be amazed at the United States of America. My love for this country is so deep and so wide that I am often accused of being blinded to her many faults. And, to be fair, I can see how it would appear so.

But that is not the case at all. My enormous love and respect for this nation does not come from a belief that she is perfect, unblemished and incapable of error. Precisely the opposite. I love her because she remains an example of what we can aspire to, down here among the Damned Human Race. I love her because she tries to be good; she wants to be. And I love America because I see that America learns from her many mistakes.

I love and respect my nation as if she were a great ship at sea. I admire the quality and genius of her construction. I admire the way she handles rough seas. I poke and prod into the smallest of her compartments and see built-in all manner of ingenious devices to keep her afloat and level. I stand in awe of her speed and power, and sometimes in embarrassment and regret at the damage caused by her great wake. And I have seen her sailed through shoals and narrows that have wrecked scores of nations before her, and seen her emerge scraped and damaged but never fully run aground.

And I admire her crew – both those that sailed her when she was young, and those that man her to this very day, and those that we will turn her over to tomorrow.

I never fail to notice – in line at my bank, or outside a movie theater, say – how different and diverse we are, how many colors and accents and histories blended together into a single line of *Americans*: arguing basketball and politics and all the rest as new people, remade.

It's a marvel.

Her achievements in science and technology, her military strength, competence and decency, her cultural vivacity and passion – all of these things mystify and amaze me, even as I contribute my small part to the effort. But nothing astounds me more than her desire to try to *do the right thing*.

I believe that sometimes, good people have to fight – and good people, by definition, do not enjoy or glory in fighting. Many peoples – such as the Germans and Japanese – have been astonished at the dual nature of American power: in one moment ferocious and ruthless in combat, then tossing candy bars from Jeeps and treating wounds and setting broken bones caused by us the very next.

Ulysses S Grant was a fighter; perhaps the most direct, heads-down, raw-power commanding General in US History. He had something to say about this startling American duality. He wrote *"If we have to fight, I would like to do it all at once and then make friends."*

That, to me, is the sound of American power. We do not enjoy sending our sons and daughters to die overseas. But when we have to fight we fight to win, and win quickly. *"War is cruelty; you cannot refine it,"* wrote Grant's friend and subordinate, William T. Sherman. You cannot refine it, indeed. You can only do it and get it over with as quickly as possible.

Those who mistake American isolationism and restraint for weakness would do well to understand this dual nature, and realize in no uncertain terms that while we will tolerate much as a nation, we will not tolerate everything; that certain actions will throw that switch in the American psyche, as it was thrown that September morning, or that December one. September 11th angered us, but the world has not seen America fully enraged since 1945. It is my fervent hope that we will not need to be that angry and that determined ever again. Because if we are, you may count on this: we will fight like furies until we **win.**

For then, and only then, can we revert to our preferred nature, which is to get on with our own lives, raise our children in the safety and freedom we will not sacrifice – ever – and go back to being the kind of big goofy place that a Sean Penn or a Barbra Streisand can again feel comfortable in, because, once again, other, better people have paid their debt for them.

EPILOGUE

Ah…you're back.

Let me close this collection with a thought that never fails to spook me, but in a good way.

Here we are, you and I, having an odd sort of conversation. As usual, I'm doing all the talking for the moment, but in a few seconds, you will fold this book and I will be silent again – for how long?

It's 12:26 am on November 12th, 2004, here in this little crystal of time I've locked away. Where are you? Somewhere downstream, that much is certain. How far? And do you have any idea how much I would like to know what you know, right now?

How far down the river of time are you from me this very instant? Perhaps, after some years pass, you might return to this book and read this passage again. You'll be further along, but I will still be here in November of 2004. I'll always be here. What I have written here is all I am allowed to know.

Stupid 2nd Law!

But you! You may know how it all turned out! All of the questions I have, all of the doubts and hopes and uncertainties – many of these will be known to you. How much did we get right? How much has changed? How many of the values that I have tried to bring to life do you cherish and retain? Or scorn? I have no way of knowing.

So here's a message from November 12th, 2004 at 12:32am:

I hope we are doing the right thing. Millions of us mean to. I have tried to show how my own views into the past color what I hope would be the right course for the future. But when it's all said and done, we did what we did on faith. I hope that the things I have fought for were best for us as a country and a species – but I don't know that they were.

You, however…somewhere down that moonlight river, beyond the bends that we can just make out through the mist…you, you lucky bastards, you will know!

My good friends Kim and Connie Du Toit gave me a book of essays from a man named Albert Jay Nock. Albert Jay and I have never met; he did most of his writing in the Thirties. His voice sounds stuffy and archaic to me…as mine will no doubt sound to you, when you are far enough down that river that I cannot navigate. But Mr. Nock and I are of a mind on many things. And one of the things he wrote about has stayed with me through the darkest moments of these often shadowy and confusing times.

Mr. Nock talks about **the Remnant** – that being an odd sort of club with neither a clubhouse nor member list. The Remnant that Nock speaks of consists of that small, silent, diamond-hard core of unconnected people who carry civilization, and decency, and freedom, in their hearts. This Remnant, says Albert, this irreducible nugget of good, will never die. They are the people that survive the fall of civilizations and quietly, stubbornly keep the flame of liberty and science and morality burning through the dark nights of history.

Such people do not ask for this, nor do they often even understand it. They just exist. They just *are*.

I, who slept through most of my life, have awoken shocked to discover that I may in fact be such a person. And if you are reading this, and you find some music in it, then very likely you are part of the Remnant, too.

Greetings, then, to you, my friend and ally – wherever or whenever you may be.

Enlarge on these ideals. Make them bigger.

For this is a story that will *never* end.

Bill Whittle
Los Angeles California
www.ejectejecteject.com

ACKNOWLEDGEMENTS

Where to begin? The beginning, I guess.

I owe a huge debt to Rachel Lucas, who not only encouraged me to start my own weblog, but went on to do days of tedious programming to get it all set up and ready to go. I wouldn't be here without her.

Likewise I remain very grateful for the support of both Kim and Connie Du Toit, who instilled in me a sense that this might be important work. The party they threw for me with the rest of the Dallas mafia – Rachel, Emperor Misha I, and many others – is not something I will ever forget. It really got me to believe that *Eject! Eject! Eject!* might in fact be worthwhile.

I am deeply indebted to every blogger out there who has ever thrown me a link, and I still blush at the kindness and generosity they display when they reference my essays. But I would probably have been left out in the cold, like so many other promising weblogs, had it not been for Steven Den Beste putting me on his blog-roll at *USS Clueless.* Thank you, Steven, for watering this plant as you watered so many others. You are sorely missed.

Along these same lines, I am deeply grateful to Charles at *Little Green Footballs,* and especially The Blogfather – Glenn Reynolds at *Instapundit* – for their links. When you are writing for free, everything comes down to page hits. That's the currency. Both of these guys, and many, many others, have repeatedly sent me their readers. There's a fair chance that you are one of them.

We've managed to develop a little community of commenters at *Eject! Eject! Eject!* It's an odd thing for an author, this instant feedback. Odd and **wonderful.** For all of you who have left comments, thank you. The support I have received from my online readers has not only kept me going, they have elevated me as a person to levels undreamed of. How can one ever repay something like *that?* Oh, and speaking of weblog comments, I owe a very large debt to my old and dear friend Steve Stipp, who cleans, maintains and field-dresses them on a daily basis, not to mention adding insights that I often steal with abandon. Thanks buddy.

As far as the actual book is concerned, it just wouldn't be here without the effort and encouragement of Amy Hooper. She has proofed and prodded and needled – I asked her to do all three – and kept at me until it finally appeared right here, in your hands. Thank Amy for me, because I'll never be able to thank her enough by myself. She is the Fairy Godmother of this volume.

My old friend Buster O'Connor at *Eye4.com* did the cover that just blew through all my expectations. Hire him. He's just the best graphics guy I've ever met, and I've met a bunch. Richard Brown's help on the text formatting was invaluable; thanks Rick.

There's a lot about my Dad in this book, and next to nothing about my Mom. Which is odd, because she's the one that put this voice into me, with her compassion and decency and tireless support. I have never in my life doubted for an instant that I could become anything I wanted. That I owe entirely to her. Is there anything greater than a gift like that? Anything at all?

I love you, Mum.

Last and *certainly* least, there would be no Bill Whittle as we know him today without the repeated support of Dr. Jerry Stipp. He thinks he has some glimmer of how much he has helped me over the course of my life, but the fact is, he doesn't have a clue.

(P.S. Hi Dana! We win!)   *Bill Whittle November, 2004*

Printed in the United States
65763LVS00005B/88-90

9 780976 405900